Published by INTERTANKO
Art Direction: Reg Wright, Creative Decisions
Printed by Connekt Colour

# A Century of Tankers

## The Tanker Story

By John Newton

# INTERTANKO

wishes to thank


Alexander S Onassis
Public Benefit Foundation


DVB NedshipBank NV


Leif Høegh Foundation


Polys Haji-Ioannou, Loucas Haji-Ioannou Foundation


for their generous financial support which enabled
A Century of Tankers to be produced

# A Century of Tankers

## The Tanker Story

…"The 'Aquidneck', a little barque which of all man's handiwork seemed to me the nearest thing to perfection of beauty, and which in speed when the wind blew, asked no favour of steamers"

CAPTAIN JOSHUA SLOCUM

Captain Slocum has a unique place in the history of seafaring by being the first man to circumnavigate the globe single-handed. He set sail from Boston on 24 April 1895 in *Spray*, a yawl-rigged sailing boat of just under 37 feet overall which he had rebuilt from a former hulk, and returned to Newport, Rhode Island on 27 June 1898, having sailed over 46,000 miles in his lone voyage which took just over three years.

During his career as a master mariner Joshua Slocum was captain and part-owner of the magnificent ship *Northern Light* which in the 1880s was considered to be the finest American sailing vessel afloat.

Later he commanded *Aquidneck* of which he was also part-owner. On 28 February 1886 the 326 ton barque with a crew of ten left New York bound for Montevideo, Uruguay with a cargo of case-oil. By his own account the weather forecast was "not encouraging" and they set sail in a NW gale which by 3 March had increased to a hurricane. In his description of the voyage Captain Slocum wrote...

*"Our barque could carry only a mere rag of foresail, somewhat larger than a table-cloth, and with this storm sail she went flying before the tempest all those dark days with "a large bone in her mouth" making great headway. Mountains of sea swept clean over the ship filling her decks to the top of the bulwarks and shaking things generally. During a lull, more sail was crowded on and the ship flew like scud, sheeting home sail after sail as required till March 5th*
*when all of her white wings were spread*
*and she fairly walked the waters like a thing of life"*.

# A Century Of Tankers

## The Tanker Story

## CONTENTS

# A Century Of Tankers

## The Tanker Story

## FOREWORD

It is with great pleasure that I introduce *A Century of Tankers* published by INTERTANKO, of which I have the honour to be the present Chairman.

It was INTERTANKO's wish to provide a book with an appeal to a wider audience than the maritime sector alone. *A Century of Tankers* traces the development of the tanker industry from its origins in the 1840s to the end of the twentieth century. It spans the period from when oil was carried in barrels along with general cargo through to the development of custom-built tankers and the advent of modern double-hulled ships with safe transportation as a major goal.

The result, I believe, is a valuable contribution to the documentation of maritime history in the nineteenth and twentieth centuries and illustrates how the world's economy prospered through the availability of oil, and the vital role of the tanker in transporting this essential commodity.

Many well informed persons have contributed to this book and I would like to thank them for their wisdom and their time. Without you, this book would not have been as valuable as we believe it is - a document of a thrilling chapter of the world history.

I hope you will find *A Century of Tankers* both interesting and enjoyable.

**Lars Carlsson**
Chairman of INTERTANKO

# A Century Of Tankers

*The Tanker Story*

# Introduction

Transportation by water has always been one of the cheapest ways of conveying goods. Even when horses provided the motive power, they could haul a much greater cargo in a canal barge than in a road-going cart.

When oil was first shipped from the US to Europe in 1861, it was carried aboard conventional sailing vessels in wooden barrels and later in cans, often together with other cargo.

As oil became a more widely used commodity, it was only a matter of time before ships were designed specifically for the transport of oil in bulk. The driving forces behind the evolution of tankers were the demand for oil and the ever-growing competition between oil companies striving for a greater share of the market for kerosene and other refined products.

At the start of the First World War the size of the largest tankers had increased to 15,000 dwt and the British Admiralty was becoming convinced that oil-fired steam propulsion was the future. The conversion of British Naval ships from coal to oil fuel also provided a stimulus for the development of the Anglo-Persian Oil Company's concessions in Iran, planting the seeds for the eventual growth of the Middle East as a major oil production region.

The economic depression of the 1930s did not encourage any expansion in the size of tankers and even during the Second World War the standard workhorse, the T-2 tanker, only had a carrying capacity of about 16,000 tons. However, the war gave a new urgency to the techniques of welding and mass production that were later to prove key elements in the insatiable drive for larger ships and the reduction in transportation costs.

The American economy grew strongly during and after the Second World War and expansion continued with the postwar rebuilding of a devastated Europe under the Marshall Plan. US and European oil companies worked at full speed to develop the giant Middle East fields to feed the new refineries in the developed world. The oil companies not only controlled production and refining but also transport and distribution. All these activities required a great deal of capital and projects were given priority based on their potential return. Gradually, as the return on transportation was much less than that of other activities, it was found advantageous to purchase the transportation service rather than buy transportation assets. To enable independent owners to finance ships, long-term charters were arranged and, with these as security, an owner could seek funds from a bank either to acquire existing ships or build new ones.

As transportation needs increased, the forward march of technological innovation, including improved materials and new building techniques, permitted the building of larger tankers both in Europe and the US and the maximum size reached about 28,000 dwt by 1949. The demand for newbuildings encouraged the traditional shipbuilding nations in Europe and also Japan to rejuvenate their yards.  In Japan, for example, American mass production and welding techniques were introduced to the former Naval Kure shipyard controlled by Daniel Ludwig. Over time, the techniques were also utilized and further developed in other yards in the country and Japan became the leading shipbuilding nation. Throughout the 1950s European and Japanese yards vied with each other for the honour of the builder of the largest tanker. Early in the decade massive orders were placed in a number of European yards by some of the better-known Greek shipowners. In 1953 a German shipyard delivered a ship of 45,000 dwt, the largest tanker yet built.

It was not long, however, before Japanese yards began to establish a lead, both in terms of the size of ship and overall tanker tonnage delivered. Japanese shipbuilders were supported by generous export schemes and enjoyed the benefits of a low-cost, co-operative and highly capable labour force. In addition, the Japanese continued to push forward the technological boundaries of shipbuilding in their modern facilities, while many European builders were frequently held back by strong unions which sought to implement restrictive working practices which did not allow yard productivity to be optimised. By the mid 1960s Japan had become the world's largest shipbuilding nation and tankers of 100,000 dwt were being commissioned at a number of the nation's yards.

During the 1960s the tanker fleet and the average size of ships continued to grow rapidly.  The Japanese, now major importers of Middle East crude, were pioneering larger ships and by 1966 they had built the first vessel of over 200,000 dwt.  The closure of the Suez Canal in 1967 reinforced the trend towards bigger and bigger ships.  Such vessels were needed to realise the benefits of the economy of scale as large volumes of Middle East oil were transported around the Cape of Good Hope to the US and Europe.  By 1968 a Japanese shipyard delivered a ship of  326,848 dwt, the largest tanker yet launched.

In 1970 the Suez Canal, contrary to all previous expectations, was still closed and, as time went by, its reopening seemed increasingly remote.  Oil consumption was projected to grow at a compound rate of 5 per cent per annum in the US, 7 per cent in the rest of the western world and 8.5 per cent in the developing countries. Because of the Suez Canal closure and the increased voyage distances, these rates in terms of ton-miles were even higher. The whole industry, including shipbuilders, oil companies and independent shipowners, embarked on capacity enlargement and by 1973 there were as many ships on order as were in the existing fleet. Although Japan had become the dominant force in shipbuilding a shortage of berths and rising prices enabled European yards, and in particular those in Sweden, to compete by using very advanced modular prefabrication techniques and high tensile steel.

In 1960 the Organisation of Petroleum Exporting Countries (OPEC) was established to oppose a reduction in the posted prices for oil. The posted prices were the benchmark of the oil industry and provided vital revenues to the producing countries. However, the import quotas America had set in 1959 to protect its domestic producers had the effect of creating an oil surplus outside the US which held down world prices throughout the 1960s. Although OPEC had made several attempts to raise prices during this period, these had been strongly resisted by the oil majors and the importing countries. Eventually, in August 1970 Libya took unilateral action to raise the posted price by 30 cents (13% increase) and increased its profit share from 50 to 55 per cent. The incident provided OPEC with an opportunity to raise oil prices in all its member countries.

This was a significant development as, in effect, OPEC was saying 'it is our oil and from now on we will be calling the shots'. In raising prices the oil producers took control of the industry from the oil majors.

In October 1973 war broke out between Egypt and Israel. OPEC instigated an embargo on oil exports particularly aimed at the US. In a space of five months, posted prices escalated from $2.90 in September 1973 to $11.65 in January 1974. A new era of high oil prices had started, dramatically reducing prospects for growth in oil consumption. Some of the tankers on order were cancelled but the major part of the new tonnage was delivered because construction work had progressed too far to cancel the orders. Tanker industry growth prospects were given a further blow by a second oil price shock in 1979 following the Iranian revolution. By 1982, despite the fact that much of the older, inefficient smaller tonnage had been scrapped, over 23 per cent of the fleet was unemployed and laid up. The earnings of even the most efficient VLCCs trading on the spot market could not cover operating costs and ships less than five years old could be purchased at close to their scrap value.

Another key effect of these developments was that the dominant integrated oil company system was fast collapsing.

Oil companies had become buyers of oil from a much wider variety of sources than in the past when they shipped oil from the fields that they controlled themselves. As a result their whole transport matrix changed and they could no longer carry out efficient transportation with their fleet of owned and long-term chartered tonnage.

A new set of players became prominent in the tanker industry - the independent oil traders. They bought oil from producers and sold it to refiners or other traders in the consuming area, chartering ships at the cheapest possible rate on the spot market. The oil companies formed their own oil trading departments and the previously independent oil company marine departments, now looking after very reduced fleets, became part of the oil trading profit centre.

In more recent years a series of mega-mergers between leading oil companies has further increased their influence on the tanker market. Among other things, this has led to a reduction in long-term charters and put greater emphasis on the spot market.

As a logical reaction to these developments, independent tanker owners have sought to improve the scope and flexibility of their transportation services, and at the same time improve their bargaining position. As part of this initiative, a number of acquisitions and mergers as well as the development of pooling arrangements have taken place amongst the independent shipowners.

Environmental issues have also had a profound effect on tanker shipping over the past two decades. The grounding of the tanker *Exxon Valdez* in 1989 with the subsequent loss of 37,000 tonnes of crude oil into Prince William Sound in Alaska was a defining moment for the industry. Stringent legislation was introduced in the US under the Oil Pollution Act of 1990 (OPA 90), including a requirement that new tankers be built with double hulls and the placing of potentially unlimited liability for an oil spill on the tanker owner. Some of the OPA 90 tanker structural provisions were subsequently adopted by the International Maritime Organization (IMO), with the result that all new oil tankers ordered since the mid-1990s are constructed with double hulls.

The use of double hulls and the implementation of a raft of other safety measures and practices by the industry during the 1990s have undoubtedly had a beneficial effect and brought further improvements to the tanker safety record. Tankers today deliver in excess of 99.998 per cent of their cargoes safely and without incident. As the new century begins, and in line with the public's expectations of nil spills, the industry continues to press ahead with further measures aimed at safe transport and delivery of oil and refined products.

This book sets out to describe the growth of the tanker industry set against the background of the oil industry and the political and economic events which have shaped its progress since the first American oil boom in the early 1860s.

In its long voyage the tanker has generated a series of contrasting images. These differing meanings show that the story of the tanker is a complex and fascinating one, reflecting not only the unpredictable nature of the industry but also the changing perceptions and expectations of the world which the tanker helps to fuel.

From sail to steam
from wood to iron and steel
from barrels to bulk

1859    Oil strike at Titusville, Pennsylvania, US

1861    First transatlantic shipment of oil in barrels

1863    First iron sailing ship purpose-built for bulk oil transport

1870    First oil wells at Baku on Caspian Sea

1878    First iron steam tanker

1886    Forerunner of modern tanker Glückauf delivered

1892    Murex first tanker through Suez Canal

1895    Oil-fired tanker built for Pacific Coast Oil

1901    Oil discovered in Mexico

1908    Major oil strike in Persia

1908    First ship built using Isherwood system

1913    First 15,000 dwt tanker built for Eagle Oil

Chapter One: Beginnings

# The discovery and early production of oil

*In 1859 Edwin Drake, one of the oil pioneers, successfully drilled the first oil well in Titusville, Pennsylvania to a depth of just over 69 feet. The oil was then transported from the site in barrels by horse and cart.*

The foundations of the modern oil industry were laid by Dr Abraham Gesner, a Canadian geologist who invented a method of extracting and refining oil from asphalt or bitumen. In 1854 he took out a US patent for the manufacture of a product which he named kerosene and described as a new liquid hydrocarbon that could be used to provide illumination.

Until Gesner's discovery oil was generally produced from coal or oil shale. This was based on a process for recovering and refining oil from coal developed by James Young, a Scottish chemist who went on to build up a successful business using this technology.

Its main product was a lighting oil called paraffin which was extensively used in Britain and met with some success when it was first introduced to the American market.

However, the prospects for Young's paraffin in America and the shale oil industry in general were cut short by an event in Titusville on the 27 August 1859. That was the day when the Seneca Oil Company's drilling rig struck oil at just over sixty nine feet down. Until that afternoon Titusville had been just another quiet little town in Pennsylvania, USA, but news of the strike spread like wildfire and started a stampede like the Klondike gold rush. Within a year there were no less than 75 wells producing oil in the area and land prices had rocketed around the locality known as Oil Creek.

Production in the first twelve months was a mere 450,000 barrels but soared to over 3 million barrels in 1861 by which time there were also some fifteen refineries operating in that part of Pennsylvania, mostly processing kerosene from crude oil. At that point Russian oil output did not amount to one-twentieth of this quantity, as it was largely controlled by monopoly and confined by geographical reasons to local markets.

Thus, kerosene became the most important product coming out of the US refineries. It was a superior lighting oil, which gave a brighter, cleaner flame for oil lamps than alternative fuels, such as whale oil. It quickly became known as 'the new illuminant'.

This made kerosene an extremely valuable commodity, not only in the US where it was effectively changing the American way of life by extending the hours of daylight, but also in Europe and other parts of the world where big potential export markets were waiting. The tantalising problem was how to deliver it, especially as seafarers were extremely nervous about the hazards of fire and explosion onboard ship.

*US crude oil production increased from 2,000 barrels in 1859 to 61 million barrels in 1896, out of a world total of 114 million barrels that year.*

In the early days the crude oil was moved from the oil well at Titusville, Pennsylvania, USA in iron-hooped barrels and taken to the mouth of Oil Creek by horse and cart. The barrels were then loaded into oil boats and floated down the Allegheny River to Pittsburg where refineries had been set up. The refined oil (kerosene) was again put into barrels and transported to the East Coast markets by railway.

In the early 1860s the Atlantic and Great Western Railroad extended its track up to the oil-producing region in Oil Creek. The crude oil could then be loaded directly onto wooden tank cars which were later replaced by boiler tank cars. But it was not long before the obvious method of dealing with large quantities of liquid was introduced and the crude oil was pumped through pipelines from the wells to the refineries. It was then barreled and transported or pumped to the railway terminal or wharf.

*It is impossible to say precisely when oil was first transported at sea, but the Newchang Junks are probaly one of the oldest. For centuries these craft had been engaged in transporting salt water in bulk up the Chinese rivers to the saltpans. Others carried live fish and in the early part of the eighteenth century some were modified to carry bean oil in bulk.*

*A typical example measured approximately 55 feet in length by 13 feet in beam and could carry some 50 tons of oil. As in more recent designs, the cargo space was divided by transverse bulkheads and provided with a trunk for the expansion of cargo.*

## The 20th century was powered by oil

Oil ushered in the golden age of travel, pioneered by the motor car and later expanded on a huge scale by the airlines, which superseded ocean liners in making international travel affordable for mass markets.

While coal had raised steam for the first industrial revolution, oil fired the second one. In the early days it provided kerosene - a superior fuel for burning in lamps - as well as lubricants to keep the latest high-speed machinery running smoothly. Next, and most importantly, came gasoline for the newfangled automobile. In the wake of this came a cascade of downstream products and petrochemical derivatives, from plastics, fibres and detergents to insecticides, paints and synthetic rubber.

In 1900 oil held a negligible share of the world energy market; 100 years later oil accounted for 40 per cent of a global energy consumption which itself had grown tenfold over the period. In contrast, coal's share of the total had dropped to 27 per cent, while gas accounted for 23 per cent. Other sources of energy made only a marginal contribution. Even nuclear power, which had initially carried such high hopes, provided only 7 per cent of world energy, its credibility undermined by accidents, radiation fears and decommissioning problems with redundant plants.

Over the last 100 years oil thus became the world's most important and versatile source of energy, fuelling everything from power stations, factories and farms to aircraft, ships, trucks and cars. By the end of the century the production of crude oil was running at 3.5 billion tonnes annually to keep pace with a seemingly insatiable demand.

Perversely, crude oil was seldom found in the places where it was most needed. The most valuable resources were often very remote from the centres of industry and, with two-thirds of the planet being covered by water, it was often said that God must be a shipowner.

This is where tanker shipping came to play its vital role.

From the start transportation was the key to the oil industry's phenomenal growth. Without the ability to deliver crude oil to refineries and distribute their products to the marketplace, the oil industry could not have developed as widely or as fast as it did. And certainly not on the international scale which was fundamental to its success.

The growth of the tanker sector mirrored events in the oil industry, with the size and design of ships evolving rapidly to meet burgeoning transportation needs.

One of the early tankers was the 416 ton *Atlantic* built in 1863 for the Petroleum Trading Company of Newcastle-upon-Tyne, England. She was a three-masted sailing ship and like her sistership, *Great Western*, had been built of iron rather than wood.

These ships were purpose-built for a newly emerging trade on the Atlantic, carrying oil (in the form of kerosene) in bulk from producers in the US to expanding markets in Europe. The cargo-carrying spaces in *Atlantic* and *Great Western* were subdivided by a central longitudinal bulkhead and transverse bulkheads and the eight cargo tanks in each ship could carry a total of 700 tons of oil. The two ships were also amongst the first to have their own pumping installations. This equipment could empty the tanks in 24 hours. A similar vessel but with a total tank capacity of 1,400 tons was also built the same year in the Isle of Man for a Mr Gibson. She was named *Ramsay* and could also carry oil in barrels in the 'tween decks.

These early iron-hulled sailing ships were among the first vessels purpose-built for the bulk transportation of oil. Previously, exporters had experimented with oil in barrels but barrels proved too costly, were prone to leakage and were regarded with some fear by the crews. Even so, there were at least 1,000 small sailing ships, ranging in size from 300 to 1,300 tons, engaged in the carriage of oil in barrels in the 1860s. One of these, the 224 ton *Elizabeth Watts*, carried the first transatlantic oil shipment in 1861 when she sailed from Philadelphia to London.

## Oil in barrels gave way to 'case-oil' before bulk shipments developed

To try and solve the problems of barrels, exporters turned to rectangular metal cans, holding five US gallons each and packed two at a time into wooden cases. 'Oil cases' or 'case-oil' proved, however, to be even more expensive than barrels and this spurred exporters to develop the concept of bulk transport. Although bulk transport soon caught on, case-oil continued to be used into the early years of the 20th century, particularly on sailing ships carrying Caspian Sea oil from the Black Sea to the Far East. In addition, the heavy demand for tankers during the First World War led Standard Oil to employ sailing ships to carry case-oil to the Pacific, Australia and China.

Besides the purpose-built iron ships, wooden sailing ships were converted to carry oil in bulk. The first known conversion of this type was the 794 ton *Charles* which in 1869 was fitted with 59 separate tanks. Despite a certain amount of waste from leakage, *Charles* traded successfully between the US and Europe until 1872 when she caught fire and was lost.

The problem of leakage prompted some shipowners to seal the wooden hulls to make them oil-tight. One shipowner, Gustav Conrad Hansen of Tønsberg in Norway, adopted a particularly ingenious approach. Captain Even Tolleffsen, one of his ship masters, developed a design in which the wooden transverse and longitudinal bulkheads installed in the wooden sailing ships to create oil compartments were insulated by tarpaulins. A hand-driven pump was installed as well as an arrangement for interconnecting the tanks.

*The Lindesnæs*
*1869 (674 tons)*

a regular Antwerp-New York service. Passengers were to be accommodated in cabins alongside the cargo tank expansion trunking. Whether or not she ever achieved this dual capability is open to question, as the US authorities would not permit passengers to be carried in such accommodation, while officials in Antwerp refused to allow the construction of storage tanks in the port. Even so, *Vaderland* is noteworthy because she was designed with features that were soon to be adopted as some of the key elements of tanker construction. Tanks were divided into pairs, for example, by a centreline bulkhead and the internal structure of the tanks formed natural cofferdams. In addition, each cargo tank was provided with a separate expansion trunk and the ship's machinery space was located aft.

## Caspian Sea oil trade also develops bulk shipping

In the second half of the 19th century, the Caspian Sea oil trade centred on the oilfields around Baku, was the only rival to that of the Atlantic Ocean shipments of US oil to Europe. Robert and Ludwig Nobel, brothers of Alfred of dynamite fame, dominated the Russian oil trade with their refinery at Baku. By 1884 there were some 200 refineries in the area and Russian oil production had reached 10.8 million barrels, around one-third the level of US production. The Nobel brothers, through their Petroleum Production Company, faced similar logistics problems to the Americans. Oil had to be shipped in barrels across the Caspian Sea in small sailing ships, then on barges up the River Volga for final delivery by rail. The operation was costly and inefficient.

In 1878, six years after *Vaderland* had been built, the Motala shipyard in Sweden delivered *Zoroaster*, an iron steamship of about 400 tons, to the Nobel brothers. Her design originally featured eight cylindrical tanks built independently of the hull which could carry a total of 240 tons of oil. Capacity was later increased to 400 tons by removing the cylinders. Another innovative feature of *Zoroaster* was the use of fuel oil instead of coal to power the engines. In 1885 Black Sea Navigation Company was set up by the Nobel brothers to build a fleet of steamers to compete with America in the supply of oil to Europe.

Gustav Conrad Hansen's vessels, *Lindesnæs, Rolf, Einar,* and *Jan Mayen*, were converted by Fagerheim Vaerft near Tønsberg, Norway. *Einar* and *Rolf* were commanded by Captains Henry Tschudi and Camillo Eitzen, respectively. These sea captains were two of the pioneers in the tanker trade and eventually founded the shipowning company Tschudi & Eitzen, still in operation today in Norway. This concept for converting wooden sailing ships into bulk carriers was successful both technically and commercially. A contract was fixed in 1877 for five years employment with French charterers for the carriage of kerosene from the USA to France. These Gustav Conrad Hansen vessels were amongst the first genuine attempts to provide bulk transportation.

The 1870s saw the introduction of iron steamships for the oil trade. The first such vessel known to be designed to carry oil in bulk was the 2,700 grt double-skinned *Vaderland*, built in 1872 by Palmers of Tyneside for Red Star Line of Antwerp. What made *Vaderland* unique is that she was built to carry passengers as well as oil on

They also took some ships on time charter, a practice which later became very common.

In the 1890s shipowners from the Greek Aegean and Ionian Islands also carried oil in barrels from the Black Sea to the Mediterranean Sea and the Indian Ocean. One notable example is the Kulukundis family who carried oil from Baku to Alexandria with their last sailing ship, *Anastassia*.

Another innovation in the Caspian Sea oil trades was the use of diesel engines to power a 245-foot long oil barge designed for use on the River Volga. *Vandal* was powered by three 120 hp diesel engines located amidships and coupled to three propellers by means of an electric transmission system. This arrangement avoided the need to run propeller shafts through the intervening oil tanks and was one of the first examples of diesel-electric drive. Built by the Nizhni Novgorod's Sormovo shipyard, *Vandal* made her maiden voyage in the spring of 1903. This was marred by engine failure but her subsequent operational performance was excellent.

A number of iron steamships for the carriage of oil in bulk were built in shipyards in Great Britain, the US and Sweden in the 1880s, while several existing ships were converted to carry oil in bulk. One of the first conversions involved the cargo ship *Ferguson* which in 1885 had two rows of iron tanks fitted and equipped with independent connections and pumps by the R Cragg & Sons shipyard in Middlesbrough, England. Separate regulating tanks as well as an overflow cistern allowed for expansion of the oil cargo. Gauze was also used to cover the tank ventilators to reduce the risk of vapour explosions. *Ferguson* was employed by the Nobel brothers' Black Sea Line operating between Batum, on the Black Sea, and Europe.

The early steamship newbuildings were based on traditional cargo ship designs, with the installation of some bulkheads to compartmentalise the internal space. However, the numerous, disparate improvements in ship construction and propulsion systems were leading towards a logical conclusion – the purpose-built petro-leum steamer. That ship was the 2,297 grt *Glückauf* built in 1886 in England.

It is interesting to note that already in 1886 elements that were to shape the design of future tankers - economics, politics, safety, cargo containment, propulsive power - were already in place. Even some of the terms such as horsepower and barrels have remained in our current jargon.

*Oil production in Baku, then a Persian town, dates from about 1300. However, records of mineral oil production prior to 1859, the year of first production in the US, are incomplete. When Baku was annexed by Russia from Persia in 1801, a refiner named Meerzoeff was granted a monopoly for the production of petroleum. By 1849 there were about 130 pit wells around Baku producing 3,340 tons of oil per year. About 3 tons of crude oil were used to produce one ton of kerosene. Even with the relatively poor distillation techniques of the period, kerosene was a superior lamp oil.*

BLACK SEA

CASPIAN SEA

BATUM

BAKU

OIL WELLS

*Barrels, having been used long enough, became the standard measurement which is still used in the oil industry today. The standard barrel is 33 inches long and 25 inches in diameter and one barrel equals 42 US gallons. In the 1860s barrels in the US were made from white oak, glued, reinforced with six or eight metal hoops, painted and fitted with a two-inch bung.*

*The barrels themselves took up to a fifth of the weight of actual cargo and with a full cargo, it was difficult to bring the ship down to her load line. Moreover, barrels were an unhandy cargo, taking a long time to load and unload and very wasteful of space. Only the first class barrels could be used for the more volatile clean products, second class were permitted for crude oil and third class only for residue. During transport they were prone to leakage, often of up to 15 per cent of the contents and, owing to the air spaces and the large areas of oil surface exposed, liable to give rise to explosive mixtures. As it was almost impossible to return the barrels after delivery, they accounted for considerable loss, owing to the their low resale price.*

# Glückauf

## the forerunner of the modern tanker

The delivery of the 2,297 grt *Glückauf* in July 1886 was a significant breakthrough in the evolution of oil tankers. The ship brought together the best features of designs available at the time and she is acknowledged as the forerunner of the modern oil tanker. *Glückauf* was the first vessel to be classified as a 'petroleum steamer' by a classification society, in this case Bureau Veritas Registration Society.

She was the brainchild of Colonel Henry F Swan, one of the leading naval architects of the day, who had such confidence in his design that he persuaded his co-directors at shipbuilders Armstrong Mitchell & Co Ltd on Tyneside in England to build the vessel as a speculative venture.

The Swan design provided an immensely strong hull structure. *Glückauf* was 300 feet long overall,

constructed partly of iron and partly of steel. The shell plating, which was boiler-riveted throughout to prevent leakage, formed the outer wall of the cargo tanks. The cargo space, which had a capacity of 3,020 tons, was divided by longitudinal and transverse bulkheads into eight separate compartments linked by continuous trunking to allow for expansion (the forerunner of side or 'summer' 'tween deck tanks) and all valves were operable from the upper deck. A cargo main ran through the bottom of all the tanks which were also designed to be used as ballast tanks for return journeys. Fore and aft cofferdams were fitted, the latter incorporating the pump room which separated the cargo tanks from the machinery space and coal bunkers. The option of a double bottom, except under the engine room, was rejected in order to eliminate the risk of dangerous

volatile gases accumulating in the under-floor spaces.

With the bridge located amidships and the engine installed aft, the overall layout of *Glückauf* also established a new trend. Barquentine-rigged, she was powered by a triple-expansion steam engine, giving a service speed of 10 knots. *Glückauf* was also fitted with powerful cargo pumps and electric lighting.

While under construction at Wallsend-on-Tyne, the vessel attracted the interest of Wilhelm Anton Riedemann, a successful German shipowner who was also the agent for the German-American Petroleum Company, a subsidiary of Standard Oil. At that time no shipyard in Germany was prepared to engage in tanker shipbuilding due to the safety risks associated with carriage of petroleum products in a single hull vessel. However, Riedemann's experienced eye was quick to see the advantages of Swan's design and he purchased the vessel on completion. The previous year, 1885, he had converted *Andromeda*, an 1,871 ton sailing ship, from barrel carrier to bulk tanker by the installation of 72 cylindrical tanks. This increased her capacity from 12,000 barrels to the equivalent of 17,000 barrels and by 1886 *Andromeda* had successfully completed two voyages between New York and Germany.

It was Riedemann who gave *Glückauf* her name, which means 'good luck' in German. She delivered her first cargo of petroleum products (kerosene) from Philadelphia to Geestemünde (today's Bremerhaven) in autumn 1886. However, her maiden voyage was not without trouble.

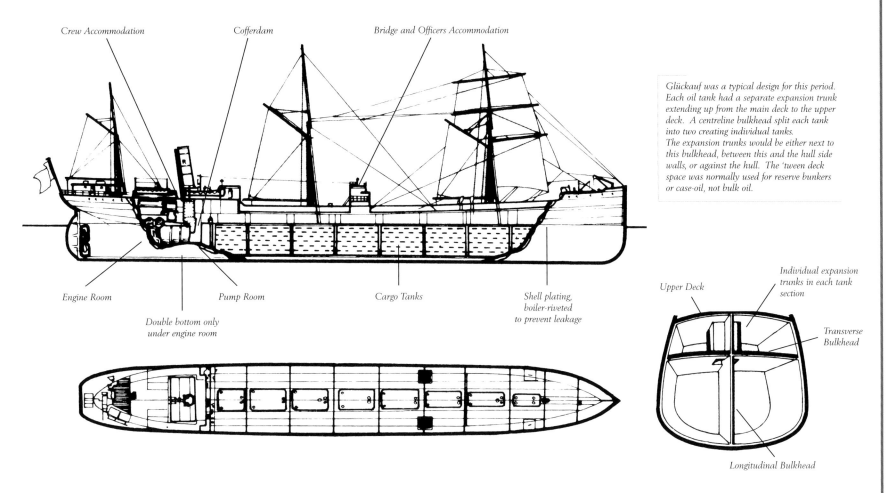

Crew Accommodation

Cofferdam

Bridge and Officers Accommodation

Engine Room

Pump Room

Double bottom only
under engine room

Cargo Tanks

Shell plating,
boiler-riveted
to prevent leakage

*Glückauf* was a typical design for this period.
Each oil tank had a separate expansion trunk
extending up from the main deck to the upper
deck. A centreline bulkhead split each tank
into two creating individual tanks.
The expansion trunks would be either next to
this bulkhead, between this and the hull side
walls, or against the hull. The 'tween deck
space was normally used for reserve bunkers
or case-oil, not bulk oil.

Upper Deck

Individual expansion
trunks in each tank
section

Transverse
Bulkhead

Longitudinal Bulkhead

Before she arrived in New York the longshoremen, and coopers were afraid that that her fast and automated loading systems would put them out of a job; so they organised a protest. They warned the population of New York of the dangers of explosions associated with a steamship that was propelled by a coal-fired engine situated adjacent to cargo tanks laden with highly flammable cargo.

Although the protests did not prevent the ship from docking, people were still sceptical. *Glückauf* had been given the nickname *Fleigauf*, or *Blow Up*, indicating the lingering doubts attached to this new type of merchant ship. Having loaded a full cargo of oil in the US, the master of the ship,

Captain Heinrich Fortmann, discovered that he was not yet out of trouble. Under pressure from the protest groups, the local coal merchants refused to supply *Glückauf* with the bunker coal needed for the return journey to Europe. The tanker was forced to proceed under sail to St John's, Newfoundland where she stocked up with the necessary coal. Following this episode, Reidemann increased the bunker capacity on *Glückauf* so that she could carry enough coal for a round-trip transatlantic voyage.

*Glückauf* continued in service until 1893 when she ran aground off Fire Island near New York. Her less famous sistership, *Vorwärts*, also delivered in

1886, was lost without trace in July 1890, allegedly destroyed by fire while enroute. The disappearance of this ship added fuel to the debate that was raging in the industry at the time - whether a single hull containment system, with the shell plating forming the outer wall of the cargo tank, was safer than a double containment standard in which the oil was carried in an independent tank within the ship's hull. On the whole, the double containment system was deemed to be less safe because of the risk of flammable cargo vapours collecting in the void spaces.

## US oil companies build up tanker fleets

In the US oil companies like John D Rockefeller's Standard Oil and Pacific Coast Oil Company had begun, somewhat slowly, developing their own fleets of tankers. Standard Oil commissioned its first bulk tanker in 1888, while Pacific Coast Oil Company ordered the first ocean-going oil-fired tanker to be built. The 461 ton *George Loomis* was constructed in 1895 by the Union Iron Works of Richmond, California and was the first

steel-hulled tanker built on the West Coast of the United States. In her early years of service she transported nearly 30 per cent of California's entire annual oil production to the Pacific Coast Oil Company's refinery at Point Alameda on San Francisco Bay.

Standard Oil, meanwhile, had built up its fleet to 78 steamships, 19 sailing ships and a large number of tank barges. This fleet carried the company's oil to the US Atlantic and Pacific Coasts, and even as far afield as Europe and Japan. In 1900 Standard Oil acquired Pacific Coast Oil Company and the latter's fleet was expanded with the addition of several tankers and barges, including one self-propelled barge and a stern-wheel steamer. In 1909 Standard Oil was broken up by the US government under the anti-trust Sherman Act into separate oil companies: Standard Oil of New Jersey (the original parent organisation known as Standard, later to become Esso and eventually Exxon); Standard Oil of New York (Mobil); Standard Oil of California (first Socal, then Chevron); Standard Oil of Ohio (Sohio); Standard Oil of Indiana (Amoco); Continental Oil (Conoco); and Atlantic which became part of ARCO and, ultimately, Sun. This break-up of Standard Oil was a major turning point in both the oil and the tanker industries.

Before Standard Oil's break-up, its virtual monopoly of the oil market had been successfully challenged by a new company which had founded itself on the transportation of oil rather than exploration, production or refining.

This new company subsequently moved into production, initially in what was then East Borneo. Marcus Samuel, an English trader in the Far East, recognised the potential growth in the oil trades and saw his opportunity in the movement of oil from the Black Sea to the Far East via the Suez Canal. Sailing via the Canal would give his tankers an enormous advantage over those of Standard Oil, since the British directors of the Canal imposed such strict safety requirements that oil was only allowed to transit in either barrels or as case-oil. Samuel planned to build a fleet of tankers with enough safety features to satisfy the Suez Canal directors, while Standard Oil tankers were forced to sail an extra 4,000 miles around the Cape of Good Hope.

## Tankers built to transit Suez Canal with Russian oil

Samuel first negotiated a supply of Caspian oil from the Rothschilds, the Paris banking house brought in by the Nobel brothers to help finance expansion of the oil trades and which by the 1890s had become the second largest Russian oil group. Samuel then ordered his first tanker.

This ship, the 5,000 dwt *Murex*, built by Gray's shipyard in West Hartlepool, England, and launched in 1892, had water ballast tanks which could be deballasted to lighten her in case of grounding. The vessel's five cargo tanks were located amidships and isolated by cofferdams from the forehold and forepeak forward and the boiler and engine room aft to provide protection in the event of a collision. To reduce lateral cargo surge, an oil-tight bulkhead ran through the centre of the tanks which were also fitted with top trunking to allow for cargo expansion and to minimise the free surface.

*Murex* also featured a pumping system that could load or discharge the cargo tanks in 12 hours and a steam tank-cleaning system which enabled the ship, after discharging its Russian oil and washing the tank walls, to carry backload cargoes from the Far East such as tea, cereals or rice. On its inaugural voyage in August 1892, *Murex* carried over 4,000 tons of oil through the Suez Canal. By the end of 1893 Samuel had had another 10 similar tankers built and within the next two years made 69 voyages through the Canal with ships he owned or chartered.

In 1897 Samuel's successful venture became Shell Transport & Trading Company Ltd, which assumed ownership of the expanding fleet and other assets.

Expansion continued through the acquisition of oilfields in East Borneo, as well as the development of storage and distribution activities in India and throughout the Far East. However, in 1900 the new company faced a serious problem when the price of kerosene slumped due to oversupply at a time when Samuel had been heavily stockpiling oil. A year later, however, Shell's fortunes seemed to have turned round when Samuel secured a 21-year agreement with the owners of a huge new oil find in the US at Spindletop, Texas to carry half their production with a minimum delivery of 100,000 tons.

*The Suez Canal authorities issued new regulations for bulk oil tankers in January 1892, having previously banned the movement of oil through the waterway other than as consignments of case-oil in cargo ships as a safety measure. The alternative route for shipments of oil in bulk to the Far East was around Africa via the Cape of Good Hope. The design features of the new Shell tanker Murex satisfied the Suez Canal authorities that this ship would be able to carry oil in bulk safely through the Canal. It is interesting to note that tanker safety and environmental protection was already an issue of strong debate in 1892.*

The first Spindletop cargo was delivered by the Shell tanker *Pinna* from Port Arthur in Texas to Europe in July 1901, but by the following year the Texan wells had run dry. Some of the tankers were converted into cattle carriers. There were also problems with tanker charters in the Far East and at one stage half the Shell tanker fleet was laid up. Having rejected an earlier offer from Standard Oil to purchase the company, Samuel eventually gave in to Royal Dutch Oil which acquired 60 per cent of his company. Transportation and ownership, including ownership of the fleet, now came under a new subsidiary, Anglo-Saxon Petroleum.

## Tanker fleet expands, steamships get larger and faster

By 1900 the world's deepsea tanker fleet numbered 145 ships amounting to around 600,000 tons, including 60 steam-powered tankers in the transatlantic trades where bulk shipments had virtually replaced parcel shipments of kerosene. By 1900 the oil trade between the US and Europe had expanded to 2.3 million tons. In contrast Russia had only limited deepsea exports to the Far East via the Suez Canal, the majority of its oil trade being restricted to the Caspian and Black Sea routes.

The cargo capacity of the largest tankers had also increased to around 12,000 tons, a figure which would be surpassed with the development of tankers in the Eagle Oil fleet. This company had been set up by Weetman Pearson, later Lord Cowdray, to explore and produce oil in Mexico. By 1912 Eagle Oil was pumping 1,100,000 barrels a day. To help distribute the oil, Pearson set up the Eagle Oil Transport Company in 1912 and a fleet of 19 new 'state of the art' tankers was ordered from British shipyards - nine ships of 9,000 deadweight tons (dwt) and 10 of 15-16,000 dwt. In practice it was found the larger ships were able to transport a ton of oil at a cost that was 10 per cent below the level of their smaller sisters on an average voyage. Until then, 9,000 dwt had been thought to be the most economical size.

The first 15,000 dwt ship, *San Fraterno*, was delivered in 1913 by the Swan Hunter yard on Tyneside in England. This caused something of a sensation at the time as it represented a huge leap in size. She was not only considered to be the biggest tanker in the world but also incorporated many novel features. Her 12 holds were divided by longitudinal bulkheads into 24 separate tanks equipped with steam-heating coils to speed up unloading which, with the most powerful pumps yet fitted to a tanker, could now be achieved at a rate of 1,200 tons an hour.

*San Fraterno* and her sisterships also represented the first large-scale adoption of quadruple-expansion steam engines, giving them a service speed of 10 knots. They had been designed to run on either coal or fuel oil but were later totally oil-fired. Safety was a big consideration, not only in their construction, but also in how they were fitted out. To increase navigational safety the new ships had the most up-to-date equipment, including sounding machines, magnetic compasses and Admiralty charts, as well as the latest telegraphy equipment. This was at a time when most masters were expected to provide their own chronometers and charts.

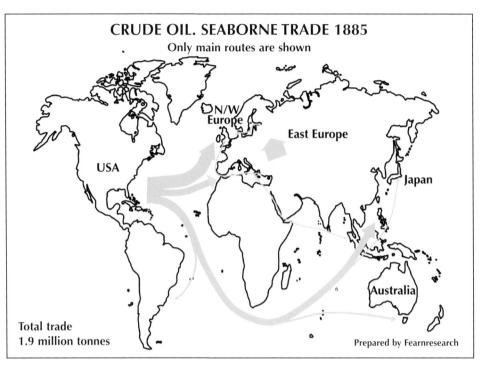

## CRUDE OIL. SEABORNE TRADE 1885
### Only main routes are shown

USA

N/W Europe

East Europe

Japan

Australia

Total trade
1.9 million tonnes

Prepared by Fearnresearch

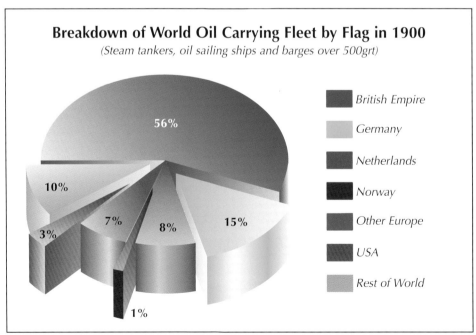

## Breakdown of World Oil Carrying Fleet by Flag in 1900
*(Steam tankers, oil sailing ships and barges over 500grt)*

56%

10%

3%

7%

8%

15%

1%

- British Empire
- Germany
- Netherlands
- Norway
- Other Europe
- USA
- Rest of World

In 1902 Thomas W Lawson - the world's only seven-masted schooner - had been built to carry coal for the US coastal trade. She was later converted to carry oil in bulk, mainly between Texas and Philadelphia for the Anglo-American Oil Company, the British subsidiary of Standard Oil.

She was constructed in steel by the Fore River Shipbuilding Company of Quincy, Massachusets, USA in 1902. Although she was a big vessel, with a tonnage of 5,218 grt, a length of 385 feet and a 50 feet beam, she could be handled by a crew of only sixteen men, as her rig and steering were operated by steam.

On her first transatlantic delivery of oil for Anglo-American in 1907 she came to a tragic end when she was wrecked near the Scilly Isles, off the south west coast of England in a hurricane.

The Eagle Oil tankers also set new standards in crew facilities. Libraries, sport and entertainment facilities were included, while the accommodation was equipped with mosquito netting and electric ventilation fans.

Refrigeration also ensured a supply of fresh vegetables and meat, even on the longest voyages. Such high standards of comfort enabled Eagle Oil to attract good crews, including officers from the big liner companies.

## Unusual 'cart-and-horse' oil carrier crosses Atlantic

In the first decade of the new century, cargoes even bigger than those carried by Eagle Oil's tankers were shipped across the Atlantic by a unique system known as the 'cart and horse'. This involved a steam tanker towing a barge, giving a combined cargo capacity of 18,000 tons.

The tanker was the 11,800 grt *Iroquois*, built in 1907 by Harland & Wolff of Belfast for Anglo-American Oil Company, the British subsidiary of Standard Oil.

The barge, named *Navahoe* was, in fact, a six-masted fore and aft rigged sailing vessel. *Iroquois* was the first large tank steamer to be fitted with twin propellers and two sets of quadruple-expansion steam engines, giving her a speed of 10 knots when laden with her tow.

*Navahoe* could slip her tow if the strain became too great for *Iroquois* and on one such voyage she proceeded under sail and arrived ahead of *Iroquois*. Between 1909 and 1917 the two made 148 Atlantic crossings, while *Iroquois* had been built so strongly that she continued in service until she was 40 years old.

In the 1890s and 1900s Anglo-American owned one of the biggest fleets of sailing vessels in the world, comprising 16 steel-hulled windjammers. While many were originally designed to carry case-oil, they were later converted for the bulk shipment of oil. One such was the 3,765 grt *Brilliant*, believed to be the world's largest four-masted vessel, built by Russell & Co of Glasgow in 1901.

These ships could sail at speeds of up to 15 knots and, before they were converted to carry oil in bulk, could carry more than a million gallons of case-oil.

The company, however, was already moving towards steam tankers. In 1898 Anglo-American took delivery from Scotts of Greenock in Scotland of what was then the largest tanker, the 6,117 grt *Tuscarora*, built with machinery amidships. She was followed by the even larger 9,196 grt *Narraganset*, with a cargo capacity of 12,000 tons and a speed of over 13 knots, making her the largest and fastest tanker of her time. She had three decks, 18 transverse and two longitudinal bulkheads, and contained 27 separate cargo tanks, each equipped with steam-cleaning. She was also designed to carry general cargo at the sides of the 'tweendecks.

On one of her best runs she made the trip from Tyneside, England to New York in ballast and back to the Thames at London with a full cargo in 27 days.

*Iroquois (the horse)*

By 1907 Anglo-American owned one of the biggest tanker fleets under the UK's Red Ensign flag, including 19 ocean-going tank steamers, four case-oil steamers and 16 sailing ships.

However an important breakthrough which would enable much larger tankers to be built was made the following year when Joseph Isherwood developed a new construction method.

*Tuscarora, built 1898*

*Brilliant*

*During the 1880s and 1890s the Anglo-American Oil Company, the British subsidiary of Standard Oil, owned one of the world's biggest fleets of oil sailers. In 1901 Brilliant, together with her sistership Daylight, were launched. Brilliant was in the record books as the largest windjammer under the British flag and the largest four-masted vessel in the world. Brilliant was a 3,765 gt barque of steel construction built by Russell & Co of Glasgow in 1901. She was originally designed to load case-oil but was later converted to carry oil in bulk. Brilliant and Daylight were named after the end uses to which their valuable cargoes would be put - lamp oil. Besides her captain, her crew consisted of 3 mates, 1 bosun, 1 sailmaker, 1 carpenter, 1 donkey-man, 2 cooks, 2 stewards, 6 apprentices and 28 able-seamen – quite a different crew from that of a tanker in 2001.*

*Navahoe (the cart)*

# The Isherwood System

## Sir Joseph Isherwood patents new stronger ship hull construction method

From the earliest days, even as far back as the Chinese Newchang junks, shipbuilders had used longitudinal bulkheads to divide tank space and make hulls stiffer.

However, the construction of tankers and the provision made to ensure the safe and economical transport of crude oil and its ever-increasing range of byproducts had been steadily improved since *Glückauf*. Nevertheless, lack of longitudinal strength remained a problem, especially when engines and machinery were placed aft to enable a continuous run of tanks, pipework and trunking through the vessel. This put enormous strain on conventional hulls, particularly when loading, discharging or in ballast, sometimes causing hulls to buckle.

As tankers became bigger, the problem got worse and the traditional form of construction - which adopted the transverse framing method used in wooden ship construction limited the size of iron and steel ships to about 12,000 tons. Placing the engines amidships was tried but this meant fitting extra cofferdams and running the propeller shaft tunnel through the aft tanks. Furthermore, the riveted hulls were prone to flexing which allowed gas to fill the tunnels.

The problem was solved by Sir Joseph Isherwood, a former surveyor with Lloyd's Register of Shipping who, in 1906, developed a longitudinal framing system which he later patented in 1908. Known as the 'Isherwood System', it has been used, with slight modification, ever since.

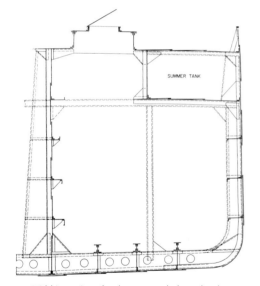

Midship section of early transversely framed tanker

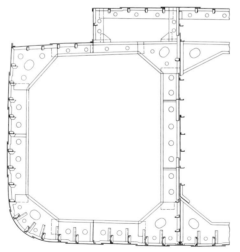

Midship section of the first Isherwood tanker, *Paul Paix*

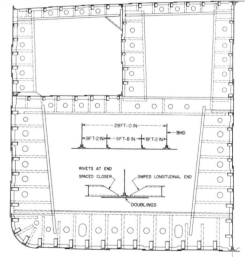

Midship section of a tanker on the Isherwood "bracketless" system

With his first application of the longitudinal framing system in 1908, Sir Joseph Isherwood had the greatest impact on tanker construction of all naval architects. His design enabled the construction of much stronger ships, able to withstand better the stresses and strains experienced by a tanker hull as it proceeds through the sea laden with cargo. It also allowed much larger ships to be built than had previously been possible. Until Isherwood introduced his concept, most ships had been built around a framework somewhat similar to an animal's rib cage. Transverse frames had been attached to a strong centre keel. These were joined at the top by beams and supported along the sides by stringers and by the shell plating or planking itself.

In contrast, the Isherwood approach utilised a number of strong, longitudinal plates, or frames, running the length of the ship and supported by a limited number of heavy, vertical, transverse frames to produce a latticework of girders. The resulting ship was not only much stronger than its predecessors, it was also much easier to build and maintain. Isherwood continued to modify and improve upon the basic design, introducing the bracketless and combined longitudinal/transverse framing systems in the 1920s.

Traditionally, tankers had been built with a single keel from which numerous transverse frames branched off to form the ribs to which the plating was attached. A longitudinal bulkhead and a number of transverse bulkheads were fitted to divide the tank space and prevent the cargo from surging when the ship rolled or pitched in a seaway as this could destabilise the vessel.

In Isherwood's design the frames ran fore and aft through the ship, parallel with the keel. The frames were joined to each other and to the keel by deep transverse floors and vertical bulkheads which also divided the tanks, and by a continuous longitudinal bulkhead.

The resulting structure was not only very rigid but also used less steel in its construction than the traditional method.

The first tanker to incorporate Isherwood's ideas was the 6,600 dwt *Paul Paix* built in 1908 by the Craggs Shipyard of Middlesbrough for John Lennard & Sons. By 1914 a further 276 ships had been built using the new system.

However, brackets were found to cause oil leakage and Isherwood later modified the system by eliminating all brackets to the longitudinals. In July 1926 the first ship with the Isherwood 'bracketless system', the 7,100 grt *British Inventor*, was delivered by Palmers, Newcastle to the British Tanker Company and she was highly successful.

Isherwood later took an interest in the shape of the outer hull and from experiments in the early 1930s developed an 'Arcform' rounded form design, the sides of the ship being arched or curved instead of straight. In 1935 the 10,627 grt *G S Walden* was the first vessel to be built to the new 'Isherwood arc' form of construction.

To demonstrate the efficiency of the system, her Dutch builders also produced a very similar ship on conventional lines, powered by equivalent machinery and designed to carry the same deadweight. Both hulls were of equal length and draught, but the Isherwood type had nearly six feet more beam and proved slightly faster.

The construction method was well received, particularly by American owners who commissioned a number of new tankers built to this new 'Arcform' system.

*1908 marked the beginning of a new era of safer and stronger tanker construction. Paul Paix was the first ship to be constructed to the Isherwood longitudinal system of framing.*

The magnificent five-masted sailing ship Preussen was built at Geestemünde, Germany, in 1902 and made regular fast voyages between Germany and the West Coast of America.

At 5,081 grt and with an overall length of 409 feet, she was the biggest sailing ship afloat when she made a world circumnavigation in 1908, during the course of which she set a record by rounding Cape Horn for the twentieth time.

Under her master, Captain R Petersen – who had been in command since her maiden voyage – she left Hamburg on 10 March 1908 for New York where she loaded a cargo of case-oil for delivery to Japan. Starting on 27 May, the trip took 112 days and she spent a month unloading the cargo in Yokohama before departing on 16 October for Chile, where she arrived on 31 December. There was a three-week stay in Chile before she left on 21 January 1909 to return to Hamburg. She was sighted off Dungeness in the English Channel on 31 March.

Sadly, she was later wrecked near South Foreland off the English coast in November 1910 when she was in a collision which carried away her foremast.

# Tonnage - of ships and cargoes

## Ships' Tonnage: Grt-Dwt-Tons

The tonnage of a ship, which provides an indication of its size, is measured in different ways. The gross register tonnage (grt) is a volumetric measurement and the basis on which ship manning and safety regulations are applied, and registration fees are reckoned. Gross register tonnage is also often used in the calculation of port charges. The cubic capacity of the enclosed revenue-earning and some additional spaces in a ship is fed into a formula to yield the grt of the vessel in tons. The other main indicator of a ship's size is its deadweight tonnage (dwt) which is the maximum number of tons of cargo and stores bunkers etc a ship can carry to bring the vessel down to its allotted loadline, as shown on the Plimsoll Mark. Another ship tonnage is net register tonnage (nrt) which is the space available for cargo and passengers. Nrt is calculated by deducting those spaces considered necessary for operating the vessel from grt. For tankers, deadweight - the maximum number of tons of oil the ship can carry - is the most relevant tonnage measurement.

This book primarily indicates the size of tankers in deadweight tons, although for many of the early oil-carrying ships the only figures available are the gross register tonnage, and grt figures are given. For a number of the early ships described in these pages, historical records fail to indicate whether the tonnage was grt, nrt or dwt. In such cases the ship is described as a vessel of so many tons, e.g. a 400-ton ship. Depending on the size and construction date of the tanker, the grt is, on average, just over half the dwt figure.

## Ships' Tonnage: Background

The word 'ton' is a nautical term derived from the 'tun', a large wooden cask in which wine was transported, originally from France to England as early as the 13th century. A tun was equivalent to four hogsheads, or 252 'old wine' gallons. The word 'tuns' from the 19th century, later became 'barrel' a measurement still used in oil transport today. The measurement of a ship in those days was by tunnage, or the number of tuns of wine she could carry in her holds. Tunnage was also the tax levied on each tun or barrel of wine imported into England, while 'tonnage' became a tax, first levied in 1303 by Edward I, on all imports brought by ship into England. Tonnage quickly became established as the charge for the hire of a ship at so much a ton of her burthen, or cargo-carrying capacity. This wine cask-based system of measuring a ship's size remained in use until the Builders Old Measurement formula for calculating the tonnage of a ship was adopted by an Act of Parliament in 1773.

Life at sea remained a hazardous occupation and many lives were lost due to overloaded ships. Such 'coffin ships', as they came to be known, were often heavily insured against loss by their owners. Samuel Plimsoll was a British Member of Parliament who campaigned for better conditions for seamen. His Plimsoll Mark, or Plimsoll Line, became compulsory in Britain under the provisions of the Merchant Shipping Act of 1876, passed after a long and bitter parliamentary struggle. From that time all British merchant ships were required to have this Mark painted on their sides amidships indicating the draught level to which the ship could safely be loaded.

The Plimsoll Mark, which is now universally accepted through the adoption of the International Load Line Convention in 1930, shows six loading levels for varying conditions of season and location, thus taking into account differing water densities. As a result of Samuel Plimsoll's efforts, the British Board of Trade was also given strict powers of ship inspection.

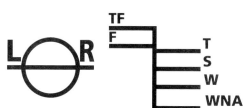

DECK LINE

TF: Tropical Fresh
F: Fresh
T: Tropical
S: Summer
W: Winter
WNA: Winter North Atlantic

## Cargo Tonnage: Tons - Tonnes

The other tonnage figure used in the book is that which indicates the magnitude of the oil trade, e.g. a global annual trade of 40 million tons. Traditionally, the ton used was the British Imperial or avoirdupois ton of 2,240 pounds. However, in line with the global shift to the metric system, in recent decades this trade has come to be measured in metric tonnes, a tonne being equal to 1,000 kilogrammes. A metric tonne is equivalent to 2,205 pounds, and so is only 1.6 per cent less than the Imperial ton. As such, the two tonnage measurements of the oil trade can be taken to be approximately equivalent.

# Oil's vital role in war, post-war expansion, global trade slump, newbuilding orders surge again

| | |
|---|---|
| 1914-18 | *First World War, oil's vital role, tankers sunk* |
| 1917 | *Prestol built with 14-knot service speed* |
| 1918 | *17,000 dwt tankers built* |
| 1919-21 | *Experimental ferro-concrete tankers built* |
| 1920 | *Largest motor tanker and first US diesel-electric tanker* |
| 1921 | *The forerunner of the so-called combination oil/bulk carrier* |
| 1927 | *Oil discovered in Iraq* |
| 1931 | *Japanese tanker records 17.5 knots* |
| 1931 | *Oil discovered in Bahrain* |
| 1934 | *Schierwater Plan adopted* |
| 1934 | *International Tanker Owners' Association inaugurated* |
| 1934 | *First cargo loaded in Arabian Gulf* |
| 1935 | *First all-welded tanker built* |
| 1938 | *Oil discovered in Saudi Arabia and Kuwait* |
| 1939 | *First large tanker fitted with turbo-electric machinery* |
| 1939 | *US tanker fleet reaches 13.7m dwt* |
| 1939 | *First Saudi Arabian crude cargo lifted* |

Chapter Two:
First World War and depression

*Sir Winston Leonard Spencer Churchill was twice Lord of the Admiralty, on each occasion at the outbreak of a world war. During the second war he then served as Prime Minister but continued to take a close interest in naval operations*

## First World War

The First World War demonstrated how vital oil had become, fuelling, as it did, navies and, increasingly, motorised armies. The conflict also showed how the control and supply of oil were essential ingredients of success.

Germany's submarines were powered by diesel-electric engines and the British Navy's latest steam-driven warships were oil-fired, as were many cargo vessels engaged in the vital work of transporting supplies. Aircraft fuelled by aviation fuel also became an important arm of the military.

## British Navy switches from coal to oil fuel before war begins

Britain's and Germany's essential supplies, including oil, had to be imported by sea. The British Navy had only switched from coal to oil just before the outbreak of war. Marcus Samuel of Shell Transport and Trading Company had succeeded in his lobbying efforts, thanks to the support given by Winston Churchill in his role as First Lord of the Admiralty. By 1911 the Navy was building a batch of 56 destroyers which were oil-fired and in 1914 *Queen Elizabeth* was commissioned - the first of five oil-fired, steam-powered battleships. In the 1914-18 war this gave the British a valuable advantage over the German Navy which was coal-burning and could only replenish bunkers from its home ports, thereby limiting the range and flexibility of its ships.

German U-boats, however, proved devastatingly effective and by the end of the war had sunk - mostly by torpedo attacks - some 2,479 merchant ships, including tankers amounting to 7,759,000 tons, with the loss of over 14,000 lives.

Tankers were among the early casualties. The Norwegian ship *Belridge*, carrying a cargo of oil from New Orleans to Amsterdam, was torpedoed and sunk in the English Channel in February 1915. Over the next three years Norway alone lost 889 ships and 2,000 seafarers, nearly all to U-boats.

Shell placed its tanker fleet at the service of the British government and suffered its first and largest loss of the war in March 1916 when the 10,000 dwt *Goldmouth*, carrying a cargo of fuel oil from Borneo, was ambushed by a U-boat on the surface about 40 miles west of Land's End, off the British south west coast. In December that year *Murex*, Marcus Samuel's first ship, was sunk and by the time the war ended Shell had lost 11 tankers totalling nearly 55,000 dwt.

Another key provider of oil for Britain was the Anglo-Persian Oil Company which, by the end of the war, was producing 18,000 barrels per day from its Abadan refinery in what was then Persia, and supplying 20 per cent of the British Navy's total fuel requirements. During the war the company decided to set up its own shipping operations - mainly because of soaring freight rates - and formed the British Tanker Company (which later became BP) to own and manage its ships. Two new 5,600 dwt tankers were ordered as the nucleus of the fleet, the first of which was *British Emperor*, built by Armstrong Whitworth & Co. Within two years the company had launched a further five new 10,000 dwt vessels, plus two of 5,000 dwt, and acquired an additional 15 tankers. Two of these were sunk in the war, but by 1919 the fleet had grown to 21 ships.

By 1917 Britain was running desperately short of oil, but in April that year the US entered the war. During April alone, 430 Allied merchant ships amounting to 852,000 tons were sunk and it was estimated that less than six million tons of shipping, including tankers, was left to bring supplies to Britain. By the end of May the British Navy was down to 10 weeks' supply of oil. The loss of six tankers from Standard Oil - including the brand new *John D Archbold* - added to the problem.

## Convoy system, higher shipyard output help turn tide

What saved the situation for Britain and her Allies were the convoy system, which had been adopted to protect merchant shipping, and increased shipbuilding output.

The former meant that by November 1917 losses had been reduced from 500,000 tons a month to 200,000 tons. In particular, it enabled two million American troops to be brought to Europe without a single loss of life. The second factor meant ships were being built faster than they were being sunk by the Germans. For example, in October 1918 approximately 511,000 tons of new shipping was launched, against 118,600 tons lost. Two of the new tankers launched about this time were unusually large for their day. The 17,000 dwt *Cadillac* and her sistership *Saranac* were built by Palmers of Newcastle-on-Tyne for the Anglo-American Oil Company. Powered by quadruple-expansion steam engines driving single propellers, they had a service speed of 10.5 knots.

## Standard ship types built, ingenious cargo expansion methods

In this race against time the concept of the 'Standard Ship' was adopted in order to speed up construction. A good example of this was the 8,000 grt 'Z' type tanker which had its triple-expansion steam engine located amidships, providing a service speed of 11 knots. A total of 34 were built, with 15 being sold to the British Admiralty and most of the remainder going to the Anglo-Saxon Petroleum Company.

A number of fast tankers were also built specifically for the British Admiralty to transport oil across the Atlantic. The 5,900 dwt *Leaf* class, which were fitted with triple-expansion steam engines placed amidships and driving twin propellers, were capable of 15 knots.

*Prestol* was an example of another type of fast tanker launched from British shipyards in 1917. Designed for fleet use by the British Navy, this tanker type provided a capacity of around 2,000 tons with a speed of 14 knots.

*In 1919 one of the first deep sea motor tankers Vulcanus, 1,194 dwt was delivered for Shell. Her diesel internal combustion engine (compared to a steam engine) was more efficient and could undertake voyages as long as 88 days without refuelling. She needed to carry, by weight, only one-fifth of the fuel that a coal-fired steamship of similar size would require and instead of 16 engine-room crew of an equivalent coal-fired ship, Vulcanus needed only 5. However it took nearly 20 years for the development of the diesel engine to become generally accepted. The Norwegians specifically built motor tankers as they quickly realised their economic advantage and the benefits of the diesel engine.*

*The tanker Belridge carrying a cargo of oil from New Orleans to Amsterdam was torpedoed and sunk in the English Channel in early 1915*

In addition to tanker newbuildings, a number of standard dry cargo ships were converted to carry oil, as were several passenger ships. The frantic scramble for more tanker tonnage even led to the conversion of a few sailing ships by fitting them with engines. Standard Oil actually utilised sailing ships to replace tankers appropriated by the British government for war service and acquired the full-rigged ships *Dunsyre* and *John Ena* for this purpose. The company also commissioned the four-masted schooner *La Merced* and used this new sailing fleet to carry case-oil around the Pacific as far as Australia and New Zealand.

The early years of the First World War also marked the emergence of the Norwegian motor tanker fleet - one of its first vessels was the 5,000 grt *Hamlet*, built in 1915 by Götaverken of Gothenburg, Sweden for Bruusgaard Kjøsterud of Drammen in Norway. This ship, after several name changes and owners, remained in service until she was 40 years old.

A highly innovative World War One idea, pioneered by Shell, was to utilise the double bottom of cargo ships to carry oil. Some 1,280 vessels were converted for this purpose and provided a capacity equivalent to 100 new tankers. From the time it was introduced in June 1917 to the end of the war, over a million tons of oil were carried to the UK by the double bottom method.

Shell also developed the idea of converting dry cargo ships to tankers by fitting cylindrical tanks in their holds. This system enabled a further 100,000 tons of oil to be delivered.

The ability of the Allies to keep the oil flowing was a major factor in their victory. In contrast, by October 1918 Germany was facing a petroleum crisis and it was estimated that the battle at sea could not be continued for more than a few months. The industries which were dependent on oil had only two months' supply; industrial lubricants were due to run out in six months; while air and mechanised land warfare would stop within two months. However, the war ended in November 1918.

At one of the most critical stages of the conflict Marshall Foch, the commander of the Allied armies, stated: "We must have oil or we shall lose the war." After the war Lord Curzon, the British Foreign Secretary, summed it up aptly: "The Allies floated to victory on a wave of oil."

The tanker industry had played no small part in providing that vital lifeline.

## Post-war boom, surge in tanker newbuildings

An immediate trade bonanza followed the end of World War One due to the pent-up demand for raw materials, foodstuffs and manufactured goods which had been in short supply for four years. This created a boom in shipping and there was a surge of newbuilding to replace tonnage lost in the war.

The oil companies not only led the way in rebuilding their own fleets - continuing to dominate the market throughout the 1920s - but they also encouraged independent operators to take a bigger role. This may not have been entirely altruistic, because when a downturn came it was usually the independents who had to lay up their ships first.

The Eagle Oil Transport Company of Mexico was in the forefront of fleet replacement to make good wartime losses of some 56,000 grt. In 1919 they started a five-year shipbuilding programme for 25 new tankers, including six of between 18,000 and 19,000 dwt each which were to be among the largest in the world at that time. Following the

Sweden's first tanker Varjag under construction at Gotaverken shipyard in 1913 - at that time the biggest ship ordered from a Swedish shipyard. She was 7,210 dwt and a new slipway had to be built to manage the job. Although the Varjag was ordered in 1913, by the brothers Nobel in Baku, the First World War prevented them from taking over the ship in 1916. She was then sold to Bruusgaard Kiosteruds D/S in Drammen, Norway and renamed Hamlet. The vessel's hull was built with two longitudinal bulkheads, a new type of design at the time and she was driven by a pair of two-stroke 'polar' diesel engines of 3200 bhp giving a 10 knots service speed. This ship, after several name changes and owners, remained in service until 1955.

retirement of Lord Cowdray in 1919, the company transferred the management of its Mexican interests - including the Eagle Oil fleet - to Royal Dutch Shell.

Royal Dutch Shell also needed to expand its own Anglo-Saxon fleet but found it expedient to buy existing ships first, including some that the company had managed during the war years. In 1919 they purchased 23 tankers amounting to 134,346 grt and the following year acquired another nine, adding a further 44,465 grt. Newbuilding commenced in 1920 and the company set a precedent by using non-British shipyards for the first time. The initial order was for eight ships, of which the first - the 5,767 grt *Acardo* - was built by Union Construction Company of Oakland, California. A further batch of nine tankers was built in 1921-22, of which four were also built by Union Construction; four by Whampoa Dockyard of Hong Kong; and one by W S Bailey & Co, also of Hong Kong.

## Anglo-Persian expands with 22 steam turbine tankers

Other oil companies, including the Anglo-Persian Oil Company, were also adding to their tanker tonnage.
Between 1921 and 1923, the subsidiary British Tanker Company built 22 steam turbine - driven tankers to a design similar to that of their 10,900 dwt *British Advocate*. By 1939, to keep up with Anglo-Persian's increasing need for oil transportation, the company's fleet had grown to 93 ships. While new ships were usually built of steel, three experimental tankers were constructed of ferro-concrete for the US Shipping Board between 1919 and 1921. The 6,144 grt *Palo Alto* and *Peralta* were built on the US West Coast, while *Dinsmore* was built by Bentley's of Jacksonville, Florida. All three were equipped with triple-expansion steam engines and designed for a service speed of 10 knots. However, they were not a great success and never found a role in regular service.

In 1921 Bethlehem Steel of the US built *G Harrison Smith* - a ship believed to be the forerunner of the so-called combination oil/ore carriers. This vessel carried ore in centrally located hoppers which were surrounded by spaces. These spaces were subdivided by bulkheads to form tanks which held oil. In service the ship was mainly used to carry Mexican oil to South America and to bring back cargoes of ore.

## Largest motor tanker built in Germany

About the same time the world's largest motor tanker made its appearance. This was the 9,932 dwt *Wilhelm A Riedmann*, a ship that had originally been launched in 1914 but was not completed until 1920. She was one of a series of large motor tankers built for the German-American Petroleum Company by Krupp of Germany and was powered by a pair of six-cylinder diesel engines of 2,800 bhp each driving twin propellers. In 1929 Krupp built *California Standard* for Socal. With a capacity of 18,000 dwt, this was the largest ship of its type in the German-American fleet.

Standard Oil also increased the size of its fleet during the 1920s. Most of the new tankers were built by Krupp, including a batch of 11 standard type vessels each of 12,000 dwt and 11 knots service speed.
By 1926 the company owned the largest diesel-powered fleet in the world, providing more than 300,000 tons of cargo capacity.

In the early 1920s Standard Oil Company of California (it became known as Socal in 1926) needed more and larger tankers to deliver new crude oil production from Mexico and serve the growing market for gasoline. Among the tankers that were commissioned was *Charlie Watson* which, when launched in 1920, was the first American tanker with diesel-electric drive. She was followed by several ships built by Bethlehem Shipbuilding Corporation of Alameda, including *F H Hillman, H M Storey, W S Rheem* and *K R Kingsbury*, all of 16,000 dwt.
The last of these was powered by a diesel engine that gave an 11 knots service speed.
This tanker carried refined petroleum from the US West Coast to US Atlantic Coast markets via the Panama Canal soon after its launch in 1921.

## Independent owners' share of fleet rises to 25 per cent

However, these new ships built or bought by the oil majors did not increase the dominance of the oil transportation markets enjoyed by these companies before the war. At the start of the 20th century oil companies had owned about 90 per cent of the total tanker fleet, while independent owners controlled 10 per cent. But during the 1920s the oil companies' share dropped to about 82 per cent, while the independents extended their share to 18 per cent.

The most significant factor in the development of the independent tanker sector was the growth of the Norwegian fleet, which rapidly became a major force in the market. By 1939 Norwegian owned tankers numbered 170 vessels.

The Standard Oil Company of California built in the early 1920s a number of larger tankers to deliver crude oil from Mexico.
The picture shows one of these vessels W S Rheem, with its war time armaments, unloading its cargo at Point Wells, near Seattle, Washington during World War Two

The Norwegians had initially been more heavily involved in whaling and whale oil, although the doyen of that industry at the time, Wilh. Wilhelmsen, had his first petroleum tanker, the British-built 10,360 dwt *San Joaquin* launched in 1913. By the end of the First World War he owned 10 similar vessels - all on long-term charter to American oil companies.

Among those who started in the whaling business before branching out into tankers were Anders Jahre and Thor Dahl, but often it was a two-way process. Occasionally, tankers came in handy for those in the whaling industry. In 1905 whalermen had converted an old tanker (also British-built) into a factory ship to allow harpooned whales to be flensed alongside, rather than being towed back to a shore station.

With the advent of the First World War, whale oil was used for lubricants and was also a key element in the production of the high explosive nitroglycerine, which made it an extremely valuable commodity. After the war more tankers were converted to factory ships by fitting stern slipways to winch whales on board for flensing on deck. This was a more efficient process and four ex-Eagle Oil tankers were acquired for this purpose. Purpose-built factory ships were also ordered. These were essentially built to a basic tanker design of around 15,000 dwt with a superimposed factory deck.

Anders Jahre A/S of Sandefjord, Norway began transporting whale oil from factory ships to Europe in 1929 in *Ranvik*, an ex-British Tanker Company ship formerly named *British Knight*. One of the first purpose-built factory whaling ships, *Kosmos*, was built in Belfast in 1929. The Viking Whaling Company - set up by whaling men Johan Rasmussen and Toger Moe with the help of a young Erling Næss - ordered a similar vessel, *Vikingen*, at the same time from the Swan Hunter shipyard on Tyneside. Thor Dahl A/S, also of Sandefjord, Norway, had been in whaling since about 1910 and owned several converted whale factory ships, including *Thorshammer*, another former Eagle Oil tanker originally named *San Nazario*. Modern motor tankers, including *Thorsholm* and *Thorshavn*, built by another British yard, Laings of Sunderland, later augmented these vintage vessels in this owner's fleet.

Back in 1905 whaler men had converted old tankers into whale factory-ships to enable harpooned whales to be flensed alongside, rather than being towed back to a shore station. With the advent of the First World War, whale oil was used for lubricants and was also a key element in the production of the high explosive nitro-glycerine which made it an extremely valuable commodity.

After the First World War more tankers were converted to whale factory-ships by fitting stern slipways to winch dead whales on board for flensing on deck.

The photograph above shows how inflated whale carcases served as fenders between the whale factory-ship and the tanker loading the whale oil.

# Panama - the 'lock' canal

Sometimes claimed to be the 'Eighth Wonder of the World', the Panama Canal connects the Atlantic and Pacific Oceans by a 51-mile long waterway through the Isthmus of Panama, saving over 10,000 miles on the route round Cape Horn. It incorporates three sets of locks that raise vessels on average 26 metres above sea level to enable them to navigate through Gatun Lake and Gaillard Cut during their transit of the Canal.

Following its completion, the Panama Canal was inaugurated on 15 August 1914 with the passage of the steamship *Ancon*. Initially, the waterway was run as a non-corporate agency of the US government.
Then, in 1948, it became a corporate agency of the US government, under the Panama Railroad Company.
The authority was renamed as the Panama Canal Company in 1951.

In 1979 the Panama Treaty was signed which established a twenty-year transition period for the transfer of the ocean-to-ocean route and neighbouring land to Panama.

The agreement enabled control of the waterway to be passed to the Panama Canal Agency of the Republic of Panama on 31 December 1999.

The first attempt to construct the Canal was made in 1881 by Ferdinand de Lesseps, the French engineer famous for having built the Suez Canal. The project was dogged with problems from the outset as the mechanical equipment was not powerful enough for the job. Even worse was the debilitating effect of tropical diseases which claimed the lives of 22,000 construction workers, primarily through yellow fever, malaria and typhoid. By 1889 the company founded by de Lesseps, Compagnie Universelle du Canal Interoceanique, declared itself bankrupt, having spent nearly $300 million and excavated more than 535 million cubic metres in an attempt to build the Canal.
It was a major financial scandal at the time and the shareholders lost all the money they had invested.

After another false start in 1894 the rights and assets of the Compagnie Nouvelle du Canal de Panama were sold to the United States in 1901. Following the granting of Panama's independence from Colombia in 1903, the US and Panama signed the Bunau Varilla-Hay Treaty which

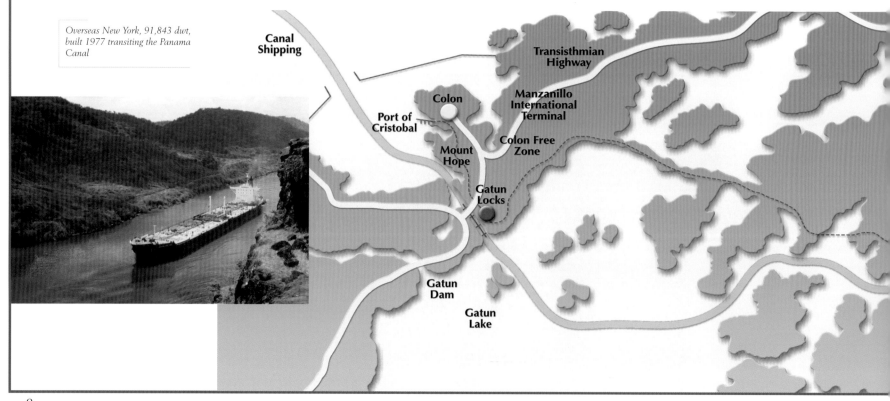

*Overseas New York, 91,843 dwt, built 1977 transiting the Panama Canal*

Canal Shipping

Transisthmian Highway

Colon

Manzanillo International Terminal

Port of Cristobal

Colon Free Zone

Mount Hope

Gatun Locks

Gatun Dam

Gatun Lake

gave the US the right to construct a locks canal through Panama and also the de facto sovereignty over a 10-mile wide corridor, the Canal Zone.

Work on the new canal began in September 1904 but, once again, progress was extremely slow. Health remained a problem until a major effort succeeded in eradicating the threat from disease-carrying mosquitoes. To speed up construction a rail network was put in to remove the vast amounts of material from the excavation sites and a supply system and housing were organised for the 60,000 workforce. The project then continued largely on schedule and in the autumn of 1913 the machinery was evacuated and the first man-made canyon was filled with water.

Completed at a total cost of $352 million, the Canal was inaugurated with the *Ancon* voyage which took 9 hours and 40 minutes to complete.

By the end of the 20th century the Canal was handling more than 13,000 vessels a year carrying nearly 200 million tons of cargo.

The limitations on the size of vessels are the dimensions of the lock chambers which are 305 metres long and 33.5 metres wide, with a maximum safe depth of 12 metres tropical fresh water. The maximum permissible length for passenger and container ships is 294 metres, and all other self-propelled vessels are restricted to 289.6 metres. Maximum beam is 32.2 metres.

The canal can handle virtually any ship of up to 80,000 dwt. The lock dimensions dictated the design of a major class of merchant vessel known as the Panamax-size, which is the largest type of ship able to transit the Canal.

Until 1999 certain types of vessel, including Panamax-size ships, were restricted to one-way passage on the narrower sections of the Gaillard Cut. However, a key section has recently been widened, allowing Panamax vessels to pass each other in opposite directions. Further work is in hand for the rest of the Cut which will increase its width to 190 metres on straight stretches and 225 metres on the curves to allow for two-way Panamax traffic, and this is scheduled for completion by 2002 at an estimated cost of $225 million.

*This photograph shows a tanker (foreground) passing through the lock system*

Madden Lake

Madden Dam

Panama City

Galliard Cut

Paraiso

Pedro Miguel Locks

Miraflores Locks

Port of Balboa

Balboa

Bridge of the Americas

During the mid-1920s a number of Norwegian ship-brokers came to specialise in oil transportation and took a very active part in the development of the tanker market. Prominent among the firms engaged in this activity were Fearnley & Eger, Hjalmar Bjørge, Lorentzen & Co, A O Andersen & Co and the Viking Shipping Agency. In addition to arranging charters and sale and purchase deals, they also helped to create new shipping companies through their close affinities with shipowners and contacts with oil companies and shipyards in Great Britain and Sweden.

In 1925 this business know-how facilitated the construction of two new tankers by the Swedish yard Götaverken for the Norwegian owner Hjelm Waage. This was believed to be the first contract in which tankers were commissioned for voyage chartering on a speculative basis. These vessels were followed by the diesel-powered tankers *Raila* - built in 1925 - and her 7,900 dwt sister ship *Bianca*, built in 1926.

This deal was the precursor of many such contracts between Norwegian owners and Swedish builders. In fact, during the 1930s over 65 per cent of Götaverken's production was destined for Norway, as was 80 per cent of Kockum's, 45 per cent of Eriksberg's and 90 per cent of Öresundsvarvet's. Much of the Norwegian tonnage was ordered against long-term charters, but there were still speculative orders amongst them, such as that for two diesel-engined tankers - one of 12,478 dwt and one of 10,476 dwt - placed by Rasmussen and Moe with Swan Hunter on Tyneside and Barclay Curle in Glasgow for delivery in 1930.

The trend toward long-term time charters had begun in 1927 when the Anglo-Saxon Petroleum Company came into the market with a chartering programme for 10-year time charters for large tankers. Virtually the entire programme was covered by Norwegian shipowners who ordered the vessels from Swedish yards with 70 per cent shipyard credit against the charters. Over the next two years many tanker orders were placed in combination with time charters, mostly arranged through Oslo shipbrokers, often together with Baltic brokers in London.

An indication of Norway's increasingly important role in the tanker industry between the wars can be gauged by the continuing growth in its tonnage, which rose from about 170,000 dwt in 1925 to more than 2.1m dwt by 1939. This placed Norway behind only Britain with 4.1m dwt and the US with 13.7m dwt in tonnage terms. Most of the growth had come from newbuildings which also reflected a growing preference for diesel propulsion over steam and resulted in the most modern fleet in the world industry.

This development was largely due to the importance of shipping to the Norwegian economy which for decades made up the shortfall in the country's trade deficit. The shipping industry's revival was helped by Norway's departure from the gold standard in 1931 which weakened the krone against the British pound. The benefits stemmed from the fact that freight rates were paid in pounds but nearly 50 per cent of running costs were in kroner. Moreover, the shipyards were keen to build so the shipowners were able to obtain favourable prices.

Thus, at an early stage Norwegian shipowners saw the opportunities in the tanker sector and made it a key part of the strategy driving the country's shipping industry-an industry which was essential to the national economy.

The initial trade boom after the First World War soon petered out and was followed by a slump. There was a brief period of stability in 1925 but even so, in terms of seaborne trade, the dry bulk cargo market, for example, was actually 7 per cent lower in 1925 than it had been in 1913. In sharp contrast to this, oil trade over the same period more than tripled from 39.5 million to 122.6 million ton-miles per annum. Extensive newbuildings had, however, created a surplus of tonnage and many tankers were laid up, while large numbers of seafarers were unemployed.

When conditions were particularly difficult, many owners chose to run their ships at slow speeds simply to keep them in operation and their crews employed. At the same time this helped extend the voyage times which reduced fuel costs and provided more time for onboard maintenance which helped to reduce repair costs.

By the 1930s, however, the world was in the grip of deep economic depression with mass unemployment, falling industrial production and a sharp decline in world trade. Trade levels shrank from US$2.9 billion a month to less than US$1 billion between 1919 and 1933.

The 1930s depression, with the abrupt reduction in trade, did not favour any expansion in the size of tankers.

The oil industry shared the general misery, its difficulties being aggravated by over-production which had cut prices to the bone. Oil transportation also went into decline, falling from 191 million ton-miles in 1929 to 175 million in 1932, its lowest ebb. This created surplus capacity in the tanker market, forcing freight rates down and causing many ships to be laid up. Among the independent operators, only a few owners with vessels on long-term time charter to the oil companies were able to buck the trend.

The slump in shipping also affected newbuilding prices. For example a 14,500 dwt tanker which had cost £155,000 in 1923, cost £166,750 in 1936, and £239,000 in 1937. But there were not many buyers.

## Trade recovery: newbuilding orders surge again

The tanker market recovered by the mid-1930s. This was partly due to an increase in world trade and partly by countries building up their oil reserves in preparation for another war. However, a further factor was the stabilising effect of a remarkable industry cooperation scheme known as the 'Schierwater Plan'.

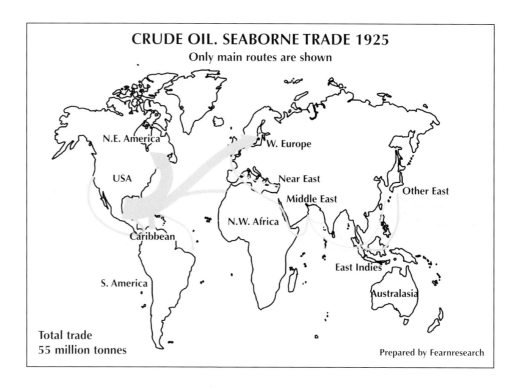

## CRUDE OIL. SEABORNE TRADE 1925
### Only main routes are shown

Total trade
55 million tonnes

Prepared by Fearnresearch

# Growth in Tanker Dwt 1900-35

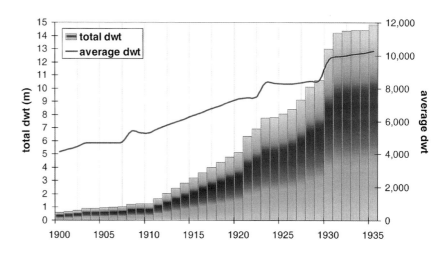

Source: SSY Consultancy & Research Ltd

# The Schierwater Plan

*The inauguration of the International Tanker Owners' Association, leading to the formation of the International Association of Independent Tanker Owners (INTERTANKO)*

In the Great Depression of the 1930s shipping and tankers in general suffered from the decline in world trade and the slump in demand for oil. By 1933 an estimated 15 per cent of the world tanker fleet was laid up, with as much as 40 per cent of independently owned tonnage out of service.

The tanker industry has largely avoided "Conferences", i.e. the cooperation agreements of the type which operate in the scheduled liner trade. Tanker chartering is cited by economists as one of the very few examples of "perfect competition" - the price is set purely by negotiation between buyer and seller of the service without regulation of outside bodies or rules. Thus, when the supply of tankers exceeds demand for them, there is nothing to stop the price negotiated by the customers - the charterers - being driven right down to the floor.

The early 1930s was such a time for the tanker owners, and adversity led them to explore ways to cooperate. An enterprising citizen of Liverpool whose own produce brokerage had been a victim of the 1929 crash, H T Schierwater, had joined British tanker owner United Molasses, later to develop into Athel Line, first in its Liverpool office and then in London.

Schierwater pioneered a plan to even out the tanker supply-demand balance by cutting the number of tankers available to trade. The Schierwater Plan involved laying up surplus tankers entered into the scheme. The tankers which remained in trade would, from the expected higher freight returns, contribute 10 per cent of their freight income to reward the owners of ships put into lay-up.

The Plan was given additional bite because the oil company charterers, concerned that the quality of the tanker stock should not fall due to underfunding, supported it and gave charter preference to ships entered into the scheme.

The seeds of a cooperation between independent owners led on to other opportunities to work together, and on 28 February 1934 the International Tanker Owners' Association was inaugurated, with Schierwater its first Chairman, *"to establish a medium for tanker owners to exchange information and opinions and to deal with the oversupply of tanker tonnage which depressed the market at the time"*, as shipowner Erling Næss reflected in his autobiography.

The Schierwater Plan was the first such scheme of active cooperation amongst tanker owners to work. Although attempts were made to repeat its formula, no other scheme had the same results. Whether its success was due to the participation of all parts of the industry, the forbearance of United States' anti-trust authorities, or the recovery of economic activity and then the onset of World War II in 1939 is open to debate.

After World War II the massive reduction of tanker tonnage through ship loses led to good times for tanker owners shipping oil from America and the Middle East to power the rebuilding of Europe. The Association was reassembled in 1949 by Schierwater, and elected R R S (Reginald) Cook of Hunting & Son, Newcastle, as its Chairman, which post he held until 1967. The Association continued to meet but in times of prosperity the meetings were more social than businesslike.

Despite the apparent success of the Schierwater Plan, there had been considerable doubts amongst some owners about its market effects. The continuing opposition resulted in 1955 in the Association, which was the Plan's custodian, deciding that a 75 per cent vote of members in favour would be required to revive a lay-up plan. In 1956 Egypt's Colonel Nasser nationalised the Franco-British Suez Canal, and it closed, vastly increasing the length of tanker voyages from the Middle East oil wells to industrial Europe, and back again in ballast. Increased demand for tanker service brought good times but in 1957 the Canal opened again, now under Egyptian control, and the freight market fell away.

**Mr Jan Hudig**
INTERTANKO Chairman
1970-1973

**Jørgen Jahre**
INTERTANKO Chairman
1973-1976

By 1962 after several years of poor freight rates the Association was actively discussing a fresh lay-up plan modelled on Schierwater. The International Tanker Recovery Scheme was offered to owners and to the oil companies to improve conditions in the industry.

The European oil companies - British Petroleum and Shell - were ready to back the scheme as the oil majors had backed Schierwater but this time the Americans were having none of it. Nonetheless, the Association pressed on with the plan and at its peak in summer 1964 some 80 tankers totalling 1.5 million tons of carrying capacity were in lay-up under the scheme. Although there was usually a short recovery during the early winter months each year, up until 1967 the tanker market was generally poor. Then in 1967 the Suez Canal was again closed by the Arab-Israel war.

Lay-up schemes were not the only objective of the Association. Erling Næss and the Norwegian shipowner Jørgen Jahre promoted a Shipbuilders and Shipowner Collaboration Scheme in the 1960s in an attempt to limit building of surplus tankers. The European shipbuilders were ready to support the scheme but the Far East builders - dominated by the Japanese - who were busy establishing themselves as the controlling force in world shipbuilding, were unwilling to back it and it failed.

The Association was active in attempts to harmonise safety requirements for tankers and to standardise equipment needs in different oil ports and terminals.

These were the days before a true international body for maritime affairs. The United Nations was only brought into being late in the 1940s. The convention creating the Intergovernmental Maritime Consultative Organisation, the forerunner of the International Maritime Organization (IMO) was drawn up in 1948 but not brought into effect until 1958-59. Shipping traffic was regulated by national rules and occasional bipartite treaties. The need for worldwide agreement on ship operation and equipment for a class of ship trading in a hazardous product to all corners of the world was readily apparent to the Association.

Following the stranding of the tanker *Torrey Canyon* on the British coast in 1967, and outcries about the clean-up of oil spills and compensation for the victims of the pollution, discussions started amongst tanker owners and oil companies to form a voluntary agreement accepting liability and providing compensation funds, through insurance.

The International Tanker Owners' Association was active in these discussions which led to the creation of the Tanker Owners' Voluntary Agreement concerning the Liability for Oil Pollution, or TOVALOP.

The International Tanker Owners' Association was headquartered in London, signifying the continued strength of the British merchant fleet. Its membership was international but the leading positions were those of the British tanker owners - Hunting's of Newcastle, Athel Line, P&O, and Erling Næss' Anglo Nordic. Stewart Browne of Athel Line, Vice-Chairman under Mr Cook, continued to serve as Vice-Chairman until the Association closed in London and Jan Hudig, Jørgen Jahre and Erling Næss, all later to become Chairmen of INTERTANKO in Oslo, were on the Association's Council.

The Association worked closely with the leading bodies of British shipping and with the London-based oil companies. Indeed, when in the 1960s the senior manager in BP's shipping operations, Houston Jackson, retired from BP, he was signed to Hunting's and elected Chairman of the Association in succession to Mr Cook. Many of the British members were liner companies with tanker departments or sections closely monitored by the United Kingdom Chamber of Shipping. This led the more specialist tanker owners to become restless and concerned that other interests were limiting the effectiveness of the Association.

The 1967 closure of the Suez Canal had rendered the Recovery Scheme unnecessary. The Association's agenda had therefore shrunk. The opportunity arose for these independent tanker owners to recreate the Association on finer lines and with more independence from other influences. Although some of the Association's members resisted it - the London ones particularly vigorously - the Association was wound up in London and, largely inspired by Jørgen Jahre, INTERTANKO, the International Association of Independent Tanker Owners, opened in Oslo at an inaugural meeting on 21 October 1970.

*Extract from INTERTANKO's 25th Anniversary Book published by INTERTANKO in 1996.*

**Mr Erling Dekke Næss**
INTERTANKO Chairman
1976 -1979

**Sir Yue-Kong Pao**
INTERTANKO Chairman
1979 -1982

## Trade recovery, newbuilding orders surge again

In the mid-1930s, to meet the requirement for larger and faster tankers, particularly from Norway, Deutsche Werft produced plans for a 14,000 dwt vessel driven by a single 4,100 bhp diesel engine which would provide a service speed of 13 knots. One of these new vessels, *Petrofina*, comfortably exceeded this when she logged 14.8 knots during fully laden trials in 1937. This was a new speed record for European-owned tankers. The design was based on a 'three-island' configuration, with a patented hull form below the waterline. Structurally, the vessels incorporated twin longitudinal bulkheads, which divided the hull space into nine sets of three tanks, and had a dry cargo hold forward. Altogether, 21 of these tankers were built - 17 by Deutsche Werft and four by Bremer Vulkan. A somewhat smaller tanker, *Moira*, was launched by Swan Hunter in 1935 - also for a Norwegian owner. Although only 1,560 grt, she is worthy of mention for being the first tanker with an all-welded construction.

Another notable vessel launched in 1935 was the 10,627 grt *G S Walden* which was the first vessel to be built to the new 'Isherwood arc' form of hull construction. (see Isherwood System on pages 34 and 35).

## Despite diesel, steam still popular

Whilst the quest for bigger ships continued, propulsion technology was also evolving rapidly, as evidenced by the growing popularity of diesel engines. However, many owners were rather conservative, remaining loyal to steam rather than switching to the newer alternative of diesel.

One of the reasons was that the diesel engines were technically difficult to operate and required expensive diesel fuel not commonly available in all ports.

The diesel engine, however, opened the door to a technological race between steam and motor propulsion that lasted until the 1980s.

The first large tanker to be fitted with turbo-electric machinery was the 11,651 grt *J W Van Dyke*, built by Sun Shipbuilding of Chester, Pennsylvania in 1939 for the Atlantic Refining Company. She was fitted with Babcock & Wilcox water tube boilers, with automatic combustion and superheat control, running at 625 psi and 832°F - the highest temperature and pressure ever used on an American ship.

The vessel had a service speed of 13.5 knots and became the forerunner of many US wartime tankers.

Some of the best-known tankers of the period were the 'Triple Twelves' or 'Three Twelves', as they were sometimes known, of Royal Dutch Shell's Anglo-Saxon fleet. Some 20 of these diesel-powered ships were built in the period 1935-37. They were so named because they had a capacity of 12,000 dwt, a service speed of 12 knots and a fuel consumption of 12 tons a day. Soon afterwards the two biggest tankers in Anglo-Saxon's fleet were delivered - the 15,260 dwt sisterships *Torinia* and *Thiara*, built on Tyneside in 1939. By this time the company's fleet accounted for almost 10 per cent of the world's tanker tonnage.

## Japanese and Americans develop faster ships

In the search for greater speed the Japanese had set the pace, literally and metaphorically, when their first fast tanker, the 9,860 grt *Teiyo Maru*, recorded a speed of 17.53 knots in ballast in 1931. To encourage the construction of more high-speed tankers, the Japanese Navy provided subsidies on the condition that the new vessels should be capable of not less than 19 knots.

In the period up to 1939 about 20 such ships were built - typified by *Tatekawa Maru* and her sistership *Nippon Maru*. Both were 13,600 dwt and designed for a service speed of 17.5 knots with a range of 21,000 miles. In fact, *Tatekawa Maru*, which was equipped to refuel naval ships at sea, actually achieved 20.5 knots on her trials. The two ships were extremely powerful vessels with double-acting diesel engines rated at 9,000 bhp driving single propellers. Structurally, they featured the conventional twin longitudinal bulkhead arrangement dividing six sets of tanks into three to provide 18 tanks in all.

These developments were noted by the Americans who responded with a similar arrangement between the private sector and the military. This was an agreement between the US Navy and Standard Oil of New Jersey whereby the oil company would build 12 high-speed tankers able to meet certain naval requirements. The extra costs of tailoring the ships to the Navy's specifications were to be covered by the US Treasury. These tankers were larger than their Japanese counterparts and the first vessel completed, the 18,300 dwt *Cimarron*, launched in 1939, had a service speed of 17 knots. During the next few years all 12 tankers were requisitioned by the US Navy and converted into escort aircraft carriers for wartime use.

*Teiyo Maru, 9,860 grt, was the first Japanese fast tanker and attained a speed of 17.53 knots (in ballast) in 1931*

## Automobiles increase demand for oil

In the inter-war period the oil trades had undergone changes in global distribution patterns, caused by a sharp decline in Russian production; the replacement of Mexico by Venezuela as the major oil exporter in the Caribbean region; and the development of Middle East supplies.

In 1927 Mexico exported only 4.6 million tons, compared with 25.2 million tons in 1922, the result of revolution and political upheaval. In contrast, Venezuela exported more than 19 million tons in 1929. Oil accounted for 76 per cent of Venezuela's export earnings in 1929 and by 1932 it had become Britain's biggest supplier of oil. Difficulties in building a pipeline and political uncertainties led Shell, one of the biggest producers, to site a new refinery 50 miles north of Venezuela on the island of Curacao. To cope with a low water depth of only 12 feet at the entrance to Lake Maracaibo in the Gulf of Venezuela Shell bought several ex-Royal Navy shallow-draught monitors and ordered 30 new tankers of 3,000 dwt each. The new ships had a draught of only 13 feet to enable them to enter the lake at most states of the tide.

Increasing demand for oil, due largely to the rapid expansion of automobile ownership in the US (by the end of the 1920s there were 23 million cars on US roads and gasoline consumption had gone up by 400 per cent over the decade between 1920 and 1930 from 645,000 to 2.58 million barrels a day) prompted governments and oil companies to join the scramble for Middle East supplies. Oil had already been discovered in Persia (modern Iran) in 1908 and petroleum products were being shipped from the Abadan refinery. In the new region of exploration one of the biggest oil discoveries was in 1927 at the Kirkuk field in Iraq which was controlled by a consortium of British, French and American oil companies.
The Armenian banker and oilman, Calouste Gulbenkian, held 5 per cent of the company. Kirkuk oil flowed via two of the first great Middle East pipelines, one of 522 miles to Tripoli via Syria and the second of 650 miles to Haifa via Jordan. The pipelines opened in 1935, by which time Kirkuk's annual production was running at 4 million tons and shortly afterwards the company completed a new refinery at Haifa.

## New big oil finds in Iraq, Saudi Arabia, Kuwait

In 1934 the first cargo of Arabian Gulf crude had been loaded in Bahrain by the Socal tanker *El Segundo* and carried to Singapore and Yokohama. Socal had acquired the local oil concession and, after striking oil in 1931, had built a modern terminal and pipeline to the harbour. In 1935 the company formed the Panama-based Foreign Steamship Company to run the shipping side and organise the transportation of Socal products to European, Russian and Pacific Rim markets. By 1938 the company's fleet numbered 22 seagoing tankers, four self-propelled river craft and six barges, which between them that year had carried a total of 65 million barrels of crude oil and finished products.

Socal also secured a concession in Saudi Arabia from King Ibn Saud and the first major oil discovery was made in 1938. A pipeline was laid to connect the oilfield to a newly constructed marine terminal at the coastal port of Ras Tanura. In April 1939 the King ceremonially opened a valve to load Socal's tanker *D G Scofield* with the inaugural cargo of oil shipped from Saudi Arabia. By this time Socal had formed a joint venture, Caltex, with Texaco to pool all their assets east of Suez. The deal gave Socal access to Texaco's marketing and distribution networks in Africa, Asia and Europe, while Texaco gained access to Middle East oil supplies.

At the same time the Anglo-Persian Oil Company, which had been forced in 1933 to renegotiate its concession in Persia with the Shah, Rezah Khan, formed the Kuwait Oil Company in a joint-venture with Gulf Oil and signed a 75-year concession with the local ruler, Sheikh Ahmad. A major oil strike was made in 1938 in the Burgan fields in Kuwait, but there was not enough time to commence production before the outbreak of war the following year when the well was capped. The Burgan fields remained dormant until 1944.

# Russian oil production and transportation

## Production

In 1864 the first oil wells were drilled in the Kuban region, one of which turned out to be a gusher that produced more than 190 tons per day in 1866. By the beginning of the 20th century Russia had become the world's leading oil producer with an output of 11.9 million tons in 1901.

Initially, oil production was centred on Azerbaidjan (Baku) but during the 1920s valuable discoveries were also made in the Northern Caucasus areas of Grozniy and Maikop. Since then there has been significant diversification of Russia's oil resources in other parts of the country.

## Transportation

Although Russia was originally at the forefront of oil transportation in bulk, their tanker fleet did not have enough capacity to handle all the country's production and, historically, a large percentage of Russian oil exports has always been carried by foreign tankers.

Traditionally, the main pattern of oil transportation involved shipments from Baku and other ports on the Caspian Sea to Astrakhan and thence up the River Volga for onward delivery to destinations in central Russia.
In 1880 the five leading Caspian Sea ports of Baku, Krasnovodsk, Astrakhan, Petrovsk and Guriev recorded cargo through put of around 470,000 tons but by 1913 their combined cargo traffic had increased by 6.8 million tons, most of which was oil.

Following the Civil War these oil supplies assumed critical importance for the country's ruined economy and between 1921 and 1940 the volume of oil cargoes carried in the Caspian Basin rose from about 3 million tons to 14 million tons.

During the Second World War, the demand for oil increased significantly. For example, in 1942 the monthly shipments from Baku/Makhachkala to Astrakhan were running at about 700,000 tons in the spring, 1.5 million tons in May and June, and between 500,000 and 600,000 tons in August and the autumn.
The flow did not stop even during the winter when ice blasting kept the River Volga open, enabling up to 100,000 tons a month to be delivered. Overall, about 30 million tons of oil cargoes were carried on the Volga - Caspian and Urals- Caspian canals during the war years. Also, 4 million tons a year were delivered to the port of Krasnovodsk on the East coast of the Caspian Sea and shipments up the River Volga were stepped-up using a special type of shallow-draught tank vessels.

The Black Sea oil trade began in 1883 when the railway from Baku to Batum was constructed across the Caucasus mountains. The largest Russian shipping company, ROPIT, bought two tankers *Sviet* and *Louch* in Sweden and Britain which, in 1888, made 47 voyages carrying 70,000 tons of kerosene from Batum to Odessa.

In 1913 the total cargo throughput of all Russian sea ports was about 36.9 million tons of which oil accounted for just under 5 per cent of the export volume. By 1925 total cargoes had increased by 40 per cent, with Baku accounting for 2.83 million tons (due to significant oil exports), Novorossiysk with 1.24 millions tons and Batum with 1.09 million tons.

In the 1920s oil exports had started from the Black Sea port of Novorossyisk. In the 1930s the Grozniy-Tuapse pipeline was built to link refineries at both ends and make Tuapse one of the most important oil exporting ports on the Black Sea. In 1940 these facilities enabled vessels of the Sovtanker fleet to carry over 5 million tons of oil cargoes from the Batum/Tuapse/Novorossiysk region.
There were also military shipments of oil from these ports to Odessa and Sevastopol during the war and lasting until 1942. Deliveries by Russian tankers were resumed in 1944 from Coustanza in Romania.

After the Second World War production increased steadily. By the end of the 1960s the Sheskharis oil terminal in Novorossiysk was exporting about 18 million tons of oil cargoes a year as a result of its connections to the Magistral oil pipeline Druzhba and also to some large oil refineries. It was subsequently augmented by the port of Klaipeda in Lithuania.

# The story of the Sovetskaya Neft

On 16 May 1932 the 12,700 dwt tanker *Sovetskaya Neft* became one of the most famous ships in the world. She had discharged a cargo of benzene at Vladivostok and was crossing the Indian Ocean bound for the Black Sea when, at 02.15 hours approaching the Cape of Guardafui, the watch officer detected a vessel on fire.

It was *Georges Phillipar*, a 21,000 grt French passenger liner carrying 676 people on board. Although *Sovetskaya Neft* was in ballast with benzene vapours in the tanks, her master, Aleksander M Alekseev, gave the order to approach the liner - which was engulfed in flames - and launch all lifeboats.

The tanker's engines were stopped and during that night her crew rescued 437 people. Later two British dry cargo vessels, *Maksud* and *Contractor*, came on the scene and saved another 160 people. But, unfortunately more than 70 lives were lost on that tragic night.

The world community was moved by the courage and professionalism of the *Sovetskaya Neft's* crew and the liner's owners, Messagerie Maritime Company, presented Captain Alekseev with a personal sextant and gold watch engraved with a message of gratitude. Eleven crew members were decorated by the French ambassador who expressed the nation's appreciation for their outstanding self-sacrifice, for which they received the highest award for bravery - the medal for saving life at sea.

The French government also granted the *Sovetskaya Neft* the right to transit the Suez Canal free of charge in perpetuity.

During the Second World War the *Sovetskaya Neft* became a military transport vessel on the Black Sea and on 26 October 1941 was torpedoed when leaving the port of Sevastopol. In spite of four cargo tanks being damaged and a 100 square metre hole in the plating the crew managed to save the vessel and their own lives.

The ship remained in operation until the 1970's and the same name *Sovetskaya Neft* was given to a new Suezmax tanker of the Novorossiysk Shipping Company in 1980.

Other Russian tankers involved in dramatic rescue operations include *Pavel Dybenko* which in 1972, when carrying crude oil from the Arabian Gulf to Europe, saved the crew of the Liberian-registered crude carrier *Karlatlantic* which was on fire in the Indian Ocean.

Another liner rescue took place on 23 December 1976 when *Lenino*, also carrying crude oil, saved 209 people from the passenger vessel *Patra* which was on fire in the Red Sea. And in 1980 *Split* carried out three salvage operations, including the saving of 30 crew members from the burning Liberian-registered tanker *Blossom*.

*Picture left:*
*The master of Sovetskaya Neft*
*Aleksander M Alekseev*

*Sovetskaya Neft approaches the liner*
*Georges Phillipar. Lifeboats are*
*already launched and heading for*
*the burning liner*

# Tanker Charterparties

The charterparty is one of the oldest forms of contract for the carriage of goods by sea. The word stems from the Latin "carta partite" which means a deed cut in two. Originally, the document was drawn up by hand and then torn in two, with each party retaining a separate part of the document. It is a contract for the hire of ship. In broad terms they can be categorised as voyage charterparties, time charterparties or bareboat (or demise) charterparties.

## Voyage charterparties

In a voyage charterparty the owner agrees to hire out his vessel for one or more voyages. In general terms the owner retains control and possession of the vessel and crew. The owner is remunerated by means of the payment of freight. The charterparty also includes an allowance for the time in which the charterer must arrange the loading and discharge of the cargo.

This is known as the laytime. Tanker charterparties generally have a fixed 72-hour period of laytime.

If this allowance is exceeded, then agreed damages known as demurrage become payable to the owner. The allocation of the risk of delay to the vessel is an important aspect to the contract.

C.F.
TANK VESSELS

**DAVIES & NEWMAN, Ltd.,**
*Ship Brokers,*
3, GRACECHURCH STREET,
LONDON, E.C.3

Telegraphic Address:—
" OILCHARTA," STOCK, LONDON.

Telephone No.:—
MANSION HOUSE 5821 (4 LINES).

2218—2/35

**TANK VESSEL VOYAGE CHARTER PARTY.**

*125*

LONDON,　8th March, 1935.

**It is this day mutually agreed** between WILH. WILHELMSEN,

Owners, of the good Norwegian　Tank Motor/Steam Vessel, called the "MONTANA" of 4411

tons nett register, having a capacity of (10000 tons 5% more or less of Oil, or thereabouts, and classed 100 A1 Lloyd's, (at Owners' option

now Oslo

and The ANGLO-SAXON PETROLEUM CO., Ltd,　Charterers of London.

　1.—That the said Vessel being tight, staunch and strong, and every way fitted for the voyage, and to be maintained in such condition during the voyage, perils of the sea excepted, shall, with all convenient despatch, sail and proceed to

**CURACAO**

or so near unto as she may safely get (always afloat) and there load from the factors of the said Charterers a full and complete cargo of **crude oil and/or fuel oil**

in bulk, not exceeding what she can reasonably stow and carry over and above her Tackle, Apparel, Provisions and Furniture (sufficient space to be left in the Expansion Tanks to provide for the expansion of the cargo), and being so loaded shall therewith proceed (as ordered on signing Bills of Lading), direct to

**one safe United States port North of Cape Hatteras, not**

**East of New York,**

or so near thereunto as she may safely get (always afloat), and deliver the same on being paid Freight at and after the rate of

**Five shillings (5/-)**

per ton of 20 cwts. of Oil intake quantity. **in London concurrent with discharge** on the Continent at the current rate
　2.—The Freight to be payable upon delivery of the Cargo in cash, without discount at port of loading and cost of insurance thereon. Cash to of Exchange or London at sight, less any advances made the Captain at port of loading and cost of insurance thereon. Cash to be advanced if required for disbursements at port of discharge at current rate of Exchange.
　3.—The dues and other charges upon the cargo shall be paid by the Charterers, and the dues and other charges upon the Vessel shall be paid by the Owners.
　4.—The cargo shall be pumped into the Vessel at the expense, risk and peril of the Charterers, and pumped out of the Vessel at the expense of the Vessel, but at the risk and peril of the Vessel as far as the rail only. The Vessel to supply her pumps and the necessary steam in all ports where the regulations permit of fire on board, as well as the necessary hands. If fires not allowed on board Charterers to find steam at their expense for loading and discharging purposes.
　5.—　　　　168　　　　running hours (Sundays and Holidays excepted), weather permitting, shall be allowed the Charterers for loading and discharging, the Charterers having the right of loading and discharging during the night,

The contract also specifies the owner's obligations as regards the performance of the vessel. Charterers are obliged to provide the agreed cargo and may be liable to owners for deadfreight if a full cargo is not loaded.

For the tanker industry the first standard form charterparty was Warshipoilvoy. This form was the basis for many modern forms, including Asbatankvoy. The most recent version of Asbatankvoy dates from 1977, but is still by far the most frequently used form today. The other standard forms in use today have emanated from the major charterers. Difficulties of interpretation often arise as, normally, the standard terms are amended and lengthy lists of additional clauses are incorporated into the charter.

## Time charterparties

A time charterparty is a contract for the hire of a vessel for a period rather than for a particular voyage. The owner retains control of the vessel and its crew but accepts to be under the employment and directions of the charterer.

The owner is paid hire, usually expressed as a daily amount. The charterer agrees to take over the bunkers on board the vessel on delivery and redelivers the bunkers remaining on redelivery. The charterer pays for all fuel used by the vessel during the charter and also pays port disbursements. One of the key clauses is the off-hire clause. This clause provides that, should the vessel not be fully efficient or has to be withdrawn from service,
then hire shall cease to be due, irrespective of fault on the owner's part. The most commonly used standard forms of time charters emanate from the major charterers.

## Bareboat charterparties (or charters by demise)

Under bareboat charterparties the owner parts with both possession and control of the vessel.
The charterer has the obligation of appointing the master and crew of the vessel, who are the agents of the charterer. The charterer also pays for the insurances (hull and P&I). In short, the owner has almost no role to play in the operation of the vessel.

# Worldscale

The system of a scale for freight is unique to tanker voyage chartering. The purpose is to enable a standard tanker to obtain the same net return per day at the same Worldscale percentage, regardless of the voyage actually undertaken. Thus, the profitability (or loss) of various voyages can easily be compared.

Before World War Two tanker voyage chartering resembled dry bulk chartering in that freight was agreed in so many dollars, pounds (or whatever currency used) per ton of cargo to be transported between two or more specified ports. If the charterer was to have the option of declaring any other loading or discharging ports, then the freight per ton for each of these optional other voyages would have to be specified and this could lead to a two or three page long addendum to the charterparty. It is much simpler to have a system (a scale) which, ideally, provides the same net return per day, i.e. freight less bunker costs, port charges, canal dues etc, irrespective of the voyage performed.

The first scale was introduced during World War Two when first the British government and later the US government requisitioned shipping and owners received compensation on the basis of a daily hire rate. Sometimes the governments made requisitioned tankers available to the major oil companies for their private use for which the oil companies paid freight (on what was essentially a time charter basis) in accordance with a schedule of rates designed to produce the same net return per day to the government. The scale was subsequently further developed and refined. The British Ministry of Transport schedule became known simply as "MOT". Similarly, the rates issued by the United States Maritime Commission, became known as "USMC".

Between 1952 and 1962 a number of different schedules were issued as a service to the tanker trade by non-governmental bodies; Scales Nos. 1, 2 and 3 and then Intascale in London and ATRS in New York. Then in 1969 came the joint London/New York production issued to replace both Intascale and ATRS called the "Worldwide Tanker Nominal Freight Scale", more usually known as "Worldscale". With the introduction of Worldscale, it became the custom to express market levels of freight in terms of a direct percentage of the scale rates instead of a plus or minus percentage. This method is known as "Points of Scale" and thus Worldscale 100 means 100 points of 100 per cent of the published rate or, in other words, the published rate itself, sometimes referred to as Worldscale flat, while Worldscale 250 means 250 points or 250 per cent of the published rate and Worldscale 30 means 30 points or 30 per cent of the published rate.

Under the older method these would have been referred to as plus 150 per cent and minus 70 per cent respectively.

During its life span, from September 1969 until the end of 1988, Worldscale was regularly revised for changes in bunker prices and port costs but the fixed daily hire element of $1,800 remained constant.

Finally, to bring the story up to date, "New Worldscale" was introduced with effect from 1st January 1989. It is generally understood that "Worldscale" refers to the new scale, while the previous scale is called "Old Worldscale".

Flat rates are roughly calculated as follows: A Standard Vessel is, in theory, sent on an infinite number of round voyages. Assumptions are made about her speed, bunker consumption when steaming, bunker consumption for purposes other than steaming, and bunker consumption in port. The basis reference has become a vessel of 75,000 tonnes capacity, with a speed of 14.5 knots using heavy fuel oil of 380 centistokes (a measure of the oil's viscosity) and a daily fuel consumption of 55 tonnes when steaming.

Furthermore, it is assumed that the Standard Vessel will have a total of 4 days' port time for the voyage from one loading port to one discharging port, and 12 hours are added for each extra port involved on a voyage.

A so-called fixed daily hire element of $12,000 is added. The Schedule will specify the price per tonne of bunkers assumed in the calculations ($149.75 per tonne for 2001) and the Worldscale Associations will have collected information about the port costs for the Standard Vessel in the various ports.

By knowing the round voyage distances (which are printed in the Schedule alongside the flat rate), it is possible to work out the total costs for the Standard Vessel based on these assumptions. This figure is then divided by the full cargo that the Standard Vessel could carry on the voyage in question, and the figure thus arrived at is the flat rate or Worldscale 100 for that particular voyage.

The effect of these calculations is that a tanker identical in all respects to the Worldscale Standard Vessel, incurring the same port charges and purchasing bunkers at the same price as assumed in the Worldscale calculations, will, if chartered at Worldscale 100, obtain the same net return per day, i.e., total freight less bunker consumption, canal dues and port charges, etc, regardless of the actual voyage performed. The daily net return will then be $12,000, i.e. the fixed daily hire element as used in calculating the Worldscale rates. Now, if the freight rate agreed differs from WS 100, the net result per day for the various voyages will not all be exactly the same, but will still be fairly similar.

The greatest distortion is likely to be found between one short voyage and another because for short voyages i.e. those where the steaming time on the laden leg is less than say seven days, the proportion of total voyage costs represented by port charges is likely to vary considerably between different voyages.

Consistency of net returns per day will not be perfect for a ship differing substantially from the Standard Vessel fixed at a rate substantially above or below WS 100, particularly for short voyages. The further away from the Worldscale assumptions, the greater the possibility that comparability will be impaired. Worldscale calculations have been made for over 280,000 voyages.

Depending on market conditions, the charterer and shipowner will agree on a percentage of the flat rate. Depending on the voyage in question, there may be some adjustments (fixed or variable differentials) to be made to the rate. Furthermore, the Worldscale Preamble contains a number of terms and conditions to which the parties to the contract may agree; in which case the Preamble will become part of the contract concluded. The terms and conditions include a list of specific port cost items that are for Charterers' Account.

Another function of the Worldscale system is that it provides a shorthand method for comparing market levels. For instance, some brokers publish weekly reports indicating what the typical Worldscale level is that week for selected typical voyages. Thus, one has a regular basis for judging the strength or weakness of the tanker market in a much easier manner than if one had to compare various fixtures expressed in US dollars per tonne.

Comparison over time is less than perfect because the Scale is only revised annually, and thus distortions occur when there have been substantial fluctuations in bunker prices and exchange rates.

The Worldscale system is a very useful tool for tanker chartering. However, it is no panacea, and a prerequisite for using it is also to be aware of its limitations.

1939-45    *Second World War and introduction of T-2 tankers*

1950        *Construction of Tapline pipeline from Saudi Arabia to
              Sidon, Lebanon*

1953        *45,000 dwt Tina Onassis built*

1956        *47,750 dwt Spyros Niarchos built*

1956        *Suez Canal nationalised, then blocked after
              British, French and Israeli invasion*

1957        *Suez Canal re-opens*

1959        *First oil discovery in Libya*

Chapter Three:
Second World War and recovery

## Oil vital to conduct of war

Apart from its sheer magnitude, the Second World War differed from its predecessor in other important respects. It was a mobile rather than a static war; it was fought on a global scale; and air power played a decisive part.

These considerations made oil much more vital to the running of the war than it had been in the preceding conflict. In the post-war reconstruction oil and tankers would play a role as important as it had in the war itself.

The key oil routes in the war were in the Atlantic (US to Great Britain), the North Sea and Arctic (Great Britain to Russia) and the Pacific (East Indies to Japan). Supplies from the Abadan refinery in Persia to Great Britain around the Cape of Good Hope were also important. German and Italian tankers were active in the Mediterranean, particularly those supplying oil to the German army in North Africa.

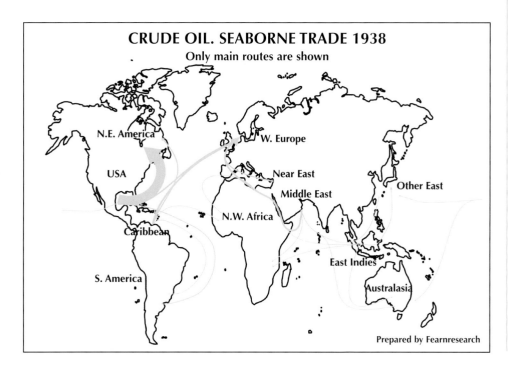

**CRUDE OIL. SEABORNE TRADE 1938**

Only main routes are shown

N.E. America

W. Europe

USA

Near East

Middle East

Other East

N.W. Africa

Caribbean

S. America

East Indies

Australasia

Prepared by Fearnresearch

## Japan's oil imports nearly all by sea

Germany itself was not heavily dependent on oil brought by sea. Instead, it relied on oil fields in Romania and the domestic production of synthetic fuel. However, Japan had to secure its supplies in South East Asia, in particular the East Indies. This became an even more vital supply when the US imposed an oil embargo in 1941 in response to Japan's invasions of Manchuria and Indochina. Before the embargo 80 per cent of Japan's oil had come from the US and only 10 per cent from the Dutch East Indies.

Great Britain was also totally dependent upon tanker shipping for its oil and was in a particularly vulnerable position after the fall of France in June 1940 when the country stood alone, facing the threat of an imminent German invasion. After Italy declared war on Great Britain, the British government's Petroleum Board, which was responsible for handling the nation's fuel supplies, decided on a 'short-haul' policy which meant that oil would be brought across the Atlantic from the US rather than around the Cape from the Persian Gulf.

However, following the Japanese air attack on Pearl Harbour on Sunday, 7 December 1941, the situation was reviewed and it was decided to increase supplies from the Gulf. The Anglo-Persian Oil Company's refinery at Abadan was put back on full production and tanker shipments increased from 426 cargoes in 1941 to 648 the following year. High octane aviation fuel was one of the most important products coming out of Abadan and out-put was steadily increased, until by 1945 the refinery was producing one million tons a year.

America, meanwhile, concentrated its Gulf Coast oil operations on providing supplies for Britain and trans-ferred many of its tankers to the North Atlantic route. A number of these, including vessels of Standard Oil New Jersey, had been registered in Panama during the late 1930s which gave them neutrality until America's entry into the war in December 1941.

The greatest risk to tankers in the Atlantic - as it had been in the First World War - was the threat from German U-boats. These vessels were even more dangerous than before, because they now had longer cruising ranges and direct access to the Western Approaches from German-held ports in northwest France.

## Tankers in the Atlantic
## easy prey for U-boats

Tankers were the U-boats' favourite targets as they were relatively slow, easily recognised, only lightly armoured and carried combustible cargoes of great strategic importance. Most of the losses on the Atlantic were sustained by the tanker fleets of Great Britain, Norway, Greece and America. In the first four months of the war U-boats claimed over 100 merchant ships, of which neutral Norway lost 58 ships amounting to 127,000 grt and approximately 400 seamen killed before the country was invaded. During 1940 Allied sinkings increased from over 55,000 tons in May to around 350,000 tons in October. But U-boats were not the only hazard; armed German raiders disguised as merchant ships sank 366,000 tons of shipping that year. The situation worsened in 1941 when the Germans switched from single U-boat attacks to wolf packs. Over 653,000 tons of shipping was sunk in April alone and Britain was reduced to only two months' supply of oil. From December 1941, when Germany declared war on the US, the attacks were also extended to the American East Coast where US shipping was harried in its own coastal waters. In 1942 the picture was blacker still; in the first few months more than four times as many tankers were sunk as new ones were built and the volume of shipping destroyed that year totalled over 6.2 million tons. This figure included almost 25 per cent of America's tanker tonnage.

At the beginning of 1943 Britain's oil stocks were at their lowest ever and still the sinkings continued. In March 108 Allied ships amounting to over 627,000 tons were sunk, of which 141,000 tons were lost in one attack when a pack of U-boats ambushed a double convoy of 77 ships, sending 21 of them to the bottom. In April a further 328,000 tons were sunk, followed by 265,000 tons in May. But in June the losses reduced to 95,000 tons and this marked the turning point of the U-boat threat.

*Sea trials of B P Newton, winter 1939/40*

*In April 1940, the Norwegian government formally requisitioned their fleet and placed it under the control of a new world-wide organisation with headquarters in London and New York - The Norwegian Shipping and Trade Mission (Notraship).*
*The tanker fleet became Norway's most important contribution to the war effort.*

*The picture shows B P Newton, one of the Notraships that sailed to England in 1940. Only her speed enabled her to out-distance the enemy. The crew were in full praise for the Chief Engineer who in the Captains's words "put a screwdriver in the engine and gave her an extra few knots". When the tanker docked in England, thirteen stowaways were found board, including a Norwegian nurse.*

These pictures show the launching of B P Newton
in 1939 which was a very special event for the
owner - as it still is today. The 16,000 dwt B P
Newton was built at Kockums shipyard in Malmö,
Sweden. Equipped with a 6,500 bhp engine she
could, if pushed to the limit, reach up to 16 knots.
This ability proved particularly useful during
the Second World War when being pursued
by the enemy.

## Tide turns with better intelligence, convoys and armed tankers

This change of fortune was due to a combination of improved intelligence work, extended convoy support and better equipment. Many tankers, for example, were converted into Merchant Aircraft Carriers (MACs) by removing the superstructure, laying a flight deck with arrester wires and crash barrier, and fitting a new bridge/control tower on the starboard side. After conversion the vessels still retained 90 per cent of their original cargo capacity. Shell was actively involved in the development of MACs and converted nine of its 'Three Twelves' tankers. The ships were armed with two Bofors and six Oerlikon guns and on the flight deck carried three Fairy 'Swordfish' aircraft equipped with rocket projectiles.

Collectively, the MACs made 323 Atlantic crossings in their two years of active service and escorted 217 separate convoys.

Convoys to Russia faced similar perils in addition to the problems caused by sub-zero temperatures, near-permanent darkness and Arctic storms in winter.

In the words of one experienced crewman who sailed on tankers in these convoys: "The conditions were absolutely atrocious and it was so cold it almost made you cry." In the summer the perpetual daylight exposed the convoys to greater risk from aircraft and surface raiders, as well as U-boats in even greater numbers. After suspension of the convoys, following convoy PQ17 where only 11 out of 35 ships survived, ships en route to Russia sailed alone using 'drop by drop' tactics and more than 2,500

*A Swordfish aircraft landing on MAC ship Amastra, North Atlantic, 1943. The Swordfish were armed with eight anti-submarine rockets and a machine-gun.*

*MAC ship Rapana. Built 1935 Wilton Fijenoord, Holland. Converted to MAC 9 1943 and returned to normal tanker service in 1945.*

vessels made these highly dangerous Arctic voyages. Many of them never arrived at their destination and during the war 103 transport vessels - including 47 American, 35 British and 12 Russian ships - were lost on this 'Arctic Bridge'.

It is worth mentioning that both Russian tankers in the PQ17 convoy survived the massive attack on 4 July 1942. *Donbass* managed to avoid two torpedoes and shoot down a German torpedo bomber. Following alone after the convoy scattered, *Donbass* saved 51 American seamen from the Arctic waters, then shot down a second torpedo plane before successfully arriving at the port of Archangel. The other tanker, *Azerbaidjan*, was hit by a torpedo in one of her tanks which contained vegetable oil.

The tank exploded in flames as high as the masts, scattering about 200 tons of burning oil over the decks.

With the main engine stopped and steering gear damaged, the tanker took on a list and began to sink. But the crew managed to save the vessel, restart the engine and, after a running battle with German aircraft, safely arrived at the Novaya Zemilia Islands.

The attacks on merchant shipping and particularly tankers undoubtedly caused great damage in terms of the loss of ships and their vital cargoes and the thousands of merchant seamen killed. There were also many individual tales of heroism and desperate courage in which the crews of merchant ships fought the enemy and battled to save their ships and cargoes. Two such tales involved the tankers *Ohio* and *San Demetrio*.

*In the Battle of the Atlantic the losses from U boat attacks were eventually overcome by providing the convoys with very long-range aircraft protection (VLRs) which extended all the way across the ocean. Another important contribution was made by British cryptologists who succeeded in cracking the U boat radio codes which enabled their communications to be intercepted, providing accurate information about U boat operations and planning.*

# Ohio

## delivering cargo at all costs

In the Mediterranean theatre during the Second World War, ships carrying supplies to Malta had to run the gauntlet of some of the fiercest attacks ever mounted against convoys. Malta was a vital strategic base for Allied units from where they could disrupt the Axis supply lines to North Africa. Because of this, the island was besieged for over three years and took a terrible pounding, particularly from bombing raids, but was vigorously defended by Allied forces and never surrendered.

*Ohio was acquired by Leif Høegh in 1947 and renamed Høegh Ray. After two further owners, she was sold to Spanish shipbreakers and scrapped in 1963.*

In one of the most critical phases of this struggle a particularly important convoy was mustered to take urgently needed supplies to Malta. Code named 'Operation Pedestal', the convoy left the River Clyde in Scotland on 2 August 1942 with an unusually heavy escort, including destroyers, cruisers, battleships and aircraft carriers. Nine days later, off the North African coast, one of the carriers was torpedoed and sunk. After that the assaults were continuous, with air raids and attacks by submarines and torpedo boats taking a further toll of the escort ships, destroying a cruiser and an anti-aircraft escort ship.

One of the vessels in the convoy was *Ohio*, a 14,000 dwt tanker carrying a cargo of kerosene and fuel oil. She was owned by Texaco, but crewed and managed by Eagle Oil. *Ohio* was one of four Panama - registered tankers and was later transferred to the Norwegian flag and renamed *Høegh Ray* in 1947. On the evening of 12 August *Ohio* was hit by a torpedo which tore a gaping hole in the main deck, shut down the engine room, breached the pump room and started fires. After several hours the engines were restarted and the following morning the ship caught up with the main convoy. In the next wave of attacks one of the bombers was shot down and crashed in flames on the tanker's decks. At the same time bombs straddled both sides of the ship and the engines stopped again. The engineers managed to restart them, but speed was reduced to about three knots and within an hour or so both boilers blew out which made another restart impossible. While waiting for a tow, there were repeated air attacks, one of which scored a direct hit, with a bomb exploding in the engine room.

*Ohio* continued under tow with a destroyer made fast to each side and a minesweeper towing ahead. Progress was painfully slow and the air attacks continued, with another hit blowing away the rudder and holing the ship near the stern, causing her to start sinking. To keep afloat some of the cargo was jettisoned and replaced by compressed air. Eventually, Malta came in sight and naval tugs took over the tow. When *Ohio* finally docked in Grand Harbour, she was almost awash, down to 30 inches of freeboard, and was a total loss. Even so, she still had 11,500 tons of precious oil in her tanks.

For their valour many of the crew were decorated. The master, Captain Mason, received the George Cross and chief engineer Wyld received the DSO. Five DSCs and seven DCMs were awarded to other members of the ship's company.

*Above - Ohio under tow entering Grand Harbour, Malta*
*Left - Ohio being supported by the destroyers Penn and Ledbury*

After two days in rain and heavy seas the 16 survivors of the San Demetrio reboarded
the vessel and brought the remaining fires under control with bucket parties.
Their heroic efforts helped to save the tanker's vital cargo of 10,000 tons of gasoline

# San Demetrio

## The remarkable voyage of the San Demetrio

*San Demetrio* was another example of the courage and seamanship of tanker crews. The 12,132 dwt vessel was part of a 37-ship convoy which, after leaving Halifax, Nova Scotia on 28 October 1940, was attacked in mid-Atlantic by the German pocket battleship, *Admiral Scheer*, on 5 November. The convoy scattered while their escort vessel, *Jervis Bay*, an ex-liner converted to merchant cruiser, took on the hopeless task of engaging the raider. Although she was sunk, along with five ships of the convoy, her heroic action allowed most of the vessels to escape. *San Demetrio*, however, had been severely hit and disabled, three of her crew were killed and the ship became a raging inferno. Because of the risk of explosion, the ship was abandoned and the crew took to the lifeboats, one of which capsized. The remaining lifeboats separated during the night and two were later rescued, but the third one found *San Demetrio* still afloat next morning with the fire much abated.

Led by the second officer Hawkins, the 16 survivors, some of whom were injured, reboarded the tanker. They found the bridge burnt out and the navigational equipment destroyed; even the glass in the portholes had melted in the heat. The fire had also gutted the storeroom, so that very little food was available. As some fires were still burning, bucket parties tackled the blaze to get it under control and the engines and generator were restarted.

After 700 miles without charts or compass, they made a successful landfall off the west coast of Ireland and on 14 November nursed the battered ship into the Clyde where they discharged the remainder of her cargo of 10,000 tons of gasoline.

*San Demetrio, 12,132 dwt*

*Picture right:*
*It was not only the Allies who suffered tanker losses during the war years. The leading German shipping company John T Essberger lost 11 of it ships, including the 8,800 dwt Biskaya captured by the Royal Navy off Greenland shortly after the outbreak of hostilities.*

*No magazine, no book, no film has portrayed the hard life of the men who worked on tankers at the beginning of the century. The ships were not beautiful, nor did they smell nice, and hardly any passengers ever stayed onboard. Almost all photos and reports come from the crew members, who wanted to make a record of their time at sea. Here we see the tanker Biskaya, built in 1927 at A G Weser in Bremen and transferred to John T Essberger in 1937, braving stormy conditions on the North Atlantic.*

*Pictures below:*
*Scrubbing the deck with a broom was a regular chore. Cleaning decks was a job that simply had to be done on tankers as on other ships. However it was a much more bearable task than the torment of washing tanks with a hot water pressure at five times greater than atmospheric pressure and temperatures of up to 70 C. After about five minutes the man had to be relieved by the next cleaner. Today tanks are washed automatically using fixed machines.*

### Japan's oil lifeline cut, 85 per cent of shipping sunk

In the Far East, American submarines played havoc with shipping along the oil supply lines between Japan and the East Indies. Japanese oil imports, which reached their highest level in the early part of 1943, were halved within the following year and by 1945 had almost petered out. During that period Japan's tanker losses were devastating. By 1944 sinkings outweighed newbuildings and ultimately more than 85 per cent of the country's merchant shipping was sunk. The resulting shortage of oil put severe limitations on Japan's ability to maintain its naval and airborne operations.

### Attacks on shipping spur safety initiatives

War often accelerates the development and application of science and technology, usually to create more destructive weapons, but sometimes to provide better means of defence and protection.

This humanitarian objective became the inspiration for a joint technical team from Shell and Eagle Oil in their efforts to solve some of the problems faced by tankers and their crews in wartime. One of their initial ideas was to use compressed air to help keep damaged vessels afloat, a method successfully demonstrated on Eagle's ship *San Delfino*, after she hit a mine early in the war. The system was then improved to deliver compressed air to any part of the ship to aid flotation in a damaged hull by forcing out water and providing buoyancy. It also had other uses, such as powering seawater pumps for firefighting, shifting cargo from damaged tanks and even steering the ship. By 1941 the system was standard in all tankers and proved its worth many times, not least in keeping *Ohio* afloat long enough to deliver her vital cargo to Malta.

The team then applied their ingenuity to one of the most terrible hazards faced by crews of sinking tankers when abandoning ship. Inevitably, a thick layer of oil would cover the sea around the vessel and sometimes it would be on fire. Those who jumped or fell into the sea trying to reach a liferaft or boat would be engulfed in oil which got into the eyes, ears, mouth and nostrils, resulting in suffocation or searing of the lungs. If the oil was burning, the chances of survival were minimal, even in a lifeboat, as it would not only catch fire but the intense flames would consume oxygen from the atmosphere, causing asphyxiation.

One of the first survival aids to be developed was a protective hood that fitted over the head and neck.

It incorporated an air valve that enabled the wearer to breathe without taking in oil or seawater and had built-in goggles with four sets of lenses. These could be removed, one by one, as and when they became coated with oil, giving several chances of retaining vision.

After getting out of the sea and into a boat, the survivor's immediate priority was to remove the oil from the skin and for this purpose a special soap was formulated which was effective in either salt or fresh water.

Turning their attention to fire protection, the team next experimented with lifeboats. This involved sitting in prototypes amidst intense flames in temperatures up to 1300°C, at which point the thermometers exploded.

It was found that wooden hulls were surprisingly effective because the wood charred and formed an insulating layer, whereas steel just melted. Top protection was provided by a canvas and asbestos canopy that covered the entire boat and was cooled by hand-operated water sprays. Whatever the level of the outside temperature, the interior of the boat never exceeded 46°C.

The experiments proved successful and wooden lifeboats were extensively converted throughout the tanker fleets, saving countless lives.

*The protective hood developed during the war by the Shell and Eagle Oil joint technical team to protect tanker crews from oil in the sea if they had to abandon ship. This illustration shows the lens changing system and the air valve to assist breathing*

*Liberty ships were mass-produced, prefabricated vessels with all-welded hulls produced in US shipyards between 1941 and 1945. Constructed to replace tonnage lost to U boat attacks a total of 2,710 of these vessels were produced, of which 62 were equipped as tankers. The original design was produced by the Sunderland Company of Newcastle upon Tyne, England and the plans were adopted by American shipyards because they incorporated simplicity of design and operation, rapidity of construction, large cargo-carrying capacity and a remarkable ability to withstand war damage. At the time, rumours developed over the safety of these welded ships, more particularly that they would break up at sea. However, these rumours were dismissed by the authorities as false propaganda by the enemy*

## Shipyards build standard designs - T-2s, Liberty ships

The main priority in shipbuilding during the war years was replacing the huge quantities of tonnage lost.

To meet the challenge shipbuilders turned to the concept of standard ships and introduced new methods of construction to produce the tonnage needed in the short time available.

The most important standard tanker of the Second World War was the American T-2 type, of which a total of 525 were produced - the largest run of tankers ever built. They were all-welded to speed up production and the majority, 481 vessels, were of the T2-SE-A1 type which was fitted with advanced turbo-electric machinery of 6,000 shp, giving them a service speed of 14.5-15 knots. The other 44 ships were A2/A3 models which had similar machinery and water-tube boilers, but had an output of 10,000 shp that increased their speed to 16 knots.

Apart from their engines, all the T-2s were virtually identical: 16,600 dwt on an overall length of 503 feet and with a draught of 30 feet. The main cargo space comprised eight sets of tanks, divided by two longitudinal bulkheads, and a short forward tank divided by a single longitudinal bulkhead. There was also a forward dry cargo hold of 15,000 cubic feet. The bridge was placed amidships, with the engine and boiler rooms located aft,

as was the main pump room which replaced the usual aft cofferdam. This was equipped with three large centrifugal pumps of 2,000 gallons per minute (gpm) capacity each and three smaller cargo-stripping pumps. The forward pump room installation consisted of one 700 gpm pump and one of 300 gpm.

The accommodation was of a higher than usual standard for the period, including individual cabins with private showers and toilets for all deck and engineering officers. Sun Shipbuilding & Engineering built 198 T-2 tankers, the most of any US shipyard, while 147 were constructed by Kaiser Company of Swan Island, 102 by the Alabama Dry Dock & Shipbuilding Co, and 34 by Marinship Corp, which also built the 44 A2/A3 versions.

At the time the T-2 came into production welding was considered a relatively new procedure for ships and, although the American Bureau of Shipping (ABS) had first included guidelines for electrical and gas welding in its 1927 Rules, these applied to relatively minor structural components within the hull. It was not until the late 1930s that all-welded merchant ships entered service. Early in the war some merchant vessels suffered inexplicable fractures that were believed to be related to welding.

The T-2s were also prone to this and one of them, *Schenectady*, experienced a spectacular structural failure following sea trials in January 1943.

The vessel was alongside the dock when the deck and both sides of the vessel suddenly fractured just aft of the bridge superstructure.

The failure was total, extending to the turn of the bilge on both port and starboard sides. Only the bottom plating held and the ship jackknifed.

Following this, in April 1943 the Secretary of the Navy set up a Board of Investigation to inquire into the Design and Methods of Construction of Welded Steel Merchant Vessels. The Board included top-level representatives from the US Navy, Coast Guard, Maritime Commission and the American Bureau of Shipping.

The investigation was extensive and cost more than $100 million. Examinations were made on various types of vessels known to have had structural failures - including 20 Liberty ships, six T-2 tankers, three C4 troop carriers and 21 Victory ships. The ships were subjected to a variety of tests, including full-scale hull bending studies in still water, determination of locked-in stresses, including those caused by temperature variations during assembly, and examination of thermal stresses while in service.

These studies found that fractures in the welded ships were caused by steel that was 'notch-sensitive' at operating temperatures which could be caused by high sulphur and phosphorous content. A notch, in this sense, was a discontinuity in the metal, resulting in high stress concentration. The research also identified design-related structural discontinuities, such as hatch openings, vents and other interruptions in the structure. Among the measures taken to prevent the problem were the fitting of 'crack arrestors', modification of the square cargo

hatch corners and the avoidance of sharp structural discontinuities or section design changes. These safety precautions helped to reduce the number of hull fractures from 140 per month in March 1944 to less than 20 per month within two years. In addition, the thorough investigation solved the brittle fracturing problem associated with the all-welded ship.

A batch of six slightly faster tankers was built in 1940/41 for Socony Mobil Oil by Bethlehem Steel Co.
These 15,900 dwt vessels were equipped with geared turbines and water-tube boilers delivering 12,000 shp, which gave them a service speed of 16.5 knots. They were later taken over for duty as fleet oilers and became the forerunners of many tankers of similar size and performance used by the US Navy.

As well as the numerous large tankers built in the war years to replace lost tonnage, American yards also produced many coastal tankers, including the 4,000 dwt T-1 class. These were diesel-powered with a speed of 10 knots and 24 ships of this type were built.

However, the best-known American vessels of World War Two were the famous Liberty dry cargo ships. Between December 1941 and October 1945 some 2,710 were built, of which 62 were completed as tankers. These 10,000 dwt ships were equipped with triple-expansion steam machinery which gave them a speed of 11 knots.
Their design was derived from *Embassage*, a vessel built in 1935 by the British shipbuilders, Thompson's of Sunderland.
After the outbreak of war, Cyril Thompson went to the US to assist the American builder Henry Kaiser, who applied mass production methods using pre-fabrication techniques and all-welded construction. This enabled a Liberty ship to be built in around 60 days and in 1943, at the height of the Battle of the Atlantic, three Liberty ships were being commissioned every day.

*Henry Kaiser, (right) explaining details of his mass production methods to President Roosevelt at the launching of a Liberty ship at Portland, Oregon in 1942*

## British designs - the 'Three Twelves' and Empire-class

British-built tankers in the war were initially based on one or two successful existing designs such as the 'Three Twelves', sometimes known as 'Ocean' type, produced for Shell's Anglo-Saxon fleet. Their internal layout was arranged on conventional lines, with nine sets of tanks divided by twin longitudinal bulkheads to give 27 tanks in all. These 12,000 dwt vessels were originally diesel-powered but later examples were sometimes fitted with triple-expansion steam machinery of 3,800 bhp.

The largest British standard tankers of the war years were the 9,819 grt Empire type which were based on *Eidanger* and her sister ship, *Sandanger*, two ships built by James Laing & Sons in 1938 for H Westfal-Larsen & Co. Originally known as the 'Norwegian type', the first two ships were fitted with 4,800 bhp diesel machinery, giving a speed of 13 knots, while their cargo space incorporated 11 sets of tanks.

In the standard Empire version which followed, the main differences from the earlier ships were the tank arrangements (six sets instead of 11) and the engines. Most were fitted with triple-expansion steam machinery of 3,800 bhp which gave 10.5 knots, while some later ships had 3,300 bhp diesels and the last few were equipped with more powerful 4,400 bhp units. Some 21 Empire types were produced, 15 of these by the original builders Laing, of which five were diesel-powered and 10 steam-driven. The remaining 10 vessels were also steam-driven and built by Furness Shipbuilding.

Both these Empire designs were superseded by the 11,900 dwt Standard Fast Tanker. Fitted with double-reduction geared steam turbines, these vessels had a speed of 15 knots and were swift enough to run independently of the convoys. Somewhat smaller in size was the 5,000 dwt Intermediate type, of which 12 were built. Another four ships (also prefixed Empire) of only 3,200 dwt were specifically designed to provide access to French ports after D-Day. *Empire Pym* was the first tanker to enter Cherbourg after the Normandy landings.

## Post-war rebuilding fired by oil

The war had left large parts of the world in ruins and in the massive task of rebuilding, led by the US, oil was to play as important a role as it did in the war itself.

The Marshall Aid plan for the reconstruction of Western Europe involved the transfer of $13.6 billion from the US, with an estimated 20 per cent being spent on oil and oil equipment between 1948 and 1952. At the same time there was a big shift to the use of oil instead of coal in power stations. In the US itself domestic oil consumption escalated as automobile numbers rose from 26 million to 40 million between 1945 and 1950. In 1948 American imports exceeded exports for the first time, while the price of oil doubled between 1945 and 1948.

To meet the ever-growing appetite for its products, the US oil industry raised production at home and made major new discoveries across the border in Canada. It also turned towards the Middle East where the international oil companies were stepping up investment to consolidate their positions and exploit the region's vast resources.

The governments of America, Britain and France were also focusing their attention on Middle East oil for strategic reasons. Quite simply, oil was indispensable to the running of their economies and any threat to supply represented a risk to national security. The dangers of the Cold War highlighted the importance of access to Middle East oil and for this reason the operations of the major oil companies tended to coincide with the wider interests of America and Western Europe.

The upsurge in the world economy and the sharp rise in demand for oil saw oil shipments more than double in the post-war period, rising from around 210 million tonnes in 1948 to more than 500 million tonnes in 1960, by which time oil accounted for about 50 per cent of total seaborne trade.

*HMS Hermione refueling in the Atlantic from the tanker RFA Dingledale, 30 January 1942*

*Tanker share of world fleet up to 32 per cent*

This created a buoyant market for tanker shipping and called for a considerable expansion in capacity. In 1938 the world tanker fleet had totalled some 17.8 million dwt and, although there were grievously heavy losses of ships and crews during the war - for example, Greece had lost 70 per cent of its merchant marine tonnage - there had also been a very effective replacement programme, particularly with American T-2 standard tankers which later became a mainstay of the post-war tanker fleets as they were sold off as surplus war equipment.

# Growth in Tanker Dwt 1900-60

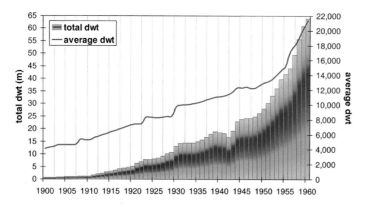

Source: SSY Consultancy & Research Ltd

Within five years of the end of hostilities world tanker tonnage rose to over 28 million dwt and by 1960 had soared to 64 million dwt, following prolific newbuilding activity. This build-up also increased the proportion of tankers in world merchant shipping, in terms of tonnage, from 20 per cent to 32 per cent over the same period.

The pattern of ownership had also been changing, as the major oil companies reduced their share of the world tanker fleet and chartered from the independents to make up their requirements. Prior to the war, the oil companies owned about 54 per cent of all tanker tonnage and the independents had 46 per cent. By 1960 the position was reversed, with the independents having increased their share of the world tanker fleet to 61 per cent. In contrast, the oil company share had slipped down to 39 per cent.

There was also a big increase in the size of new tankers coming off the slipways. In the 1930s, ocean-going tankers had generally been in the 12-14,000 dwt size range, but during World War Two the advent of the T-2 raised the level to over 16,000 dwt. The next big jump came in 1948 with the launching of the 30,011 dwt *Bulkpetrol*.

Then Greek rivalry came into play when Aristotle Onassis launched the 45,230 dwt *Tina Onassis* in 1953, one of the first 'supertankers'. Not to be outdone, Stavros Niarchos launched the similar-sized *World Glory* in 1954 and followed this with the slightly larger *Spyros Niarchos* in 1956. At 47,750 dwt, this was the largest merchant ship built in Britain since the war.

This photograph shows the compartments forward of the cargo tanks. These compartments are generally used to contain fresh water for boiler or domestic purposes, dry cargo or stores, and a deep tank for bunker fuel.

Velutina, built 1950, 29,648 dwt, one of the first four V-class tankers built for Shell which were at that time the largest tankers that had ever been built in Britain.

## Dawn of the VLCC, Middle East exports and economies of scale, Greek owners lead independents

| | |
|---|---|
| 1959-60 | *Daniel K Ludwig has first 100,000 dwt tankers built* |
| 1960 | *OPEC is formed* |
| 1965 | *First oil/bulk/ore (OBO) carrier* |
| 1966 | *First VLCC, Idemitsu Maru* |
| 1967 | *Oil discovered in Alaska* |
| 1967 | *Torrey Canyon runs aground off southwest Britain* |
| 1967 | *Six-day war, Suez Canal closed again, this time for eight years* |
| 1969 | *Oil discovered in North Sea* |
| 1969 | *Delivery of 332,000 dwt Universe Ireland* |

*Daniel K Ludwig*

## Quantum leap in sizes to 100,000 dwt

The 1950s ended with a quantum leap in tanker size through Daniel K Ludwig's *Universe Apollo* and *Universe Daphne*. Constructed in 1959 and 1960, these were the first tankers to exceed 100,000 dwt. Their debut opened up new possibilities for future tanker designs and heralded the era of the supertanker, a term which admittedly had been used for earlier barrier-breaking tankers (as with some in the 1930s). However, the term struck a chord in the 1960s when many things were 'super'.

Ludwig's tankers, built at his leased shipyard in Kure, Japan, introduced the pre-fabrication of tanker sections on a massive scale and set new standards for quality of construction. His highly efficient approach led to lower construction costs and quicker delivery times, while the structural integrity of Ludwig ships ensured that some of his 1970s built tankers were able to continue trading until the end of the century with minimum maintenance. Not surprisingly, Daniel Ludwig became a legend in the industry for well-built tankers with enviable 'on-hire' records. He is also acknowledged as an innovator of modern ship financing techniques, leveraging the equity in existing vessels to finance new ones. In the process he built his National Bulk Carriers company into one of the biggest in the US.

Driving the trend towards ever-larger tankers was the matter of basic economics. Bigger ships could transport oil more cheaply than smaller ships. The application of the 'square-cube rule' meant that increasing the surface area of a tanker, i.e. its main dimensions of length, breadth and draught, by a factor of two expanded its volume by a factor of eight. In other words, doubling the overall dimensions of a tanker increased its earning power by eight times, but only raised the construction costs by a factor of four.

Another advantage with larger tankers was the fact that power required to drive a ship did not rise in direct proportion to the increase in size, but only in the ratio of two-thirds of the increase in displacement. In practice, about 16,000 hp would drive a 60,000 dwt tanker at 15 knots laden, compared with about 42,500 hp needed for tankers of 260,000 dwt, i.e. less than three times the power for more than four times the size of ship.
This brought proportional savings in fuel consumption, as the smaller vessel's 53 tonnes a day only went up to 140 tonnes a day for the larger ship.

There was also the benefit of reduced manning costs with larger tankers, particularly as they became more automated and could be handled by fewer crew than their predecessors. These considerations were not lost on shipowners ordering new tonnage.

The increase in tanker size was also influenced by events in the Middle East which showed how vulnerable western economies had become to disruptions to oil supplies.
While the short-lived nationalisation of Iranian oil production had only a temporary effect, the closure of the Suez Canal in 1956 had far greater repercussions. By 1955 over 60 per cent of oil bound for Europe passed through the Canal, while tankers accounted for one-half the total shipping using the waterway on a tonnage basis.
The invasion of Egypt by British, French and Israeli forces in 1956 led to the scuttling of ships in the Canal which remained blocked until the following year.

Earlier, in 1951, the Anglo-Iranian Oil Company had been nationalised and its concession repudiated by the Iranian government under new prime minister, Dr Mossadegh. An embargo on Iranian oil exports followed and oil processed at Abadan, the world's biggest refinery, fell from its 1950 level of 666,000 barrels per day to around 20,000 barrels per day in 1952, causing an international shortage.
The embargo was enforced by British armed forces and in one incident a Panamanian-flag tanker, *Rose Mary*, was forced by the Royal Air Force to divert to Aden to discharge her cargo. However, Mossadegh was overthrown the following year after which the Shah returned and by November 1953 Iranian production had risen to six million tons a year. The crisis, however, led to the end of the monopoly of Anglo-Iranian. A new company was set up in which the big five US oil companies, Shell and the French state oil company were shareholders.

Political instability and the threat to vital transport arteries also served to increase the size of tankers. Oil was increasingly being shipped as crude for refining in the main consuming regions of North America, Europe and Japan. The growing requirement to ship Middle East Gulf crude oil around the Cape of Good Hope dictated economies of scale on tankers. To a lesser extent, oil was also carried by pipeline from the Gulf states to terminals on the Mediterranean or Red Sea. In 1950, for example, the $100 million Trans-Arabian Pipeline (Tapline) was built to carry Saudi Arabian oil more than 1,000 miles overland to Sidon in Lebanon. It not only cut thousands of miles off the traditional sea voyage but also avoided the payment of Suez Canal dues. Pipelines, however, were to prove just as vulnerable as canals to political disruption. Tanker design also became more specialised. Not only was there a need to build larger and more efficient crude oil carriers, but also specific types of vessel for the transportation of refined products, chemicals, liquefied natural gas and liquefied petroleum gas.

During the mid-1950s Russia reappeared on the world scene and began exporting oil to the West. By 1961 the USSR had overtaken Venezuela as the world's second largest producer after the US, with an output approaching 60 per cent of the total Middle East production. Russian oil and the expansion of independent oil companies, such as Getty Oil with its Saudi Arabian concession, (and its most productive 'neutral zone' concession between Saudi Arabia, Kuwait and Iraq) forced prices down in the oil markets. When the major oil companies tried to force the price cuts to producers in the Middle East, the hostile reaction resulted in the creation in 1960 of the Organization of Petroleum Exporting Countries (OPEC) whose members at the time were the source of about 80 per cent of total world oil exports.

## Emergence of new oil producers changes market

In the next few years the situation changed again, with the emergence of North and West African countries as major oil producers. First, oil was discovered in Libya which,

by the end of 1960s, had an output greater than Saudi Arabia's and was exporting three million barrels a day. One of Libya's most prolific strikes was made in 1966 on a concession won by the American oilman Dr Armand Hammer for his Occidental Petroleum Company. Known as the Idris field, it produced more than 800,000 barrels a day and helped to transform Occidental into one of the world's biggest oil companies. Large oil reserves had also been discovered in Algeria in the late 1950s by French interests and by 1961 Algeria was providing nearly 100 per cent of France's oil requirements.

Oil was also being exported from West Africa following discoveries in Nigeria by Shell and BP in the 1950s, although the volumes were not as significant as those flowing from North Africa.

In overall terms oil imports by the major industrialised regions soared between 1960 and 1970. Annual Japanese imports expanded almost fivefold during the decade, from 34 million tons to 213 million tons, while for Western Europe the figure more than tripled, from 206 million tons to 636 million tons.

Meanwhile, exploration efforts in Alaska and the North Sea were about to result in major new sources of oil.

In 1967 massive reserves were discovered at Prudhoe Bay on Alaska's North Slope. This turned out to be the largest oilfield ever discovered in America, although it did not start producing for some years. In the North Sea, which Britain and Norway had divided between them, the first offshore success came in 1969 when Philips Petroleum made a major find in the Ekofisk field in the Norwegian sector.

## War in the Middle East, Suez Canal closure

These new discoveries acquired greater importance when Israeli forces attacked Egypt in June 1967 - the Six Day War. This gave OPEC the first real opportunity to flex its muscles by using the oil weapon. The Organization instantly placed a ban on oil exports to "countries that were friendly to Israel" which mainly affected America and Britain. Within days, the flow of Middle East oil to the West was reduced by 60 per cent. This was their first oil embargo.

# The Suez Canal

**Maximum Draught**

| Year | | Draught |
|------|---|---------|
| 1869 | | 6.76 m (22.2') |
| 1914 | | 8.84 m (29') |
| 1961 | | 11.28 m (37') |
| 1980 | | 16.16 m (53') |
| 2001 | | 19.07 m (62') |

*Since the Suez Canal first opened to shipping in 1869, it has periodically been enlarged to accommodate the increasing size of ships. From its original depth of 6.76 metres it was deepened to 8.84 metres in 1914 and then to 11.28 metres in 1961 which gave passage to fully-laden vessels of up to 70,000 dwt. In 1980 the depth was increased again to 16.16 metres which accommodated fully-laden ships of up to 125,000 dwt, including the so-called Suezmax class. The latest enlargement came in 2001 which gave a depth of 19.07 metres and allowed fully-laden vessels of up to 150,000 dwt to transit the Canal. In 1996 the Canal Authority revised the escorting arrangements for ships using the Suez Canal net tonnage (SC nt) as the scale for charges. This covered ULCCs, VLCCs, LNGs, LPGs and certain other types of vessel and stipulated that: loaded vessels from 70,000 to 90,000 SC nt and vessels in ballast over 130,000 SC nt escorted by one tug; loaded vessels over 90,000 SC nt and vessels in ballast with a beam exceeding 71 m escorted by two tugs.*

Acknowledged as one of the greatest feats of hydraulic engineering of all time, the Suez Canal links the Mediterranean Sea at Port Said with the Red Sea at Suez through the Isthmus of Egypt to provide the shortest maritime link between Europe and the Indian and Western Pacific Oceans.

Its construction was a milestone in the development of shipping and world trade. The project was launched in 1854 when the French engineer Ferdinand de Lesseps was granted a concession to build a canal by the Viceroy of Egypt. A second Act, passed in 1856, gave the Compagnie Universelle du Canal Maritime (Suez Canal Company) the right to operate a canal for 99 years after its completion.

Work on the project began in 1859 and was scheduled to take six years. However, due to climatic difficulties, a cholera epidemic and labour problems, it actually took 10 years to finish. At first the excavation relied heavily on manual labour, but later steam shovels were used and, after some flooding of the terrain, dredgers were also brought in.

The Canal was completed in August 1869 and when it first opened for navigation the 103-mile long waterway was about 26 feet deep (except over the Serapeum Rock), 72 feet wide at the bottom and 200 to 300 feet wide between banks, with passing bays at 5 to 6 mile intervals. The Serapeum Rock was a serious obstacle at the Suez end of the Canal. It reduced the depth to 19 feet until it was removed in February 1870.

The initial transit times averaged 40 hours for individual ships which used passing bays to allow vessels to pass each other in either direction. From 1947 a convoy system, under pilotage, was introduced which cut transit times to around 14 hours.

In the early years of operation there were many groundings. However, over the years the Canal was periodically enlarged to take bigger ships. By the 1960s the channel depth had been increased to 40 feet at low tide, with a minimum width of 179 feet at a depth of 33 feet along its banks, allowing passage to fully laden ships of up to 70,000 dwt. The Suez Development Scheme, completed in 1980, provided a depth of 53 feet which could accommodate vessels of up to 125,000 dwt, including the so-called Suezmax type, and the depth was later increased to 62 feet.

During its first year of operation the Canal handled 2,014 transits and by the mid-1990s the figure was 929 transits. In 2000 the Canal handled 1,753 tanker transits totalling 87.7 m dwt and 53 m cargo tonnes.

The closure of the Canal during the Suez Crisis of 1967 was a major influence on the development of VLCCs and ULCCs. These large tankers were designed to carry oil in very large quantities to minimise the cost of taking the longer route round the Cape of Good Hope and thus realise the benefits of economies of scale.

The Canal was originally financed by a share issue, of which French investors took up 52 per cent and the Viceroy of Egypt 44 per cent. In 1875 the Viceroy sold his holdings which were purchased by the British government, making it the major shareholder, and at the same time 7 per cent of the shares were allocated to Egyptian investors who were also represented on the Board of the company. In 1956 the Canal was nationalised by President Nasser and the Egyptian government has been in control since that time.

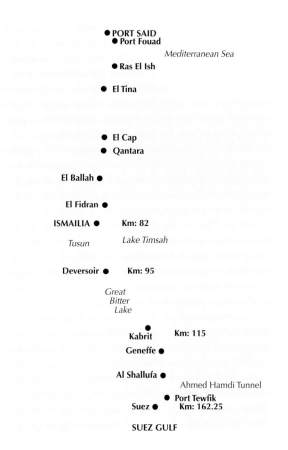

## Suez Canal Oil Flows

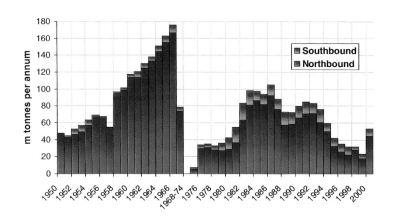

Source: Suez Canal Authority/SSY Consultancy & Research Ltd

The closure of both the Suez Canal, which this time remained shut until 1975, and the pipelines to the Mediterranean, meant that whatever oil was transported to Europe had to be shipped round the Cape of Good Hope. This virtually doubled the distance from the Arabian Gulf to ports in northern Europe and created a surge in demand for tanker capacity and a welcome increase in freight rates.

The OPEC embargo proved short-lived, as the deficit was easily made up by increased production from non-OPEC sources. However, the closure of the Suez Canal boosted tanker demand by 70 per cent on oil trade routes to the West and by 20 per cent on world oil trade routes overall. This again emphasised the benefits of the bigger tankers coming into service, with their ability to reduce the unit costs of transporting crude over long distances. These ships were originally designed to carry large volumes of Middle East crude to new refineries in Europe which had been built close to the markets they served. Instead of mainly carrying clean or dirty products from Texas, Curaçao, Aruba and Abadan, tankers started to carry crude oil to refineries in Europe and Japan. This growing trade in crude oil called for the loading of cargo in much bigger lots.

## Bigger tankers vindicated on long-hauls

The building of new ships was also encouraged by the improvement in freight rates. The new generation of supertankers fully proved their effectiveness on the long haul routes around Africa and on the route from the Arabian Gulf to Japan, where imported oil had displaced coal as the main source of energy.

The Arabian Gulf continued to increase its share of world oil output during the 1960s. In contrast to the start of the decade, when it accounted for 36 per cent of world seaborne oil trade with 90 million tons, by 1970 Gulf exports had grown to 566 million tons, representing 43 per cent of the trade. This trade involved long sea routes: 4,000-8,000 miles for western trades via the Suez Canal and some 11,000-12,000 miles around the Cape of Good Hope.

## Delivery of world's first VLCC

As a result, the Ludwig ships of over 100,000 dwt, built at the beginning of the decade, were soon overtaken by larger vessels and by the mid-1960s the first very large crude carriers (VLCCs) were coming into service. The 206,106 dwt *Idemitsu Maru*, built in 1966, is credited as being the first VLCC. Built by Ishikawajima-Harima Heavy Industries in Yokohama, she had a length of 1,129 feet, a beam of 163 feet and a fully laden draught of just over 58 feet. Steam turbines gave her a speed of 16 knots. Another early example was the 170,800 dwt *Esso Mercia*, Exxon's first VLCC which, on her maiden voyage, delivered 150,190 tons of crude oil to the company's refinery at Milford Haven, the largest cargo ever brought to the UK up to that time. Shortly afterwards Shell launched the 205,800 dwt *Megara*, one of 15 'M' class vessels. Other notable tankers built earlier in the 1960s included the 91,400 dwt *Rimfonn* for Sigval Bergesen and the 95,386 dwt *Næss Sovereign* and the 71,183 dwt *Næss Norseman*, both of which were built for Erling Naess. *Næss Norseman* was the first true oil-bulk-ore carrier or OBO.

By 1969 tankers of over 200,000 dwt were no longer a novelty. Newbuildings that year included the launch of the 213,000 dwt *Energy Revolution* for C Y Tung's Island Navigation Corporation; the 216,490 dwt *Olympic Athlete* for Onassis; the 210,822 dwt *Bulford* which was handed over to Blandford Shipping of London by Sasebo Heavy Industries of Japan; and the 212,000 dwt *J A McCone*, one of four sisterships built for Chevron by Kockums of Sweden. The *J A McCone* was notable in being the first ship design to be subject to finite element analysis (FEA), a technique that up until then had only been used for aircraft structures. The vessel was Chevron's first VLCC and the company commissioned the American Bureau of Shipping (ABS) to analyse the new design using the latest technology available for structural evaluation and stress analysis. The finite-element analysis carried out by ABS enabled a structure too complex to analyse as a whole to be broken up into tiny finite parts, each of which could be analysed and then linked back together to represent the whole.

*Næss Sovereign, 95,386 dwt, launched in 1960 built by the Mitsubishi Shipbuilding and Engineering Company, Nagasaki, Japan. In her first year of operation the Næss Sovereign carried 11 cargoes of crude oil, aggregating nearly 950,000 tonnes*

Because the number of elements ran into the hundreds of thousands, the calculations could only be done on a computer. At the time this was breaking new ground and ABS had to develop a special computer program called 'DAISY' (Displacement Automated Integrated System) and write the system's pre-processing programs. This defined hull form geometry, calculated hull girder bending moments and shear forces, developed the ship structure finite element models and the sea loads, and then created a data file read by 'DAISY' to calculate the stresses and deflections in the ship structure.

Before the end of the 1960s Daniel Ludwig had had six VLCCs of 327,000 dwt each built in Japanese shipyards and backed by charters to Gulf Oil. They were initially used to serve Gulf Oil's new Bantry Bay terminal in Ireland.

Between 1960 and 1970 the overall world tanker fleet grew from 64 million dwt to over 155 million dwt. During this period Greek shipowners gained a dominant share of the independent tanker market and by the end of the 1960s controlled a tanker fleet of 26 million dwt.
This was followed by Britain with 22 million dwt and Norway with 17 million dwt.

## Russia builds world-ranking fleet

At the same time Russia, one of the world's leading oil exporting countries, was developing an impressive new-building programme for seagoing tankers. In July 1946 the entire Russian transport fleet had consisted of 730 vessels totalling 2.1 million dwt, of which 55 per cent were aged 15 years or older. The government then took a special decision on shipbuilding with a priority for tankers. The idea was to build dozens of sister ships to speed up construction and simplify technical management and to place multiple orders with a particular shipyard to reduce building costs.

In 1951 Russian yards started to build *Kazbek*-type tankers, flexible handy-size vessels of 12,000 dwt with 4,000 hp diesel engines. During the 1950s 51 *Kazbek*-type tankers were built which helped the Russian tanker fleet to become the sixth largest in the world in terms of gross tonnage by 1960.

Next came the 32,030 dwt *Pekin*-type with steam turbines giving the tankers a service speed of 16.4 knots. Seven of these ships were built by the Admiralteiskiy Shipyard, Leningrad during the period 1959-1962. These were followed by 22 *Sophia*-type tankers of 54,000 dwt also powered by steam turbines and built by the Baltiyskiy Shipyard of Leningrad. The 19,000 hp turbines provided them with a service speed of 14.9 knots.

The Russians also ordered from overseas yards. These included six *Leonardo da Vinci* types of 50,720 dwt each built in Italy; 22 *Lisichansk/Lugansk* types of 36,684 dwt from Japan; and 33 *Split*-type product carriers of 22,330 dwt built in Yugoslavia between 1965 and 1970.
Altogether 141 tankers totalling 3.9 million dwt were built to these six ship types.

Other types, including the *Velikly Octyabr*-type of 16,500 dwt, the *Baskunchak*-type of 1,500 dwt and shallow-draught tankers, brought overall Russian tanker tonnage up to 5 million dwt by 1972.

This large tanker fleet was multi-purpose and capable of providing coastal trading to the Arctic and the Far East; bunkering of fishing vessels around the world; exports of crude oil and petroleum products from Russian ports; and serving the international cross trades.

To some extent there was an underlying political aspect to these tanker operations in that they helped to provide oil supplies to 'friendly nations'. For example, at the end of the 1960s the annual volume of Soviet-Cuban trade was in excess of 10 million tons, most of which was in oil and petroleum products. This involved Novoship tankers in regular round-the-world voyages: Black Sea to Cuba with oil cargoes, Cuba to Venezuela in ballast, Venezuela to Japan via the Panama Canal with crude oil, Japan to Nakhodka in ballast, Nakhodka to South or South East Asia with oil cargoes, South Asia to the Arabian Gulf in ballast, Arabian Gulf to the Mediterranean with crude oil and Mediterranean to Black Sea in ballast to complete the cycle.

# Growth in Tanker Numbers 1900-70

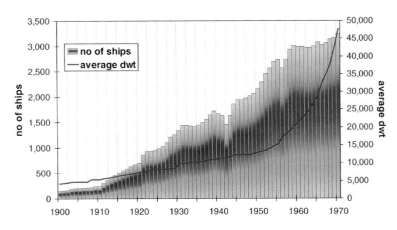

Source: SSY Consultancy & Research Ltd

*Nisseki Maru, 372,698 dwt, built 1971*

Larger tankers were sometimes used for special projects. For example, in June 1961 *Pekin* towed a large floating dock with a lift capability of 60,000 tons from Kronshtadt on the Baltic to Ilyichevsk on the Black Sea.

This was a three-month towing operation around the European continent. Other towing operations followed, using large tankers to haul huge floating docks or crane vessels between the Baltic and Black Seas to Far East ports, including Vladivostok and Nakhodka.

## Onassis, Niarchos lead Greek tanker expansion

Much of the Greek tanker fleet expansion was due to a new generation of owners, personified by Aristotle Onassis and Stavros Niarchos. Unlike the more established Greek shipowning families who financed new ships out of profits, the newcomers ordered vessels on credit backed by 5-10 year charters to major oil companies.

By assigning the charter income directly to the lending institution, the credit risk was virtually eliminated.

This was based on a method originally devised by Norwegian shipowners and later developed by Daniel Ludwig but the Greeks then expanded the concept by placing multiple orders, mostly supported by long-term time charters, but leaving some tonnage available for the spot market. By placing a series of orders with a particular shipyard, building costs could also be reduced. The orders were also very beneficial in helping to rejuvenate the war-torn shipyards of Germany, Britain, Holland, Spain, France, Japan and other countries.

The Greek resurgence had its origins in the 1940s when some of the leading shipping families moved to New York for access to the major oil companies, notably Manolis Kulukundis, Stavros Livanos, and the Goulandris brothers from London, Aristotle Onassis from Buenos Aires and Stavros Niarchos from Greece. Their involvement in oil transportation was soon shared by other leading Greek shipping companies, including those of Costas Laimos, Lykiardropoulos and the Chandris brothers, who contributed to the post-war expansion of Greek tanker ownership.

They were later followed by the 'new guard' of Greek owners like G.P. Livanos, Haji-Ioannou, Martinos brothers, Angelicoussis, Tsakos, Alafouzos and Eletson who brought a deep knowledge of tankers and their management.

The rise of the Greek tanker fleet was in contrast to the position of Norwegian owners who, in the 1950s and early 1960s, were hampered by a strict licensing system for newbuilding orders placed in foreign shipyards.

The Norwegian government was ostensibly seeking to preserve foreign exchange reserves but the restriction also applied to owners who could finance their orders by as much as 100 per cent. During this period it became harder to obtain credit and interest rates increased, making it difficult for Norwegian shipowners themselves to finance the ships 100 per cent, particularly as building prices had increased. However, the most important consideration was the 'flying start' gained by foreign shipowners in obtaining cheap tankers. Norwegian owners were thus unable to fully participate in the expansion of the oil companies' fleets through the use of time charters and were forced to watch such potentially lucrative contracts awarded to owners from other countries.

For Norwegian owners the timing could not have been worse because in June 1950 war broke out in Korea which drove up oil tanker freight rates and generated big profits for the tanker industry. Norwegian owners were unable to take advantage of the situation but the burgeoning Greek fleets were ideally placed to exploit the opportunity.

It is estimated that it took at least 10 years for Norway's tanker owners to overcome the setback caused by the licensing restriction.

By the end of the 1960s independent tanker fleets were being operated from the British colony of Hong Kong where Y K Pao and C Y Tung were emerging as major figures in the independent tanker sector. They built up significant fleets, geared mainly to the Japanese oil trade and backed by major Japanese trading houses.

Their success was often attributed to the 'shikumisen' system whereby Japanese shipping companies and trading houses used the Hong Kong owners to build and operate tankers more cheaply and efficiently. Shikumisen is a Japanese term for 'tie-in ships' which had been used earlier to facilitate the expansion of Hong Kong - owned dry cargo fleets and then adopted for tankers in 1962 when Y K Pao made what is claimed to be the first shikumisen deal with the Yamashita KK shipping line.

Aristotle Onassis

Stavros Niarchos at the launch of one of his many ships

World Concord, 31,805 dwt, built 1952

# OPEC - a major force in the world oil market

By 1960 some 80 per cent of oil traded internationally was exported from the Middle East. Although the ultimate owners of this oil were the Middle East states, in practice concession agreements permitted oil companies to establish their own development programmes, customer portfolios, production levels and, most importantly, their own pricing policy. "Posted prices" had been published in the Middle East since the early 1950s to denote the price at which crude oil was ostensibly available for sale on the open market and to provide a basis on which royalties and taxes payable to producing governments could be calculated - the so-called 50/50 sharing of profits. However, most oil was not traded on this market but rather was transferred within or between the major producing oil companies. With the dramatic increase in Middle East oil production as the 1950s progressed, combined with greater output from Russia, Venezuela and the US, the price at which oil could be sold fell well below the posted price.

In August 1960 posted prices were reduced to reflect the surplus production capacity. Oil-producing governments, faced with a reduction in their revenues, responded quickly. In September 1960 the Organization of the Petroleum Exporting Countries (OPEC) was formed at a conference in Baghdad, Iraq. The five founding members - Iran, Iraq, Kuwait, Saudi Arabia and Venezuela - were later joined by eight other countries: Qatar (1961), Indonesia (1962), Libya (1962), United Arab Emirates (1967), Algeria (1969), Nigeria (1971), Ecuador (1973) and Gabon (1975). Ecuador and Gabon withdrew from OPEC in 1992 and 1994, respectively.

The establishment of OPEC started a process whereby the strength and commercial freedom of manoeuvre enjoyed by the oil companies was steadily eroded. The power shift began with 'participation', whereby governments took over a proportion of the production interests, together with responsibility for an equivalent percentage of developments costs. The process culminated in October 1973 when Arabs and Israelis again went to war. In the midst of the ensuing oil production cutbacks, temporary supply embargoes on selected consumer countries and a massive increase in crude prices, producing governments assumed full ownership of oil production in their territories.

This effectively brought to an end oil companies' control over the development, production and pricing of oil. In the aftermath of the 1973 war OPEC was able to restrain production levels and help its member governments achieve their production and revenue ambitions. By January 1974 the price of crude oil exported from OPEC countries was five times higher than the price paid in January 1971. The essential nature of oil, i.e. there are no adequate substitutes, coupled with its limited number of suppliers, make it the ideal product for cartelisation.

Since the early 1980s OPEC members have often been faced with a difficult choice - either cut prices to regain markets or cut production to maintain price. In general, OPEC countries have been reluctant to reduce prices for fear that such action would undermine their whole pricing structure; lose their great economic and political gains; and so diminish their political influence. Over the years OPEC members have not always aligned on a united front to confront this pressure. For example, Saudi Arabia, whose oil production far surpasses that of other member countries, has often supported lower prices in order to secure a larger market share in the face of opposition from fellow members.

Looking back at the overall impact of this union of oil-producing nations, it is clear that the success of OPEC in the 1970s triggered conservation, substitution and new, non-OPEC sources of oil production in the 1980s. However, these new non-OPEC sources are relatively small and are likely to be depleted rapidly over the next 10 years. Although OPEC countries currently account for only 40 per cent of world oil exports, they hold the major share of the oil that is still in the ground. Oil prices are at relatively low levels in real terms, and it is clear that the global demand for oil will continue to rise. With the lack of major new oil finds over the last 10 years, the non-OPEC supply of oil is likely to grow only slowly. Unless a cheap alternative source of energy is discovered in the meantime, this combination of effects will serve to increase the role and strength of OPEC in the future world oil market.

## Oil shocks after biggest tanker fleet expansion, world recession, war in the Gulf

| | |
|---|---|
| *1970* | *Oil strike in North Sea forties field* |
| *1970* | *Libya gains 30 per cent rise in oil price* |
| *1973* | *Yom Kippur War* |
| *1975* | *First US-built gas-turbine tanker* |
| *1975* | *Suez Canal re-opens* |
| *1976* | *Argo Merchant sinks off US East Coast* |
| *1976* | *Norway sets up refinancing scheme* |
| *1978* | *Amoco Cadiz grounding off France* |
| *1980* | *Iran-Iraq Gulf War* |
| *1983* | *MARPOL Annex I comes into force* |

Chapter Five: A time of crisis

While the early 1970s still promised continuing economic growth and strong demand for oil, there were already warning signs that the glut of cheap oil the world had been enjoying for so long was not going to last much longer. Demand was already threatening to outstrip supply and an oil shortage was being forecast.

## Tanker fleet more than doubles 1970-77

Unaware or undaunted and encouraged by healthy profits and optimistic predictions for further 8 per cent per annum increases in oil production and consumption oil companies and independent tankers owners alike went on a buying spree which increased the world tanker fleet from about 154 million dwt in 1970 to some 338 million dwt by 1977.

This was the largest and fastest expansion ever experienced by the tanker fleet. Unfortunately, this unbridled expansion was followed by a major collapse in demand. Further events later in the decade only exacerbated the situation. The result was a huge surplus of tanker tonnage that overhung the market for most of the following 25 years.

The collapse of the tanker market was the result of the massive increase in newbuildings coinciding with a severe slump in oil demand. The price of oil rose from around $1.80 a barrel in 1970 to over $35 in 1980. Political tensions in the Middle East had much to do with the oil price increases. Key events were the attack on Israel by Syria and Egypt in October 1973 (the Yom Kippur War); a subsequent OPEC embargo on Arab states' exports to the US (the second one); the revolution in Iran and overthrow of the Shah in 1979; and, finally, the Iran-Iraq war in 1980. As a result of the two "oil shocks" of 1973 and 1979-80, oil prices soared.

The Iran-Iraq war removed a significant amount of oil from the market, as together the two countries accounted for 15 per cent of OPEC production. At the outbreak of the Iran-Iraq war oil prices rose to $42 a barrel and OPEC production fell from 30 million barrels a day to 21 million in 1981. However, world oil production and consumption continued to rise during the 1970s and 1980s.

Before these oil shocks, the post-war development of the tanker market had largely followed an orderly pattern of supply and demand, with the oil companies dictating the terms. In 1950, when the price of Middle East crude was as low as $1.60 a barrel, the cost of shipping it to Western European refineries was about the same, so transportation accounted for a high proportion of the end-user price.

As the oil trade grew, the oil companies were able to cut transportation overheads by reducing their own fleets to levels which provided them with optimum utilisation. They then made up the balance of their transport requirements by chartering ships from independent shipowners at competitive rates. During this period each new stage in the evolution of tanker design provided ships of increased size to enable oil to be carried in larger quantities at lower prices.

In the 1960s, when the oil companies owned about 40 per cent of the world tanker fleet and time-chartered another 50 per cent, the market was in a reasonable state of equilibrium. As newbuildings were generally linked to long-term time charters, this helped to ensure that fleet growth was geared to underlying demand, but provided enough spot market capacity to cover any sudden fluctuations.

This situation prevailed until the early 1970s when tanker demand soared by a further 200 million dwt in 1973. This caused a corresponding rise in VLCC freight rates.

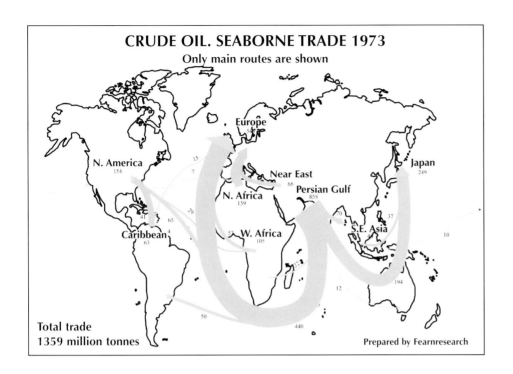

**CRUDE OIL. SEABORNE TRADE 1973**
Only main routes are shown

Europe
N. America 154
Near East 66
N. Africa 159
Persian Gulf 858
Japan 249
Caribbean 63
W. Africa 105
S.E. Asia 194

Total trade
1359 million tonnes

Prepared by Fearnresearch

## Oil Price Development 1970-80

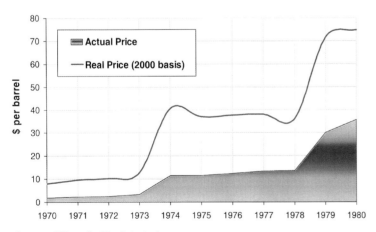

- ▓ Actual Price
- — Real Price (2000 basis)

$ per barrel

1970 1971 1972 1973 1974 1975 1976 1977 1978 1979 1980

Source: Gilbert Jenkins/Intertanko

## Growth in Tanker Dwt 1970-80

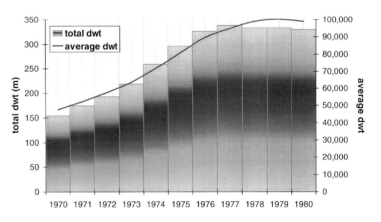

- ▓ total dwt
- — average dwt

total dwt (m)

average dwt

1970 1971 1972 1973 1974 1975 1976 1977 1978 1979 1980

Source: SSY Consultancy & Research Ltd

*Aftermath of the build up of surplus tonnage in the early 1970s - tankers in lay-up*

The result was an additional rush of speculative newbuilding to meet expected increases in demand on top of an existing large orderbook. This increased the world tanker fleet to 330 million dwt in 1980. Initially, demand grew so fast that it absorbed the new tonnage, but when demand fell there was a world tanker surplus and some new vessels went straight into lay-up from delivery.

After rising to 234 million dwt in 1974, demand had plunged to half this level between 1979 and 1985 because of economic slowdown. In addition, the European and Japanese energy markets had entered a period of maturity and slower growth, as the transition from coal to oil for power generation was largely complete. Even worse, the high price of oil was causing some power stations to revert to coal.

The diminished need for long-haul transportation put freight rates under heavy pressure. The abysmally low rates, both for the spot market and long-term charters, coupled with inflationary overheads, particularly fuel prices which escalated from under $20 a ton in 1970 to over $200 by 1981, put tanker owners between a rock and a hard place.

They were also hit by the reduced value of their ships; second-hand VLCC prices fell from a high of over $82 m in August 1973 to around scrap value in the early 1980s.

Tankers were also put on slow-steaming to help absorb the surplus tonnage. This practice also reduced fuel consumption by around 25 per cent. Some ships were used as floating oil storage vessels, particularly by the Japanese, and by October 1981 around 32 million dwt of tanker shipping was deployed for this purpose.

Another way some owners cut overheads was to transfer ships operating under high-cost national flags to 'open registers' like Panama and Liberia which, among other things, enabled operating costs to be reduced. Switching flags was not easy, because the most powerful maritime unions were associated with American, North European and Japanese flags. As early as 1948 these unions had launched a worldwide campaign against what they labelled 'flags of convenience'. Boycotts of flagged-out ships were staged where local laws were favourable, but owners often preferred to avoid such boycotts by signing special crew agreements with the unions.

Some of the expansion of the tanker fleet had been financed by banks, shipyards and government institutions with limited experience of ship finance. After the collapse in ship demand, the shipowners were blamed entirely for over-ordering new tonnage, while owners in turn blamed the lenders for being too ready to supply easy credit.
In the mid-1970s the world tanker fleet carried a debt of around $35 billion, but its second-hand value was only about $25 billion, assuming the ships could be sold.
Not surprisingly, many owners were driven into bankruptcy when the market crashed and the banks had to write off a considerable amount of bad shipping debts.

To give its own tanker industry some breathing space, the Norwegian government in 1976 introduced the Norwegian Guarantee Institute for Ships and Drilling Vessels which enabled many Norwegian shipowners to re-finance their vessels. However, the take-up was more extensive than had been envisaged and the scheme was discontinued in 1982.

While this scheme saved many companies from going under, as did some banks who supported other owners to avoid bringing on an industry-wide failure, it could be argued that it was not in the best overall interests of the industry. This is because the scheme also prevented surplus tonnage being scrapped and new orders from being cancelled.

# Tanker flags and open registers

As signatories of International Maritime Organization (IMO) conventions, flag states are the ultimate arbiters of the safety of ships registered in their country. When these IMO conventions were originally drafted, most ships flew the flags of the world's major maritime and trading nations, in which their owners were domiciled, and the enforcement of standards was robust and immune from commercial pressures. Today, however, this is no longer the case. Most countries now operate flag administrations and maintain so-called 'open' registers under which owners from other countries can flag their ships. Owners have been attracted to these registers due to attractive tax and other fiscal arrangements, while others have often been enticed by a regime in which the enforcement of applicable international standards is less rigorous than that practiced by responsible maritime states.

Although the majority of open registers are now operated to the required high standard, the lack of uniform enforcement of applicable rules and regulations worldwide has left the door open to so-called substandard flag administrations. These less-committed registers have tainted the concept of open registry and raised questions about the ability of flag state control to prevent substandard shipowners and operators from plying their trade.

## Tanker Fleet by Flag

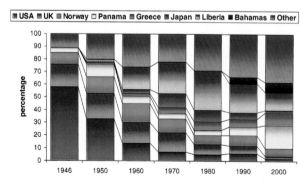

Source: SSY Consultancy & Research Ltd

## Flags of convenience

The first open registers were branded 'flags of convenience'. This phrase first came into shipping parlance in reference to a Honduras registration during a hearing of the US Senate committee on interstate and foreign commerce in 1950. However, sailing under a foreign flag was practiced long before that - as early as 1812 when the US and Britain were at war. At the time some US merchant vessels sailed under Portuguese colours to evade American and British restrictions. Also, in the first half of the nineteenth century slave trading ships owned by American and Latin American interests used various foreign flags to circumvent slave trade suppression treaties.

## Panama to the fore

The growth of Panama as a flag state began in 1916 when it opened its registry to ships owned by Panamanian corporations that were themselves owned by foreign entities. American owners soon started to take advantage of the facility as it offered low taxes and lenient conditions of employment and operation. This, in turn, allowed owners to recruit lower-paid international crews and trim operating costs. Further benefits to American owners included the availability of an American service agency to deal with administration and documentation; the ability to carry out legal and commercial transactions in English; a currency based on the US dollar; and proximity to the Panama Canal.

Buyers of many US-flag ships surplus to requirements of World War One chose to register the vessels in Panama which, among its other advantages, relieved the owners of continued boiler and hull inspections by the American Bureau of Shipping (ABS) and lessened the requirements for crew quarters and subsistence. This enabled owners to reduce overheads and made it possible for them to compete on international routes with shipping operating on a similar cost, non-US base, e.g Japanese owned tonnage.

In 1925 Panama increased its registration fees to provide more state revenue and revised the provisions of registry to attract more foreign shipping and take into account certain concerns of US shipowners. By 1939 52 tankers totalling 0.7 m dwt were registered in Panama. About one-third of these were owned by US corporations, including a number of Standard Oil tankers. The biggest transfer came in 1935 when Standard Oil New Jersey (Esso) switched all 25 tankers totalling more than 230,000 dwt, of its Baltic subsidiary, Bapico, from the Danzig register to Panama. A new operation was formed for this purpose - Panama Transport Company - which brought the vessels under US ownership and control. These moves were encouraged by the US government in anticipation of the need for neutral tonnage if war came to Europe.

During the Second World War vital cargoes of petroleum and food were shipped from the US to Britain in American-owned vessels registered in Panama which were technically neutral. Even so, around 150 Panama-flagged merchant ships were sunk or captured during the conflict. After the war Panama registration helped American merchant shipping to remain competitive by reducing costs to levels comparable with those of its rivals.

By forming Panamanian subsidiaries, tanker owners did not have to pay taxes until they declared dividends to their US parent companies which enabled them to re-invest their earnings indefinitely, allowing faster repayment of mortgages.

Under the 1946 American Ship Sales Act some 1,113 ships were sold to foreign flags. In the case of war-built T-2 tankers, the US Maritime Commission ruled that these could only be sold to American-owned firms. As a result 152 of these vessels were acquired by US owners and registered in Panama, although some of the firms were actually controlled by foreign owners.

The number of vessels sailing under the Panamanian flag increased from 80 tankers, totalling 0.9 m dwt in 1946 to 182 tankers, totalling 2.3 m dwt by 1948.

This success caused a backlash from the seafaring unions which led to boycotts of Panamanian-registered vessels, as well as opposition from established European maritime states. These difficulties were compounded by a deterioration in post-war relations between the US and Panama, instability in Panamanian politics and glimmerings of dissatisfaction among US tanker owners. The situation was not helped by Panamanian consuls charging for maritime services to generate additional revenue.

## Enter the Liberian register

Panama's problems created the opportunity to develop an open register in Liberia, which would eventually become the world's largest maritime flag state, in terms of total registered tonnage, although Panama later regained the lead.

When Liberia was founded in 1847 as the first African republic, it already had strong ties with the US through liberated American slaves and freemen who had settled there from 1822. After the Second World War Liberia's economy was in poor shape and an American firm - Stettinius Associates - developed the basic structure of a ship registration facility.

The first vessel entered with the new Liberian registry was the Niarchos owned tanker *World Peace* in 1949. Within a year there were 12 tankers on the register and by 1958 Liberia had increased this to 407 ships totalling 10.5 million dwt. The growth continued and by 1978 the Liberian registry accounted for 784 tankers totalling 103.4 m dwt, compared with around 124 tankers with 9.6 m dwt for Panama. The success of the Liberian registry was mainly due to it being tailored specifically for the needs of US shipowners by incorporating the best features of the Panama system but with the addition of a highly efficient business administration.

In spite of sustained political pressure and legal actions brought by international transport unions and governments of the traditional maritime states of Europe, ship owners successfully defended the principles of open registers to ensure their continued existence. By 1982 around 33 per cent of the world tanker fleet sailed under open registers.

*The bulbous bow section of a tanker under construction. This is an important part of the vessel which is heavily reinforced with transverse stringers, frames and beams to withstand the considerable stresses which occur during service. Originally introduced in the early 1960s the bulbous bow improves the vessel's hydrodynamics by counteracting the normal bow wave effect to assist progress through the water. The benefits are a speed gain of 0.5 knot, on average, and a reduction in engine power requirements*

## Reksten, Burmah Oil among the victims

High-profile financial casualties of the tanker market collapse included Norwegian owner Hilmar Reksten, who went out of business through over-dependence on the tanker spot market; the Israeli firm of Maritime Fruit Carriers which was unable to meet its obligations for a large order for tankers from UK yards and crashed; and Burmah Oil which had to abandon an ambitious plan for a fleet of tankers and new VLCC terminal in the Bahamas to service the US East Coast and write off its shipping interests.

Shipyards were also in a bind. Having geared up to meet growth in demand for new tonnage of more than 8 per cent a year, they were stuck with underutilised capacity when orders dwindled away. The development of the South Korean shipbuilding industry added to the difficulty.

In some cases government aid was injected to keep yards going. Aid encouraged tankers to be built in excess of real market needs, but at temptingly low prices. This increased the tanker glut, which in the early 1980s was double the demand requirement, and sent up to 30 per cent of the tanker fleet to be scrapped or into lay-up. Independent tanker owners found themselves in a deeply worrying situation. The excess capacity, particularly of modern tankers, encouraged charterers to increase their use of the spot market, to the detriment of time charters. In the early 1980s the spot market had accounted for only about 20 per cent of total tanker chartering, but within the next 10 years this share grew to 70 per cent. To be competitive owners had to cut overheads to the bone. Some, mainly traditional established owners, kept up their existing maintenance programmes and crewing levels. However, all too often vessel maintenance was reduced to the barest minimum. This led to widespread corrosion and structural problems later in the lives of the ships, although tankers in long-term lay-up were less susceptible to such damage.

## Heavy scrapping reduces tanker surplus

In a serious attempt to resolve the overcapacity problem, the tanker industry embarked on a heavy scrapping programme that reduced tanker tonnage from about 308 million dwt in 1982 to 243 million dwt by 1987.

This brought supply more into line with market needs and allowed freight rates to start rising again after the low levels in the 1980s. The poor trading conditions had encouraged some owners to trade ships rather than cargo and for a few years such asset play was, in the form of ship sale and purchase, profitable.

## Design challenges

The dramatic decline of the tanker market had been accompanied by an equally dramatic rise in the size of the ships which, in itself, had presented technical challenges. Initially, the shipyards and classification societies were cautious in their approach to design and conservative in their choice of steel dimensions for the new breed of giant ships. In the early 1970s tankers were generally built with relatively high margins against fatigue and corrosion. Later, improved methods of calculation enabled classification societies to lower their requirements on longitudinal strength.

The basic types of static and dynamic forces which act on a ship's structure had been known for years, but naval architects were unable to quantify the loads precisely or carry out the stress analysis needed on a theoretically sophisticated basis until the development of computer systems in the late 1960s. As design experience grew and the technology for building large steel structures improved, potential savings in weight and cost began to be identified. This led to the greater use of high-tensile steel by shipyards as it enabled the dimensions of material to be reduced and the strength increased. First utilised in the ship's longitudinal structural members, high-tensile steel was later extended to transverse applications as well. Some 20 years of experience have subsequently shown that problems arise when too great a percentage of high-tensile steel is used in the construction of large tankers.

*Artist: Brian Entwisle*

The demand for tanker tonnage had accelerated the shift to new shipyard capacity in the Far East which, in turn, brought tough competition to established shipyards in Europe and the US. These new players offered considerable cost-saving programmes to ship-owners, including the incentives of minimum ship weight/steel consumption.

Despite the economic setbacks, during the 1970s and 1980s tankers continued to increase in size. Norwegian owner Anders Jahre took delivery of the 380,000 dwt *Jarmada* in 1976, while the A P Møller fleet welcomed seven 'K' class ships of 338,000 dwt each during the 1974-77 period, including *Karen Maersk*. In 1977 Esso launched the ultra-large crude carrier (ULCC) *Esso Pacific* of 508,300 dwt.

The fast-growing tanker interests in Hong Kong were also ordering new ships. Y K Pao's World-Wide Shipping launched the 411,500 dwt *World Petrobras* in 1977, while the Island Navigation Corporation of C Y Tung added 16 VLCCs to its fleet between 1974 and 1980. These included the 380,000 dwt *Titus* purchased from Wilhelm Wilhelmsen and renamed *Energy Explorer*. Both Hong Kong shipowners amassed large fleets, comprising mostly ships built in Japanese shipyards which were tied to extended time charters to Japanese oil companies.

By 1980 Sir Y K Pao, who had been knighted in 1978, owned 15 million dwt of tanker shipping and C Y Tung had 9 million dwt. They jointly represented about 7 per cent of the total world tanker fleet.

In 1976 Chevron launched the 406,000 dwt *Chevron North America*, one of three sisterships from Mitsubishi Heavy Industries of Japan.

The previous year Chevron had launched the 35,000 dwt refined product tanker *Chevron Oregon* from the FMC shipyard at Portland, Oregon. She was not only double-hulled but also the first tanker built in the US to be powered by gas turbines.

*Kristine Mersk, 337,000 dwt, built in 1974/5*

These photographs show the rescue of 27 Vietnamese boat people by the
tanker Jamunda on 16 October 1979 in the South China Sea

The overcrowed little vessel in which the Vietnamese boat people made their voyage

*The world's largest tanker was originally built for Nomikos as the 420,000 dwt Oppama by Sumitomo Heavy Industries of Japan in 1976. She was then purchased in 1979 at the shipyard by C Y Tung who had her lengthened and the deck raised to increase her size to 565,000 dwt after which she was renamed Seawise Giant. She was later burned out after being hit by an exocet missile in the Iran-Iraq War but then repaired at a cost of $60 million. She is still sailing today as Jahre Viking.*

## Tanker sizes still increase but some vessels cropped

In 1976 Sumitomo Heavy Industries of Japan had built the 420,000 dwt *Oppama*. She was later acquired in 1979 by C Y Tung who lengthened her, which increased her capacity to 565,000 dwt and renamed *Seawise Giant*.

A victim of the Gulf War when she was bombed in an Iraqi raid on Larak Island in 1988, she was sold the following year and repaired and rebuilt in Singapore at a cost of over $60 million. She was acquired by Norwegian owner Jørgen Jahre in 1991 and renamed *Jahre Viking*. The largest tanker in the world fleet at the end of the 20th century, she is capable of carrying four million barrels of oil.

Since the size of *Jahre Viking* is the result of a conversion project, the title of the biggest ships built belongs to a quartet constructed at the French shipyard of Chantiers de l'Atlantique in 1976-77. These were 555,000 dwt giants, each powered by four steam turbines geared to twin propellers. Two - *Batillus* and *Bellamya* - were built for Société Maritime Shell and the other two - *Pierre Guillaumat* and *Prairial* - for Compagnie National de Navigation, a subsidiary of the French oil company, Total. Three of the four were scrapped relatively early in their lives but the fourth, the *Prairal*, was saved from the breakers when, in June 1985, she was bought by Greek owner John Latsis for a reported $8.2 million and continued trading as the *Hellas Fos* to the end of the century.

Many other ships were enlarged to increase their capacity - a technique which had been started by extending T-2 tankers after the war. *Høegh Gannet* in 1967 and *Høegh Gandria* in 1968 went through a three-dimensional increase of their main measurements of length, width and draught. This increased their deadweight tonnages by 69 and 87 per cent, respectively. It was a unique operation at the time and still would be today.

An interesting variation on this theme was 'cropping' to reduce the size of vessels. During the early 1980s, when the industry was in the grip of recession and there was a surplus of VLCCs, Chevron took the unusual step of shrinking four of its ships that were in lay-up.

The 212,000 dwt *Bower* and three sisterships had been built to transport crude from the Middle East to refineries on the US East Coast, but when the refineries were sold the ships were no longer viable.

They were converted by removing about 100 feet from the centre section and rejoining the ends. The operation reduced them to 150,000 dwt and at the same time they were overhauled and modernised - all for a fraction of the cost of building new ships. In their reduced state the ships were more versatile and could access a wider range of ports, particularly in Indonesia and West Africa.

## Size creates access problems - SBMs and special terminals

Port access had become something of a problem as tankers increased in size and the draught and sheer bulk of VLCCs and ULCCs put many ports out of reach. One solution was the introduction of the single buoy mooring system (SBM) which was developed for tankers in the 1960s from a technique previously used by the Danish Navy.

This involved securing a tanker to a very substantial buoy in deep water offshore that was connected by an undersea pipeline to shoreside storage tanks. Flexible pipeline connections enabled the tanker to load or discharge cargo and the installation had to be strong enough to hold a laden tanker, allowing it to swing around the buoy under wind and current changes and to accommodate any rise and fall of tide. One of the first SBM installations was at Idd el Shargi in Qatar, the world's first completely offshore oilfield. The Louisiana Offshore Oil Port (LOOP) in the US Gulf is probably the most important SBM in the world from the point of view of volume of oil handled.

Another method of overcoming port restrictions is the technique of lightering at sea which enables a deep-draught tanker to unload part of its cargo into a smaller tanker tethered alongside so that it can then enter the port.

This is a delicate operation, particularly in rough weather or if there is a heavy swell, and to prevent damage to the hulls enormous rubber fenders are placed between the ships' sides. Depending on the circumstances, lightering operations can be carried out with the vessels either at anchor or underway at sea. Lightering is an important technique which was originally devised in the early days of VLCCs and first used in the US and Gulf of Mexico and later adopted in the English Channel area for increasing access to North European ports.

The use of floating storage units (FSUs) was also adopted for many offshore oilfields. These utilise tankers that are permanently moored to SBMs and to which the offtake vessel attaches for the transfer of cargo.

Where the volume of traffic warranted it, special port facilities were built. Rotterdam Europoort is an outstanding example. This includes a trans-shipment terminal where 300,000-500,000 dwt tankers can discharge cargoes from the Arabian Gulf for subsequent loading into smaller vessels for delivery to other European refineries which do not have sufficiently deep water to take the largest tankers. A similar terminal capable of taking tankers up to 300,000 dwt is located at Sullom Voe in the Shetland Islands where North Sea oil is handled.

## New oil sources undercut OPEC

Oil production from the North Sea had increased during the 1970s following the first success in November 1969 when Phillips Petroleum made a major find in the Ekofisk field in the Norwegian sector. Further major discoveries included BP's Forties field and the Brent field discovered by Shell and Esso. Oil from Alaska also began flowing after the building of the 800-mile Transalaskan Pipeline by Arco, Standard Oil New Jersey and BP. By 1978 the pipeline was carrying 1 million barrels a day from the North Slope to the port of Valdez. This later increased to over 2.1 million barrels a day.

*A shuttle tanker at a loading buoy in the North Sea*

These new sources and others in Mexico, Nigeria, Egypt, China and Indonesia meant that by 1982 OPEC's output had been overtaken by non-OPEC producers.

Over-production and competition from alternative energy sources, such as coal and natural gas, put oil prices under pressure. Towards the end of 1985 the price of oil fell to $10 a barrel and below, as producers competed for volume and market share. The free-for-all was curtailed at the end of the following year, when both OPEC and non-OPEC producers agreed on a reference price of $15-18 a barrel.

For the next four years there was a period of relative calm as Middle East producers sought to restore confidence and maintain adequate production levels. The discovery of extensive new reserves around the world created fresh optimism for the future of oil as a dependable resource and OPEC acknowledged that the price mechanism had to be fair to both producers and consumers in the interests of long-term stability.

*A VLCC discharging cargo at a single-point loading buoy at the LOOP (Louisiana Offshore Oil Port) in the Gulf of Mexico. The Port consists of three single-point mooring buoys used for the offloading of crude tankers, and a marine terminal with a two-level pumping platform and a three-level control platform*

# Tanker war in the Gulf

## Iran-Iraq conflict 1980-1988

The war between Iran and Iraq, which lasted from 1980 to 1988, is often known as the First Gulf War. However, to many in the industry it was the "Tanker War", as both sides attacked oil installations and tankers, often when fully laden.

As the conflict progressed, the two warring sides extended their efforts to damage each other's vital oil production and supply routes, and neutral shipping in the Gulf became a main economic target. Merchant shipping had been first embroiled in the conflict when more than 70 ships were trapped in the Shatt-Al-Arab waterway near Basrah in Iraq. Also ships in the northern Gulf were attacked; for example, the Greek-flag, general cargo vessel *Litsion Pride*, was hit by a rocket and sunk while enroute to Bandar Khomeini.

*The first fire-fighting tug approaches World Petrobras*

The first tanker attack in the Gulf occurred in 1982. Later, in 1984, the Saudi Arabian 357,000 dwt *Safina Al Arab* was hit by an Iraqi missile. One crew member was killed in the fire and explosion that followed and the tanker was declared a constructive total loss. Other attacks by both sides followed; during 1984 some 34 tankers totalling 5.7 million dwt were hit, with the loss of 37 crew members' lives.

At an early stage in the war INTERTANKO appealed to both sides to cease attacking innocent shipping and raised the matter at the UN, later hosting a meeting with the Secretary General to discuss the situation. A cease-fire was eventually agreed.

During the conflict the Association also published a guide for tanker operators listing maritime exclusion zones, explaining the types of attack against tankers and advising on safety precautions.

From April 1984 to July 1988 ships in the Gulf were attacked by aircraft firing Exocet missiles or dropping bombs, as well as by surface craft, land-based missiles and mines. While many tankers suffered severe damage, there were a number of cases in which ships suffered direct hits by missiles which subsequently failed to explode.
This may have been because, following penetration of the hull, the impact of the missiles was absorbed by the oil in the cargo tanks which would also have been protected by inert gas. Improved market conditions and rising second-hand values also resulted in many damaged tankers being repaired when they would otherwise have been scrapped. The Iran-Iraq war did not disturb the oil markets unduly after the first shock at the outbreak, when the price of oil jumped to over $40 a barrel. This was due mainly to a glut of oil and the ability of Saudi Arabia to act a "swing producer". As the number of tankers hit increased, the outside world also seemed to take less interest.

The Tanker War, like the land war between Iran and Iraq, seemed self-contained, presenting no real threat to the rest of the world - even after Iraqi jets attacked the US frigate *Stark* with the loss of 37 lives, and the US destroyer *Vincennes* accidentally shot down an Iranian passenger jet, killing 290. The US also attacked Iranian forces in a number of minor engagements in the Gulf.

A typical attack on a tanker is recounted by Captain Bruce Ewen, master at the time of World-Wide Shipping's 412,000 dwt ULCC *World Petrobras*, which was bombed by Iraqi jets on 22 December 1987. At the time the tanker was providing floating storage off Iran's Larak Island in the northern part of the Strait of Hormuz. Two Russian-made 500 lb bombs with parachute drogues attached dropped onto the main deck during the attack by Mirage jets, which also hit two other tankers off the island.

*World Petrobras* was at the time transferring oil from one tanker, *Free Enterprise*, into another, *British Respect*. "When the bombs struck," Ewen recalls, "the rubber hoses attaching us to the *British Respect* were set afire and a large amount of shrapnel from our deck fittings blew through the side of the *British Respect*. Since we were both inerted and had our inert gas plants running, an explosion was avoided. However, we needed to get *British Respect* away from us so we could get firefighting tugs alongside.

"We cut her aft ropes and her master went ahead on the engines and ran the forward ropes off the reels. When she parted the hoses, a large amount of oil was dumped into the water which caused a large fire and set the rubber fenders ablaze. Although this rendered our lifeboat and the liferaft on the port side beyond use, the current was fairly quick so the danger passed in a fairly short time."

Normally, there would have been at least four crew members on the deck where the bombs struck, but a launch had just arrived with crew relief and mail, drawing everyone away from the danger area. "We were very lucky," continues Ewen. "Nobody suffered even a light scratch." There was still the fire to deal with, however,

*Looking aft from the departing British Respect. The Free Enterprise can be seen on the starboard side of World Petrobras.*

and, a decision having been taken not to evacuate, it took 11 firefighting tugs seven and a half hours to extinguish it. The tanker's own firefighting supplies had run out in a few minutes.

*World Petrobras* was able to resume operations 42 hours after the bombs had struck, the crew having to cope with a lack of electric power on the cargo control console and the fact that about 15 feet of the main inert gas line had been blown away. Ingenuity and the use of sticky labels, a wire cage and some canvas solved the problems. "In that way we discharged and crude oil washed the ship so that by early February she was ready to go to drydock." The tanker was repaired at the ASRY yard in Bahrain and returned to her station at Larak, but by then Captain Bruce Ewen had left for another posting. The ship was later sold to Vela International of Saudi Arabia.

Many other tankers and crews were not so lucky. In all 62 tankers of 10.9 million dwt were lost during the Iran-Iraq war and 250 lives were lost. These tanker losses were 'constructive total losses' rather than actual losses and what is truly remarkable is that although over 500 tankers were hit, none of them sank. The damage was greatly reduced by the use of shipboard inert gas systems. As in the two world wars, the use of convoys supported by naval escorts from America, Britain, Netherlands, Italy, France and the Soviet Union reduced the threat to tankers. Salvage firms were also able to save tankers which had been hit and were on fire.

One of the most prominent victims of the tanker war was C Y Tung's ULCC *Seawise Giant* which in 1988 was hit by Iraqi bombs while acting as a storage tanker *at Larak Island.

*Seawise Giant in a ball of flames after Iraqi bombs*

## Surplus reduced, anti-pollution laws, a question of age and a new boom

1986    Price of oil below $8 a barrel

1988    End of Iran-Iraq war

1989    Exxon Valdez oil spill in Alaska

1990    US enacts Oil Pollution Act of 1990

1990    Iraq invades Kuwait, Gulf War

1992    Aegean Sea hits rocks at La Corunna, Spain

1993    Braer spill off Shetland Islands

1996    Sea Empress spill off Milford Haven

1999    OPEC cuts output, tanker rates slump

1999    Erika spill off Brittany

2000    OPEC raises output, tanker rates boom

Following the tonnage oversupply crisis which hit the tanker market in the 1970s, the industry struggled for years to cope with the legacy of the massive over-ordering which had virtually destroyed asset values and put sustained downward pressure on freight rates.

High levels of scrapping and low levels of newbuilding through the 1980s led to a new mood of optimism in the late 1980s and early 1990s. Orders began to increase again, as owners also came to believe there was a need to modernise the ageing tanker fleet. Between 1989 and 1991 nearly 57 million dwt of tankers were ordered.

After the *Exxon Valdez* oil spill in March 1989, new regulations, in particular those enshrined in the US Oil Pollution Act of 1990 (OPA 90) which mandated that tankers trading in US waters in future be double-hulled, suggested that only modern and "quality" tankers would find work. Although this was not always the case, increasing emphasis was placed on ship quality following this accident. OPA 90 also put the entire responsibility for an oil spill on the tanker owner and introduced the threat of unlimited liability. This legislation, which was subsequently mirrored to a large extent in international rulemakings, was to have a significant effect on tanker design, ownership and operation for the following decade.

## Seaborne trade in oil in 1990s rises 24 per cent

On the whole, the world economy enjoyed a sustained period of growth through the 1990s, with the 'Asian crisis' of 1997 causing only a pause. Oil production and consumption showed steady increases during the decade, apart from the temporary drop in output during the Gulf War in 1990-91. Between 1990 and 1999 seaborne trade in oil increased from 1,526 million tonnes a year to 1,970 million tonnes. In 1990 the world tanker fleet (of vessels over 10,000 dwt) stood at nearly 289 million dwt. By 1999 it had risen to just over 303 million dwt.

*Berge Banker, 323,100 dwt, built 1979*

The oil industry and its relations with the tanker market also underwent changes during 1990s. The threat of exposure to public criticism and huge liabilities in the wake of oil spills prompted some oil companies to reduce their own fleets, largely to the benefit of independent owners. These included many US oil companies prompted by OPA 90 which stipulates that the shipowner is liable for an oil spill, not the charterer or cargo owner. At the same time oil companies went through a series of mergers - Exxon and Mobil; BP, Amoco and ARCO; Total, Fina and Elf; and subsequently Chevron and Texaco - which increased their influence as charterers on the tanker market, particularly the spot market. In response, independent tanker owners sought greater negotiating strength by takeovers and mergers of their own or through pooling tonnage. Efforts to increase market share, particularly in the large tanker sector, have seen the name of Frontline, controlled by Norwegian owner John Fredriksen, assume increasing importance.

The continuing overhang of tonnage meant that charterers of tankers were able reduce their dependence on long-term time charters. By the mid-1990s only 30 per cent of the independent tanker fleet was on long-term charter, compared with around 80 per cent in the mid-1970s.

## Double-hull versus single-hull

In the aftermath of *Exxon Valdez*, owners of modern tankers argued that "1970s vintage" tankers should be scrapped or at least not chartered, while owners of such elderly tonnage counter-argued that their ships were built to last. The 1970s-built tankers were constructed as single-hull vessels. Despite US and IMO rulemakings introduced in the 1990s calling for new tankers to have double hulls and for the orderly phaseout of single hull tankers, the phaseout schedules were structured to ensure that there would be no disruption of energy transportation.

The arguments against old tankers reached a particularly high pitch during periods of depressed freight rates. These occurred in 1992 when VLCC time charter equivalent rates fell to under $6,000 per day.

In 1999 cutbacks in OPEC production led to a slump in demand and old VLCCs earned less than $10,000 per day in September of that year. The arguments were also reinforced by the break-up and sinking of the 25-year-old tanker *Erika* with subsequent heavy pollution of the coast of northwest France in December 1999.

Although *Erika* was a 37,240 dwt product tanker carrying fuel oil rather than a VLCC, the accident prompted a range of proposals from the European Union - covering, for example, the accelerated phase out of single-hull tankers and increased pollution compensation limits.

Within the industry itself the *Erika* spill influenced charterers' attitudes on ship age to varying degrees, irrespective of the size of tanker.

## Tanker rates rocket in new boom

The debate on ship age, quality and operating reliability had been more muted in early 1991 when the tanker market enjoyed a freight rate peak of $47,000 a day and again just before the Asian crisis in 1997 when $44,000 was achieved. In 2000, when OPEC reversed its production cutbacks to offset the depressed demand caused by rising oil prices, the tanker market enjoyed conditions not seen since the boom of the 1960s and early 1970s. Spot market rates for modern VLCCs in November 2000 reached just over $85,000 a day and it

*Built to OPA 90 standards, an ARCO crude carrier under construction at Avondale shipyards in Louisiana. Double hulls are seen to present an environmentally safer way of carrying oil which, in part, is often why there is a two tier 'structure' in rates normally paid by some oil majors in favour of modern double hull vessels*

was estimated that VLCC spot rates were 150 per cent higher than the average for the 1990s. At the same time spot rates for Suezmax tankers were more than 170 per cent higher than the average of the previous decade.

The 1970s-vintage single-hull crude oil tankers enjoyed the market boom as much as their more modern counterparts. In December 2000 there were 94 VLCCs built on or before 1976 still trading. Time was running out for most of them, however, as the new international regulations introduced under the Marine Pollution Convention (MARPOL) meant they would have to be phased out. After single-hull ships reach 25 years of age, their owners have the options of scrapping them, finding alternative employment, fitting segregated ballast spaces or adopting hydrostatically balanced loading (HBL) if they want to keep them employed up until 30 years of age. Because no structural alteration was needed, although there was often only a small reduction in cargo capacity, HBL had already been adopted by some owners in advance of the international regulations.

However, the stance of oil company charterers on this method of containing oil after a hull rupture has been uncertain, with some accepting it, others against and a certain percentage apparently ambivalent.

In 2000 a total of 31 per cent of the VLCC fleet was aged 20 years or over, and the Suezmax fleet had a similar age profile. Decisions taken by the owners of such single-hull ships as regards the timing of their phaseout would have far-reaching consequences for the rest of the market which had been trying to anticipate the outcome. Newbuilding orders had already been increasing. For example, the orderbooks for VLCCs in December 2000 stood at 21 per cent of the existing fleet, while the Suezmax orderbook was equivalent to 22 per cent of the existing fleet.

## Million barrel tankers in demand

While VLCCs enjoyed a renaissance in terms of both spot market rates and newbuilding orders in the 1990s, their bigger sisters, the ULCCs, appeared to have fallen out of favour. Many were scrapped, laid up or given employment as storage tankers. This was largely due to changes in transportation needs - for example, the development of the Rotterdam spot market for oil products and the emergence of independent oil traders in buying and selling oil cargoes. Cargoes often changed hands in lots of 500,000 barrels which led to the demand for 'million barrel' tankers of around 140,000 dwt that could conveniently handle two consignments. The enlargement of the Suez Canal to take laden 'million barrel' tankers was another factor in favour of ships of the Suezmax size.

Another consideration was the changing patterns of production and distribution - the new patterns requiring smaller and more versatile ships. The development of new refineries near oilfields in the Middle East - in Saudi Arabia and Kuwait, for example - meant that more refined products were being exported, along with additional grades of crude oil. These called for more specialised product and chemical tankers with the ability to transport a variety of different products without the risk of cross-contamination.

In addition, growing environmental concerns during the 1990s prompted refiners to make products with smaller percentages of constituents known to be air pollutants. In order to do this they needed to process and blend various grades of crude and, therefore, to purchase their crude oil in smaller lots than previously. These factors served to decrease the numbers of charterers interested in crude consignments of the size which need to be carried in ULCCs.

In contradiction of this trend towards relatively smaller crude carriers, Majestic Shipping, a joint venture between Hellespont Steamship of Greece and the Loews Corporation of the US, placed an order in 1999 with Daewoo in South Korea for two ULCCs with an option for other vessels. The 440,000 dwt ships were ordered with high specifications and an intended lifespan of 40 years without the need for steel replacement or major repairs. Similar specifications were adopted for a series of 302,700 dwt VLCCs ordered by the same owner from Samsung of South Korea.

*Hellespont Capital, 388,042 dwt, built 1976*

## Offshore oil creates new types of tanker

The development of offshore oil production in the North Sea and other areas gave rise to a new type of vessel - specialised shuttle tankers, generally with bow-loading facilities to enable cargo loading in the open sea. Shuttle tankers are used to lift crude oil from deepwater single-point mooring installations or floating production, storage and offtake vessels (FPSOs) for delivery to refineries. The demand for FPSOs prompted several owners to convert older single-hull tankers which might otherwise have become redundant under the new regulations governing the phaseout of single hull ships.

## Designed for safety

Safety considerations have also influenced the design of new tankers and many owners have already been incorporating features which go beyond the mandated legislation, particularly in respect of structural integrity, the reduction of engine exhaust and cargo emissions, systems redundancy, and the use of advanced coating technology and new corrosion resistant materials.

For example, the 313,000 dwt double-hull V-Max type VLCC developed by Stena and Concordia Maritime of Sweden provides high levels of redundancy, including two separate engines (with emission levels well below those specified in international regulations), two propellers and two sets of steering gear and rudders to give improved manoeuvrability. Known as the 'floating Volvo', the new class also incorporates high levels of anti-corrosion protection. Assigned on long-term charter to Sun Oil, the shallow-draught V-Max is designed to access the Sun refinery on the Delaware River and navigate waterways with limited depths, such as those found in parts of Indonesia, Vietnam, Thailand and China.

## Concern over corrosion and fatigue

Increasing attention is being paid in new tankers to anti-corrosion protection. The classification societies have been studying the question of structural fatigue, while groups like the Tanker Structures Cooperative Forum - which was formed in 1982 - have investigated material selection and identified the critical areas relating to structural integrity and corrosion. One of the aims is to ensure accessibility for the inspection of areas in double-hull tankers which are prone to corrosion, including water ballast spaces. One specific problem which has arisen is pitting corrosion in the bottom of uncoated cargo tanks after as little as three or four years in service. The possible causes of this problem have been under investigation and one of the factors may be a particular type of high-tensile steel used in hull construction which itself is now the subject of a major study being carried out by Japanese shipbuilders.

Throughout the 1980s and 1990s the tanker industry, along with the rest of shipping, came under increasing scrutiny from charterers, insurers and port state control authorities. The number of different inspections to which a ship is subjected, either prior to a charter or on arrival in port, has caused concern for owners. Some success was achieved when oil companies, represented by the Oil Companies' International Marine Forum, agreed to a unified system of inspection reporting, reducing the need for each company to vet a tanker. This is the Ship Inspection and Reporting (SIRE) system.

A number of new regulations also came into effect in the 1990s. The International Safety Management (ISM) Code implemented for tankers, bulk carriers and certain other ships in July 1998, requires companies to have clear lines of command and responsibility which have been audited and certified by recognised bodies. Requirements governing the training and certification of crew were also revised under 1995 amendments to the Standards of Training, Certification and Watchkeeping (STCW) Convention. The STCW 95 requirements call on owners to gauge the competence of their crews according to the new criteria and to ensure crew qualifications are recognised by the relevant flag states. New rules also came into effect governing minimum and maximum hours of work and rest for crews.

*Tanker lifting from a single buoy mooring in the North Sea*

### Sharing the burden of safety

One of the most encouraging developments in the tanker industry towards the end of the 1990s was the growing realisation that the obligations for safety and quality did not rest entirely in the hands of shipowners, but that others involved in oil transportation also have to share the responsibility.

This concept was widely accepted by flag and port states, classification societies, charterers, insurers and terminal operators, among others.
It means that all the parties in the so-called chain of responsibility could cooperate in upgrading and enforcing the regulatory regime in a number of critical areas, including tanker design, operations, navigational safety, environmental protection and the ship-to-shore interface.

One of the key issues that has been identified is the need to achieve greater levels of transparency on ship data from an industry that has traditionally been secretive. This is vital because lack of such disclosure has helped to support substandard ships and penalise quality operators. The secrecy problem was highlighted by the *Erika* disaster. Following the spill, it was found that the vessel was one of a series of eight sister ships reportedly built to minimum scantlings and that another three of these tankers had also suffered structural and/or corrosion problems. However, under the existing system at the time of the incident there was no means of cross-referencing survey or inspection reports between classification societies, port states, flag states or charterers to provide an overall assessment of the condition or fault pattern of a particular class or vessel.

Much of the credit for the new initiative to increase levels of transparency and share the burden of ensuring safe shipping amongst all responsible parties has been due to INTERTANKO. The Association developed the idea into a workable scheme under the concept of the 'Chain of Responsibility' and successfully campaigned for an industry-wide approach which resulted in its adoption by the European Commission in its 'Quality Shipping' campaign and by the US Coast Guard.

### Surplus of 1970s – built tankers heading for scrap

At the end of the millennium the tanker industry appeared to have put the tonnage overcapacity crisis of the 1970s and 1980s behind it, although there were fears that over-ordering could once again jeopardise future prospects for a reasonable balance between supply and demand.
While a significant proportion of the 1970s-built VLCC fleet was still trading, it was widely believed that the new rules on the phaseout of single-hull tankers and the increasing reluctance of charterers to take ships over a certain age would accelerate the delivery of older tonnage to the shipbreakers.

The freight rate boom of 2000 created a new optimism and once more demonstrated the resilience of the tanker industry. While the volatile and uncertain oil market continues to present challenges and opportunities for tanker owners, their continuing success will be closely linked to their ability to resist the temptation of over-ordering new ships and maintaining the delicate balance between demand for capacity and supply of tonnage.

*Libertad, built in 1995 at AESA's Sestao shipyard, Spain*

# Chemical Tankers
## a Speciality Breed

| | |
|---|---|
| 1940s | *Petrochemical industry develops on US Gulf Coast* |
| 1948 | *T-2 tanker converted for US domestic routes* |
| 1949 | *One of the first bulk liquids chemical tankers* |
| 1950s | *Early chemical shipments from US Gulf to Europe* |
| 1955 | *Stolt-Nielsen conversion of the parcel tanker Freddy* |
| 1959 | *Parcel Tankers Inc begins trading Stolt Avance* |
| 1960s | *World demand for petrochemicals expands rapidly* |
| 1970 | *First purpose-built chemical parcel tanker Stolt Norness delivered* |
| 1971 | *IMO adopts Code for the Construction and Equipment of Ships Carrying Dangerous Chemicals in Bulk* |
| 1987 | *Annex II to the MARPOL Convention, covering the control of pollution from chemical tankers* |

Chapter Seven: Chemical Tankers

Anco Stream, built 1967

Picture right, Dutch Progess, built in 1984

Picture right: Whether it's warm or cold, day or night, work on board a chemical tanker is not determined by weather or time of day, but exclusively by the cargo. Serving on a chemical tanker is a particularly responsible and difficult job, and officers and crews are hand-picked.

## Chemical tankers - a speciality breed

In the years following World War Two, a new industry based on oil and gas - petrochemicals - began to take shape on the US Gulf Coast. Oil and gas were much more flexible and cost-effective feedstocks for the production of industrial chemicals than coal or fermentation products. Petrochemical plants began to proliferate on sites adjacent to the Texas and Louisiana oil refineries and natural gas fields. The rapid development of markets for plastics, manmade fibres, adhesives, paint, synthetic rubber, detergents, solvents, films, pharmaceuticals and insecticides - all derived from petrochemical intermediates - ensured that the chemical industry would be one of the great success stories of the post-war years.

Initial shipments of chemicals from the new plants to customers on the US Atlantic Coast were made in drums, portable tanks and rail tank cars but, as the demand for these products began to increase significantly in the 1950s, a more extensive and sophisticated means of transport was required. For a while, deep tanks in dry cargo ships carried limited quantities of chemicals, but mainly vegetable oils and latex. However, the need to ship large volumes of the many new intermediate chemical products coming onto the market - the majority of which possessed one or more hazardous properties - soon made it apparent that a new type of seagoing ship was required.

The first chemical tankers were converted, war-built T-2 tankers. In 1948 the 16,600 dwt *R E Wilson* was converted on behalf of Union Carbide and Carbon Corporation by fitting a double bottom and deepwell pumps in the cargo tanks - a unique arrangement for tankers at that time. Her centre tanks allowed the carriage of nine different chemicals while petroleum products could be carried in the wing tanks. *R E Wilson* shuttled chemicals from US Gulf to the East Coast ports until 1971, at which point she was sold for scrap but not before her deepwell pumps were removed and installed in another chemical tanker. *Marine Chemical Transporter* was also a notable T-2 conversion. This ship was modified in 1955 with the installation of two large insulated centre tanks for the carriage of molten sulphur, along with three stainless steel tanks for the transport of chemicals.

## Dawn of the international era

The international seaborne transport of chemicals also had its origins in the early 1950s, with relatively small ships carrying cargoes from the US Gulf to Europe. A pair of Dutch brothers, Jacobus and Bastiaan Broere, put their first ship, the 400 dwt *Elizabeth B*, into service in October 1949 delivering US cargoes to North Sea ports. This was followed by the 2,880 dwt *Elizabeth Broere*, a ship with 15 tanks delivered in 1954. Such small ships were soon forced out of the transatlantic trades, however, due to the

more competitive rates offered by larger vessels. At about the same time as the Broeres were getting started, A O Andersen in Norway and H W Collingwood in London launched a transatlantic operation - eventually known as the Anco Tanker Service - utilising four tankers.

The first three ships were built in Sweden to an A O Andersen design in which the cargo-carrying space was divided into many small tanks, allowing the carriage of a multitude of bulk liquids. The first of the trio, the 8,800 dwt *Svanaas* delivered in August 1949, is said to be the world's first bulk liquid parcel tanker. The Anco ships carried a variety of cargoes, including petroleum products, solvents, lube oils and some chemicals.

The era of the chemical parcel tanker-ships dedicated to the carriage of a range of chemical products but also able to carry other liquid cargoes such as vegetable oils and lube oil additives - was initiated by Jacob Stolt-Nielsen Jr in 1959 with the 13,500 dwt *Stolt Avance*. Like other first generation chemical parcel tankers, *Stolt Avance* was a converted, single-hull petroleum product tanker.

In fitting the ship out for her new role, Mr Stolt-Nielsen utilised the experience gained when he and two partners installed 19 deepwell pumps in the 12,000 dwt tanker *Freddy* in 1955 as part of her conversion for the carriage of solvents, tallow and lard. *Stolt Avance* had deepwell pumps and coated cargo tanks. She entered into service at the beginnings of the US chemical export boom and in her first year of operation carried 110,000 tonnes of chemicals from the US Gulf to Northern Europe. The ship marked not only the start of the chemical parcel tanker era but also the start of a major commitment by Stolt-Nielsen to chemical transportation activities. By 1976, the company operated 23 purpose-built chemical parcel tankers designed and built with stainless steel cargo tank capacity on worldwide routes and today the Stolt fleet comprises some 142 deepsea, shortsea and inland waterway tankers totalling 2.5 million deadweight.

A crew member connecting a cargo hose ready for discharging cargo on Bolero, a 45,998 dwt tanker for chemical and oil products

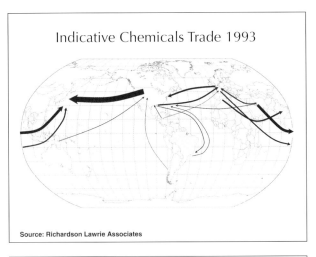

## Indicative Chemicals Trade 1993

Source: Richardson Lawrie Associates

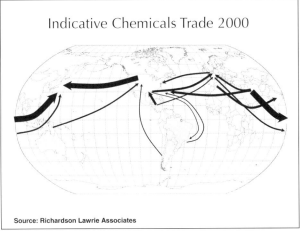

## Indicative Chemicals Trade 2000

Source: Richardson Lawrie Associates

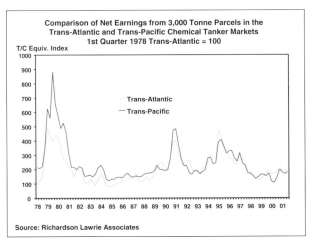

**Comparison of Net Earnings from 3,000 Tonne Parcels in the Trans-Atlantic and Trans-Pacific Chemical Tanker Markets 1st Quarter 1978 Trans-Atlantic = 100**

Source: Richardson Lawrie Associates

Other notable pioneering chemical tankers were the purpose-built 2,400 dwt *Lind*, which was delivered to Odfjell in 1959 and featured stainless steel cargo tanks. Odfjell went on to place strong emphasis on stainless steel tankage in building up its chemical tanker fleet. By 1972 the Odfjell chemical tanker fleet numbered 24 ships, 14 of which offered stainless steel capacity to some extent.

In 1990 Odfjell formed a strategic alliance with National Chemical Carriers Ltd (NCC) of Saudi Arabia and by 2000 Odfjell had merged with Seachem/Ceres. Over the years, the major operators had added complementary logistics options, such as onshore storage and tank containers, to the extent that they now offer full logistics service packages to their chemical producer customers.

# Dedicated regulatory regime

During the 1960s the worldwide demand for chemicals was growing dramatically. As the US was the primary producer of these chemicals, the accompanying expansion in the seaborne movement of chemicals was placing heavy demands on the US Coast Guard's programme of ship plan review and inspection for all the chemical tankers visiting US ports. In 1967 the Coast Guard approached the International Maritime Organization (IMO) with a request for action on an international basis. IMO initiated the task of developing suitable design criteria, construction standards and other safety measures to minimise the risks involved in loading, transporting and discharging such cargoes. In considering the flammability, toxicity, corrosivity, reactivity and other hazards posed by a long list of chemicals transported in bulk by sea, the IMO member states based their regime on the need to ensure the integrity and reliability of the ship's cargo containment system.

In 1971, IMO adopted the Code for the Construction and Equipment of Ships Carrying Dangerous Chemicals in Bulk (BCH Code). The BCH Code and its successor, the International Code for the Construction and Equipment of Ships Carrying Dangerous Chemicals in Bulk (IBC Code, which applies to ships built after 1 July 1986), stipulate design and equipment standards for chemical tankers. These international standards specify three degrees of physical protection, or ship types, i.e. IMO Types 1, 2 and 3. IMO type 1 ships provide the highest degree of protection and are designed to survive a high level of prescribed damages.

Those cargoes whose properties pose significant hazards but do not have such wide-reaching and deleterious effects as IMO 1 cargoes when released are specified for carriage in IMO 2 type ships. Both these types require double hulls. IMO 3 type ships, designed to carry products of sufficient hazard to require a moderate degree of containment to increase survival capability in a damaged condition, only require single hulls. IMO 2 ship type cargoes represent the predominant type of chemical products carried by chemical parcel tankers.

The BCH and IBC Codes also include standards for cargo transfer, materials of construction, cargo temperature control, cargo tank vent systems, environmental control, electrical installations, fire protection and extinction, ventilation in the cargo area, instrumentation and personnel protection. In recognition of the hazards associated with handling particular cargoes, the Codes specify additional special requirements. For example, the IBC Code lists 12 special requirements for phosphorus because of its self-igniting hazard. The BCH and IBC Codes also incorporate design and equipment requirements to implement Annex II of the International Convention for the Prevention of Pollution from Ships, 1973, as modified by its 1978 Protocol (MARPOL 73/78), which entered into force in 1987. With the inclusion of Annex II marine pollution considerations, the Codes were extended to provide a comprehensive set of standards for the safe shipment of bulk hazardous cargoes by sea.

The exemplary safety record built up by the global chemical tanker fleet over the past several decades has demonstrated the effectiveness of the BCH and IBC Codes in addressing the hazards facing such ships. The Codes are constantly revised and updated by IMO to reflect both the introduction of new technology and new chemical products added to the list of liquid hazardous cargoes transported in bulk by sea.

*Chemical tanker Multitank Britannia is active in European waters*

*Sunny Blossom, 22,567 dwt, built 1981*

## First purpose-built parcel tankers

The hazardous nature of the cargoes and the demands of the chemical parcel trades - most notably, the need to heat cargoes and clean tanks rigorously between cargoes of increasing variety, complexity, sensitivity and value - were the key determinants in the design of the first purpose-built chemical parcel tankers.

Designed by Jacob Stolt-Nielsen and delivered by the Boelwerf yard in Belgium in the early 1970s, the *Stolt Norness* class ships were the first, true chemical parcel tanker newbuildings. In designing the most versatile cargo carrier possible, Stolt-Nielsen took into account the wide range of cargo densities to be accommodated as well as the fluctuating trends in trading patterns over the service life of the ship. *Stolt Norness* was the first of a series of seven tankers built from the keel up as a chemical parcel tanker. This later set the standards for the parcel tanker market and IMO regulations for the chemical trade.

The first purpose-built chemical parcel tankers incorporated double bottoms throughout the cargo tank space and double sides in most of the cargo area to provide the required level of containment for the more hazardous

| 10P 481 | 9P 454 | 8P 627 | |
|---|---|---|---|
| 13C 1047 | 12C 1117 | 11C 757 | 10C 775 |
| 10S 481 | 9S 454 | 8S 627 | |

*Cross section of cargo tanks above the double bottom of a chemical parcel tanker with double hull sides, two longitudinal cofferdams and horizontally corrugated bulk heads*

products. Structural members were placed outside the cargo tanks in the double hull spaces to provide flush tank walls, thus facilitating effective and efficient tank cleaning operations. Furthermore, to ensure full cargo segregation capabilities, each cargo tank was provided with its own deepwell pump and separate line to the cargo manifold. These first purpose-built parcel tankers had clad stainless steel centre tanks and wing tanks coated with zinc silicate and/or epoxy-based paint systems. Other tank lining systems based on phenolic epoxies or polyurethanes were subsequently introduced.

## Modern chemical parcel tankers

The design of the chemical parcel tanker has continued to evolve over the past 30 years, so that today it is by far the most sophisticated bulk liquids ship afloat.

The cargo-carrying space on a typical  top of the range parcel tanker of 35-40,000 dwt is subdivided to carry over 50 different cargoes simultaneously in a fully segregated manner, including deck tanks. Solid stainless steel is used extensively in the construction of cargo tanks, and many of the new ships have stainless steel tanks throughout.

Tank plan (from left to right):

| 7P 68 | 6P 618 | 5P 590 | 4P 180 | 3P 745 | 2P 505 | 1P 481 |
|---|---|---|---|---|---|---|
| 7CP 21 | 8C 1509 | 7C 1442 | 6CP 177 | 5C 758 / 4C 758 | 3CP 562 | 2C 616 / 1C 616 |
| 7CS 32 | | | 6CS 185 | | 3CS 593 | |
| 7S 68 | 6S 618 | 5S 590 | 4S 180 | 3S 745 | 2S 505 | 1S 481 |

Stainless steel is compatible with the vast majority of cargoes carried aboard such ships and this material enables speedy tank cleaning operations to a very high standard. The combination of shallow pumpwells and well-positioned, highly efficient deepwell pumps with an efficient stripping capability also helps to ensure that cargo residues are kept to a minimum following discharge operations.

Many chemical cargoes require special attention, including accurate temperature control. Cargoes can be heated via heating coils using hot water, steam or thermal oil, while cooling systems can be provided to permit the carriage of semi-gaseous chemicals in certain tanks.

A dedicated nitrogen generator onboard provides high-purity nitrogen for blanketing cargo and purging tanks, thus reducing atmospheric pollution and increasing the quality of cargo care.

The sophistication inherent in a modern parcel tanker entails a major commitment from the shipowner in terms of capital cost, administrative backup and life cycle maintenance programmes, in order to run a viable fleet which can meet the demanding requirements of a wide range of charterers. Parcel tankers cost two to three times that of an equivalent-sized oil tanker and the ships are designed, built and operated with a service life of 30 years or more in mind.

## Total trade in chemicals

In addition to the sophisticated parcel tankers, another type of chemical tanker has evolved to serve the global chemical industry. This is the relatively simple chemical/product tanker built to carry commodity chemicals such as benzene, xylene, toluene, methanol and caustic soda solution, as well as petroleum products. Such chemicals are not as demanding in terms of carriage requirements as speciality chemicals and are transported in comparatively large-sized parcels. As a result, simple chemical tankers have coated, rather than stainless steel, cargo tanks and there are fewer cargo tanks than on a parcel tanker. Simple chemical tankers can move with relative ease between oil products and commodity chemicals, and do so as market conditions fluctuate.

Even though IMO 3 ship type chemicals are permitted to be carried in single-hull ships, shipowners invariably specify a double hull configuration when ordering new commodity chemical carriers to ensure the flexibility to transport oil products.

The combined global chemical parcel tanker fleet transports about 60 million tonnes of chemicals each year and about 40 million tonnes of other bulk liquids, predominantly vegetable oils, lube oil additives, alcohols and molasses. Today the world chemical parcel tanker fleets consist of 311 ships totalling 6 million dwt, the largest owners being Jo Tankers, Odfjell and Stolt-Nielsen.

# Features of a modern chemical parcel tanker

(Tanker of 37,000 dwt)

There are two types of chemical tanker engaged in the deepsea trades worldwide - the chemical parcel tanker and the less sophisticated chemical/product tanker built to carry "easy" chemicals such as benzene, xylene, toluene and caustic soda solution, as well as a full range of petroleum products. This profile concentrates on the chemical parcel tanker, modern versions of which are able to carry upwards of 50 different "parcels", or cargoes, simultaneously.

These cargoes range from chemicals, vegetable oils and lube oil additives to acids and other speciality liquids. Most parcel tanker cargoes require careful handling and the predominant type of cargo - speciality chemicals - often pose a range of hazards to personal health and the environment. Such hazards include toxicity, corrosivity, flammability and reactivity, while many cargoes are also classified as marine pollutants. Handling large numbers of cargoes with different chemical and physical properties on a single voyage means a busy workload for the crew. To minimise port turnaround times and to streamline cargo-handling operations, modern parcel tankers are equipped with highly automated cargo control and monitoring systems. These are fully integrated with navigational systems and linked to company administration and communication networks. Under the Marine Pollution (MARPOL)Convention, it is permissible to transport chemicals with a low hazard rating in single-hull ships. However, all modern parcel tankers are built with double hulls to provide the flexibility to carry oil products and to maximise the potential to carry hazardous chemicals.

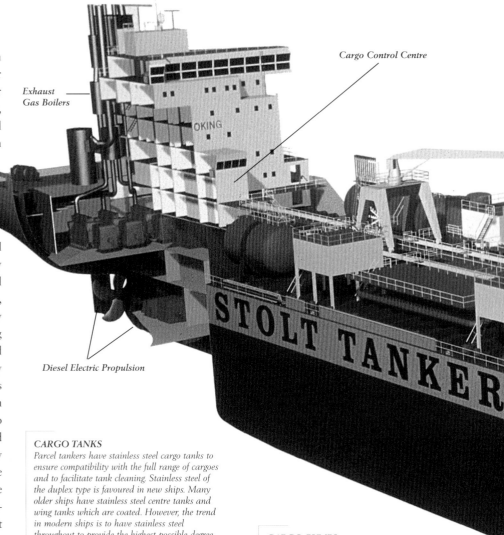

Exhaust Gas Boilers

Cargo Control Centre

Diesel Electric Propulsion

STOLT TANKER

### CARGO TANKS

Parcel tankers have stainless steel cargo tanks to ensure compatibility with the full range of cargoes and to facilitate tank cleaning. Stainless steel of the duplex type is favoured in new ships. Many older ships have stainless steel centre tanks and wing tanks which are coated. However, the trend in modern ships is to have stainless steel throughout to provide the highest possible degree of cargo-handling flexibility. The absence of internal stiffeners and other structures in the tank reduces cargo loss, speeds operations and facilitates cleaning. Cleaning is accomplished by means of fixed, tank cleaning machines. The complement of 50-plus cargo tanks on a parcel tanker can include deck tanks to provide additional capacity for the carriage of small-volume parcels.

### CARGO PUMPS

Each tank is equipped with its own stainless steel deepwell cargo pump. The one pump, line and manifold crossover per tank arrangement ensures that each tank can carry a different cargo in a fully segregated manner. Pumps are positioned to the aft of each tank in suction wells and either to port or starboard to allow optimal tank emptying. The combination of shallow pumpwells and highly efficient pumps with a stripping capability also helps ensure that cargo residues are kept to a minimum following discharge.

## SHIP PROPULSION AND MANOEUVRABILITY

Until recently, the most popular propulsion system for parcel tankers, as with most other tankers, was a slow-speed diesel-engine driving a fixed-pitch propeller. However, the ship shown is the first chemical parcel tanker to be equipped with diesel-electric propulsion, and this power option has since been chosen by other shipowners. With four medium-speed diesel engines driving an electric motor, the diesel-electric propulsion system provides four times the redundancy of conventional main engines and the opportunity to maximise fuel economy while in port. Such a propulsion system causes less air pollution, noise and vibration than slow-speed diesels. An electrically driven bow thruster is fitted for increased manoeuvrability.

## OTHER CARGO-HANDLING AND SAFETY FEATURES

Many cargoes require special attention, including close temperature control. A dedicated nitrogen generator provides a high-purity product for use in blanketing and purging cargoes, thus reducing atmospheric pollution and increasing the level of cargo care. Cargo can be heated using hot water, steam, thermal oil or a combination of these. Also, cargo cooling systems can be provided to permit the carriage of semi-gaseous chemicals. Radar-based level gauges are favoured in parcel tankers and independent high level and overflow alarms are provided. Other ancillary equipment includes multi-level temperature and ullage space pressure monitoring devices as well as a closed cargo sampling system and a gas detection system for the void spaces. Modern chemical tankers incorporate many other distinctive safety features as standard, some of which are itemised below:

- High level of bridge automation increases safety levels while ship is in confined waters
- Fully automatic vapour emission control system prevents atmospheric pollution during cargo loading and discharge
- In this ship all fuel tanks are located aft, and double hull protection is provided around such tanks, to safeguard against possible spills

*Stolt Perseverance, 36,700 dwt, built 2001*

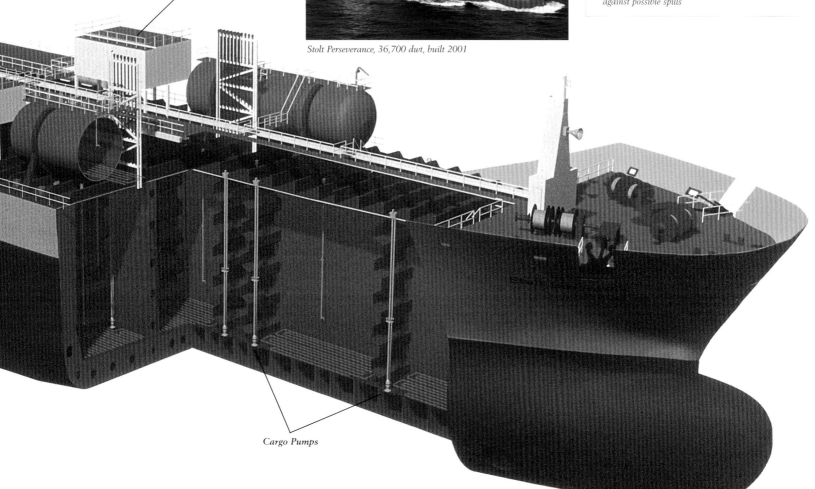

Cargo Cooling System

Cargo Pumps

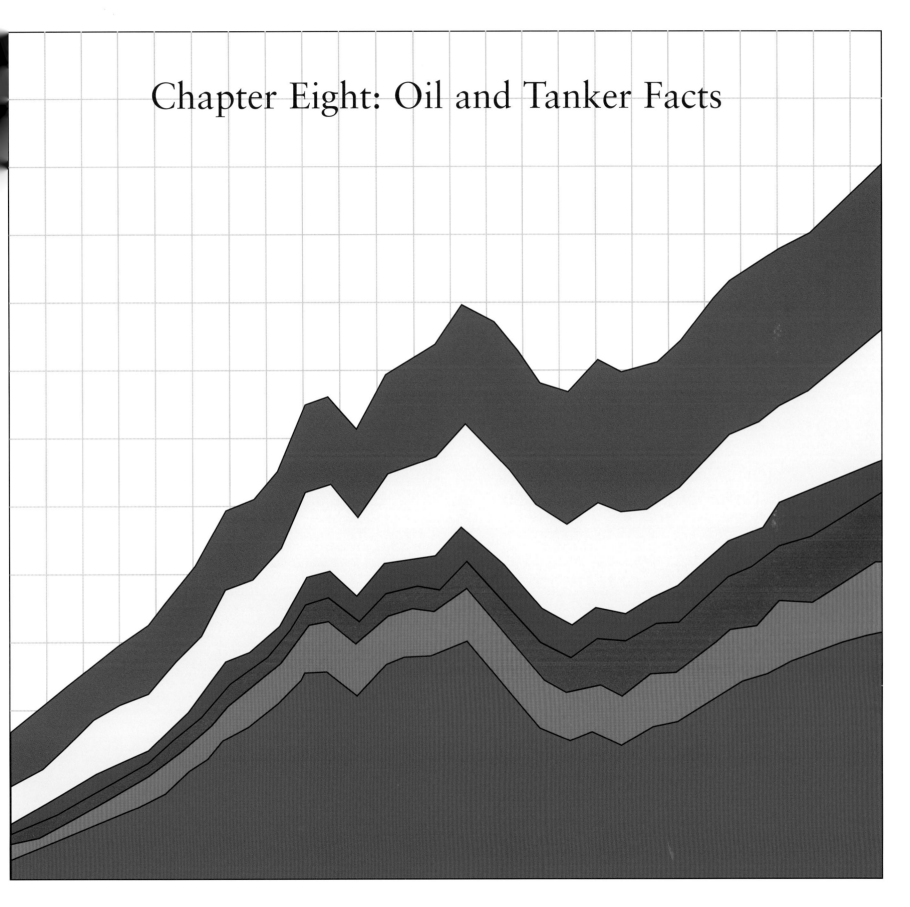

Chapter Eight: Oil and Tanker Facts

# The Freight Rollercoaster

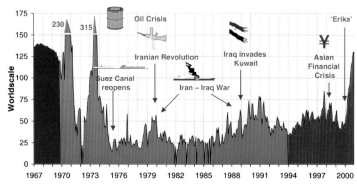

Source: E A Gibson Shipbrokers Ltd

*The Freight Rollercoaster*

*The dramatic effects of world events on tanker freight-rates expressed on the Interscale and Worldscale show that between 1945 and 1960 rates for 30,000 dwt tankers peaked. During the early 1960's rates for tankers in the 30,000 / 40,000 dwt category were generally below the 100 mark, then picked up to around 250 during the 1967 Suez Canal closure. They then increased to nearly 300 in the early 1970's, reaching a new peak of over 300 in 1973 for first generation VLCCs. The subsequent surplus of tanker tonnage then kept the rates below 100 until the year 2000.*

# VLCC Freight - War & Peace

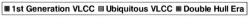

Source: E A Gibson Shipbrokers Ltd

*VLCC Freight - War and Peace*

*VLCC freight-rates fell from their peak of over 300 Worldscale in 1973 to below 50 in 1975. They fluctuated, mainly below 50, during the 1980's until climbing above the 75 level following Iraq's invasion of Kuwait. There was a slight uplift during the mid-1990's but it was not until 2000 that Worldscale recovered to reach over 125.*

# Tanker Timecharter Rates 1960-2000

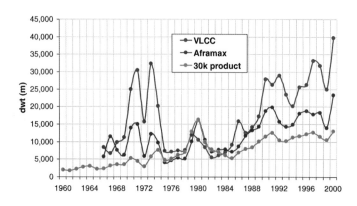

Source: SSY Consultancy & Research Ltd

*Tanker Timecharter Rates*

*After reaching the first peak in the early 1970s it took some 20 years to get back to a similar level. i.e. the higher things go the further they have to fall.*

# The Cost of Tanker Transport

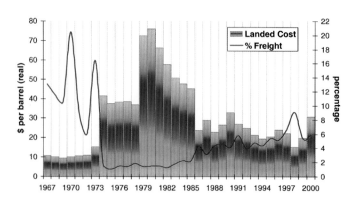

Source: Gilbert Jenkins/SSY Consultancy & Research Ltd

*The Cost of Tanker Transport*

*This clearly shows the cost of transportation as a proportion of the total cost of oil. Increases in tanker size during the late 1960s and early 1970s brought economies of scale which benefited charterers and owners. Despite substantial price increases, transportation represents a modest percentage of landed oil costs.*

## Growth in Tanker Numbers

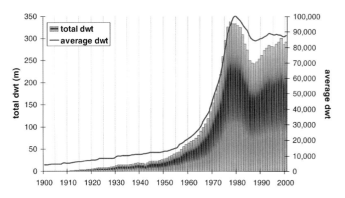

Source: SSY Consultancy & Research Ltd

### Growth in Tanker Numbers

*At the start of the century there were just under 150 ocean-going tankers. The world fleet increased steadily, reaching over 3,500 vessels by the late 1970s. From this peak it declined to under 3,000 in the mid-1980s before rising again to almost 3,500 in the late 1990s. During the same period, the size of the average tanker grew slowly from about 5,000 dwt in 1900 to 100,000 dwt in 1979, after which it declined slightly before levelling out at around 88,000 dwt in 2000.*

## Growth in Tanker Dwt Capacity

Source: SSY Consultancy & Research Ltd

### Growth in Tanker dwt Capacity

*In response to over-optimistic expectations of future oil demand tanker capacity reached a peak of almost 338 million dwt in the mid-1970s. Over the next decade it fell to under 245 million dwt as scrapping reduced some of the surplus capacity in the market. During the 1990s capacity grew from 262 million dwt to 292 million dwt. The average tonnage of tankers followed a similar pattern, ranging from about 5,000 dwt at the start, reaching a level of some 100,000 dwt in the early 1980s then declining to just under 90,000 dwt by 2000.*

## Tanker Deliveries - Changing Sizes

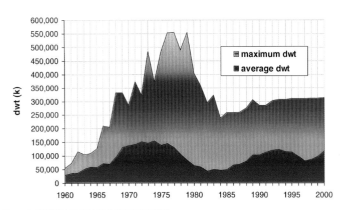

Source: SSY Consultancy & Research Ltd

### Tanker Deliveries- Changing Sizes

*The maximum size of tankers increased from just over 50,000 dwt to some 550,000 dwt by the late 1970s. Sizes diminished to around 250,000 dwt in the early 1980s then rose to 314,000 dwt by 2000. Average tonnage followed a similar pattern, starting at 30,000 dwt in 1960, increasing to 138,000 dwt in the 1970s but then dropping to under 50,000 dwt in the early 1980s in the shipbuilding slump. The average increased to 100,000 dwt at the start of the 1990s then fell back to about 80,000 dwt before finishing at 117,000 dwt at the end of the century.*

## VLCC Deliveries

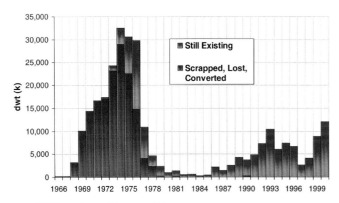

Source: SSY Consultancy & Research Ltd

### VLCC Deliveries

*After the introduction of VLCCs in the late 1960s newbuilding soared, reaching a peak in 1974 when more than 32.5 million dwt of VLCC tankers were built. Much of this tonnage was subsequently scrapped or converted to other uses to reduce the surplus of tanker capacity which was depressing freight rates. The low freight rates also held down newbuilding during the 1980s. The current VLCC fleet consists mainly of ships built since the early 1980s but also includes over 39 million dwt of tankers constructed in the 1970s, many of which were built to very high standards.*

# World Oil Production

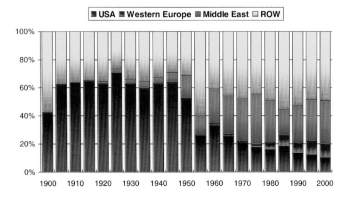

Source: BP/IEA

# World Oil Production

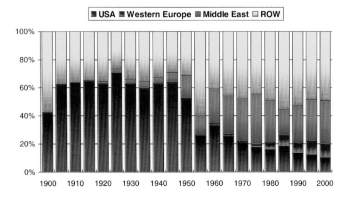

Source: BP/IEA

*World Oil Production*

*Between 1900 and 2000 world oil production increased from 0.4 million bpd to 74.5 million bpd. Declining US production was picked up by non-OPEC production. Middle East production declined after the mid - 1980s. The Middle East later lost market share to producers closer to main markets - Western Europe increased from 0.4 million bpd in 1965 to 7 million bpd in 2000 - and, as the oil price increased, new offshore production sources were developed.*

# US Oil Consumption by Source

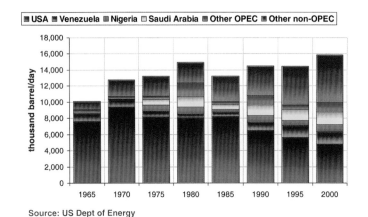

Source: US Dept of Energy

# US Oil Consumption by Source

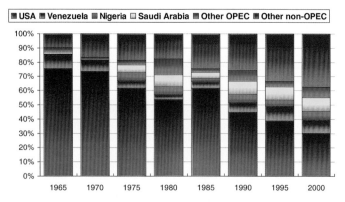

Source: US Dept of Energy

*US Oil Consumption by Source*

*In the second half of the century the US became increasingly dependent on imports, which increased from around 25 per cent in 1965 to about 70 per cent by the end of the century. Venezuela initially accounted for around half the US imports but then Saudi Arabia and other OPEC countries took a larger share. By 2000 OPEC accounted for about 32 per cent of US imports.*

## Refinery Capacity (Crude)

Legend: Europe, FSU, North America, Latin America, Asia/Australia, Africa, Middle East

y-axis: thousand barrel/day (0 to 90,000)

x-axis: 1940, 1950, 1960, 1970, 1980, 1990, 2000

Source: Oil & Gas Journal

## Refinery Capacity (Crude)

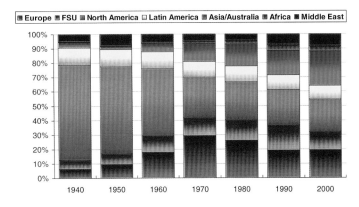

Legend: Europe, FSU, North America, Latin America, Asia/Australia, Africa, Middle East

y-axis: 0% to 100%

x-axis: 1940, 1950, 1960, 1970, 1980, 1990, 2000

Source: Oil & Gas Journal

*Refinery Capacity (crude)*

*Up until 1960 the US held the major, but declining, share of world refinery capacity. However, by 1970 Europe had caught up with the US, each producing around 13.5 million bpd (approximately 30 per cent). By 1980 the US and Europe had each increased their production to some 20 million bpd but by this time Asia / Australia was playing a significant part. In the last decade of the century, Asia/Australia refining had further increased its share to around 24 per cent and Europe had declined to 19 per cent. These figures reflect the trend to locating refineries closer to the markets for oil products and the increasing consumption of oil in Asia/Pacific. The cost of maintaining refineries to meet environmental demands also contributed to the decline in some areas.*

## US Energy Consumption

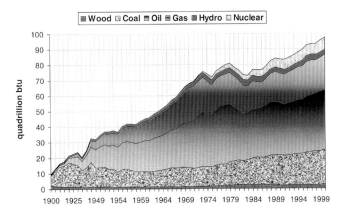

Legend: Wood, Coal, Oil, Gas, Hydro, Nuclear

y-axis: quadrillion btu (0 to 100)

x-axis: 1900 1925 1949 1954 1959 1964 1969 1974 1979 1984 1989 1994 1999

Source: US Dept of Energy

## US Energy Consumption

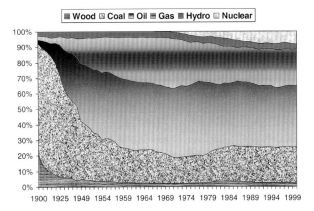

Legend: Wood, Coal, Oil, Gas, Hydro, Nuclear

y-axis: 0% to 100%

x-axis: 1900 1925 1949 1954 1959 1964 1969 1974 1979 1984 1989 1994 1999

Source: US Dept of Energy

*US Energy Consumption*

*Coal was the main form of energy until the advent of oil, which became, and still is, the prime source of energy. Gas was the other significant provider, with hydro and nuclear power taking minority shares.*

## Oil Price Development

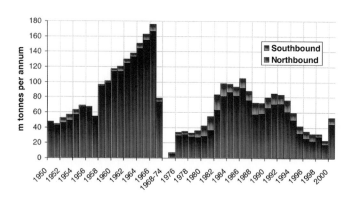

Source: Gilbert Jenkins/Intertanko

*Oil Price Development*

*The sharp rises in oil prices in the 1970s and 1980s (the oil shocks) were caused by OPEC increases in posted prices, the effects of the Iran- Iraq War and Arab states oil embargoes. By 2000 the price reached $28.98 per barrel which was actually 53 per cent higher than the average real price of $19 per barrel for the century.*

## Suez Canal Oil Flows

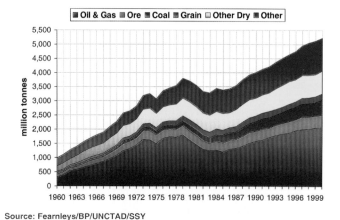

Source: Suez Canal Authority/SSY Consultancy & Research Ltd

*Suez Canal Oil Flows*

*Oil traffic through the Canal, which is predominantly northbound, increased steadily between 1950 and 1968 apart from a blip following the first closure of the Canal from November 1956 to April 1957. The second closure, between June 1967 and June 1975, brought about a prolonged diversion of tankers around the Cape of Good Hope which stimulated the building of VLCCs and ULCCs and had a more lasting effect on the volume of oil traffic through the Canal.*

## World Seaborne Trade

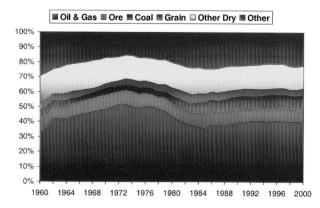

Source: Fearnleys/BP/UNCTAD/SSY

## World Seaborne Trade

Source: Fearnleys/BP/UNCTAD/SSY

*World Seaborne Trade*

*Changes in world economic growth patterns were reflected in seaborne trade, which rose from the 1960s through to the late 1970s when high oil prices led to the depression which lasted through most of the 1980s.*

# World Shipyard Output

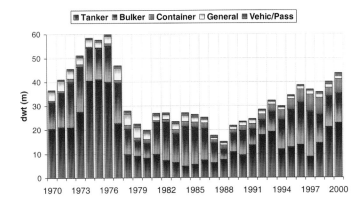

Source: LR Fairplay

# World Shipyard Output

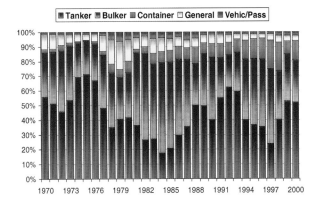

Source: LR Fairplay

## World Shipyard Output

*The massive ordering levels of the early 1970s created a huge surplus of tanker tonnage and was followed by at dramatic decline in newbuilding during the 1980s. There was an increase in newbuildings towards the end of the century as double hull tankers were built to replace older ships being phased out and as oil freight rates improved. Tankers have remained the most important vessel type for shipbuilders world-wide and accounted for 50 per cent of the dwt built in 2000. At times of low tanker ordering the production of dry bulk carriers increases.*

# Tanker Fleet by Flag

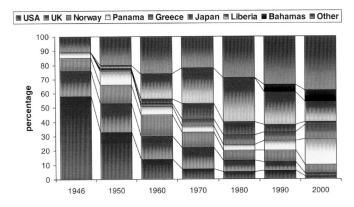

Source: SSY Consultancy & Research Ltd

# Inactive Tankers

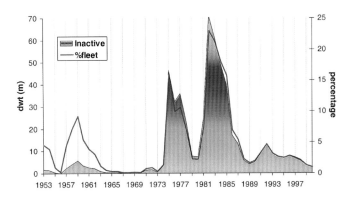

Source: E A Gibson Shipbrokers Ltd

## Tanker Fleet by Flag

*Up until the end of World War Two tanker fleets were generally registered in their own maritime and trading countries. The availability of open registers, which offered attractive tax regimes and other cost saving features, led to the increasing popularity of Panama, Liberia and the Bahamas which, between 1946 and 2000, increased their registered tonnage from 4 per cent to around 40 per cent of the world tanker fleets*

## Inactive Tankers

*The collapse in tanker demand of the mid 1970s and early 1980s coupled with massive oversupply, left many modern tankers with no employment prospects and some tankers went straight from the yards into lay up. At its nadir in 1982, the collapse put 23 per cent of the total fleet out of work.*

## Tanker Ownership

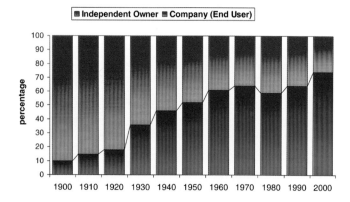

Source: SSY Consultancy & Research Ltd

## Tanker Fleet Ownership

Source: SSY Consultancy & Research Ltd

### Tanker Ownership/ Tanker Fleet Ownership

*Tanker ownership was at first dominated by the oil companies but later became mostly in the hands of independent owners. This was partly due to the ability of independent operators to provide transportation more economically than the oil companies themselves, but also because oil companies were able to get a better return on non-tanker investments which further encouraged them to charter. Later, the liability implications of the Exxon Valdez spill and the OPA 90 legislation also influenced oil companies to further reduce their ownership of tankers.*

## Tanker Fleet Age

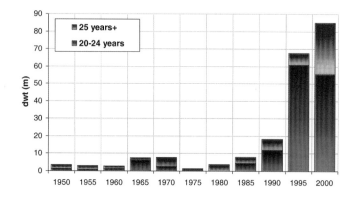

Source: SSY Consultancy & Research Ltd

## Tanker Fleet Age

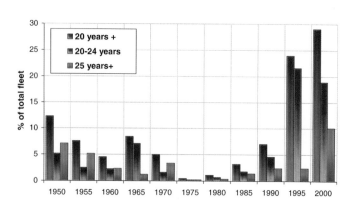

Source: SSY Consultancy & Research Ltd

### Tanker Fleet Age

*Between 1950 and 1975 the age of tankers steadily reduced as new tonnage was introduced, reaching its lowest level in 1975 as the intensive newbuilding of the early 1970s came into service. By the end of the century nearly 30 per cent of tankers were 20 years old or more, nearly 20 per cent were aged between 20 and 24 years, and over 10 per cent were over 25 years old (and would be unable to continue trading beyond 30 years).*

# Tanker Orderbook

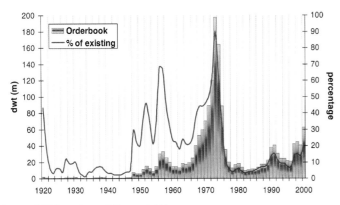

Source: SSY Consultancy & Research Ltd

## Tanker Order Book

*At the end of 2000 the tanker order book was equivalent to about 21 per cent of the existing fleet in terms of dwt. This compared with the building booms of the 1950s and 1970s, of 68 per cent and 90 per cent respectively, causing, for the latter period, a surplus of tonnage that overhung the market for the following 25 years.*

# Tanker Deletions

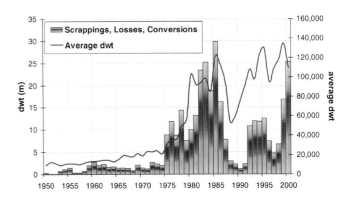

Source: SSY Consultancy & Research Ltd

## Tanker Deletions

*The rush of newbuilding in the early stage of 1970s caused a huge surplus in tanker capacity. Despite record levels of lay up and the use of tankers for floating storage, the massive surplus could only be addressed by scrapping. Consequently, almost 100 million dwt of tankers were permanently removed from the fleet between 1982 and 1985. The period of depressed freight rates in the early 1990s also encouraged scrapping of older tonnage to bring tanker capacity into better balance with demand for oil transportation.*

# Combined Carriers

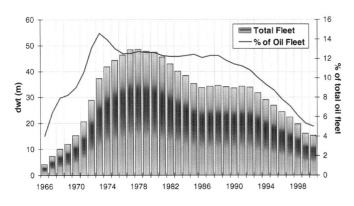

Source: SSY Consultancy & Research Ltd

## Combined Carriers

*Combined carriers were introduced to offset ballast voyages of tankers by enabling them to carry backhaul cargoes. After some initial success their earnings failed to offset the extra cost of production, and they also fell out of favour with a number of oil companies.*

# Tanker Building 1970-2000 by Area

Legend: ■ Japan ■ Korea ■ Other Asia □ Americas ■ Europe

dwt (m)

Source: LR Fairplay

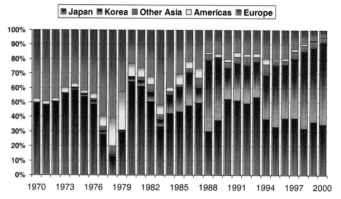

# Tanker Building 1970-2000 by Area

Legend: ■ Japan ■ Korea ■ Other Asia □ Americas ■ Europe

Source: LR Fairplay

**Tanker Building 1970-2000 by Area**

*The charts show the increasing share of tanker construction taken by the Japanese and Korean shipbuilding industries between 1970-2000 and the effects of this on shipyards in Europe, the US and other parts of Asia. European shipbuilding was in steady decline, falling from over 60 per cent of the market in 1970 to around 5 per cent by 2000. Japan also lost share, reducing from 50 per cent to 35 per cent over the same period. In contrast Korea grew from about 5 per cent in the early 1980s to over 55 per cent by the end of the century. In terms of tonnage, Europe and Japan each constructed about 10 million dwt in 1970, then in the newbuilding boom of the mid 1970s European yards increased production to 17 million dwt but this was comfortably exceeded by Japanese yards with around 22 million dwt. Not until 1988 Korea did reach the 4 million dwt level but by 2000 accounted for almost 13 million dwt compared with almost 8 million dwt from Japan.*

# Tanker Building Japan vs Korea

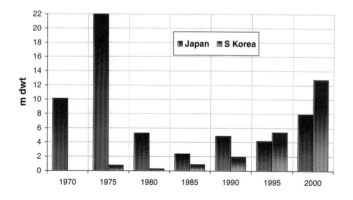

m dwt

Legend: ■ Japan ■ S Korea

Source: LR Fairplay

# Top 10 Tanker Builders 1970-2000

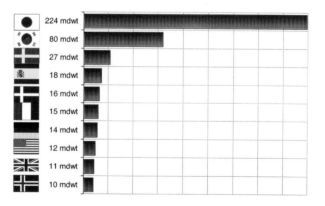

224 mdwt
80 mdwt
27 mdwt
18 mdwt
16 mdwt
15 mdwt
14 mdwt
12 mdwt
11 mdwt
10 mdwt

Source: LR Fairplay

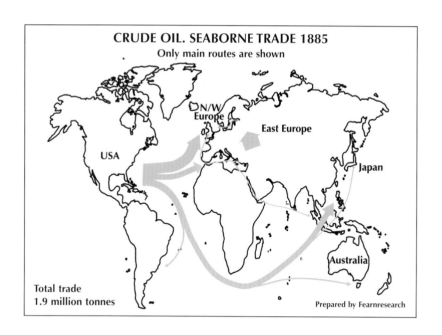

**CRUDE OIL. SEABORNE TRADE 1885**

Only main routes are shown

N/W Europe

East Europe

USA

Japan

Australia

Total trade
1.9 million tonnes

Prepared by Fearnresearch

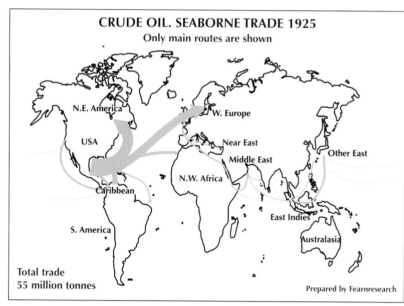

**CRUDE OIL. SEABORNE TRADE 1925**

Only main routes are shown

N.E. America

W. Europe

USA

Near East

Middle East

Other East

N.W. Africa

Caribbean

S. America

East Indies

Australasia

Total trade
55 million tonnes

Prepared by Fearnresearch

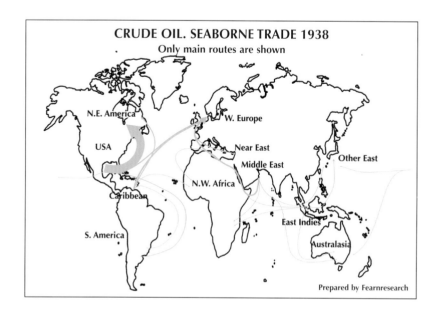

**CRUDE OIL. SEABORNE TRADE 1938**

Only main routes are shown

N.E. America

W. Europe

USA

Near East

Middle East

Other East

N.W. Africa

Caribbean

East Indies

S. America

Australasia

Prepared by Fearnresearch

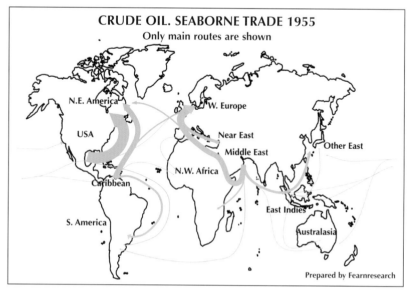

**CRUDE OIL. SEABORNE TRADE 1955**

Only main routes are shown

N.E. America

W. Europe

USA

Near East

Middle East

Other East

N.W. Africa

Caribbean

East Indies

S. America

Australasia

Prepared by Fearnresearch

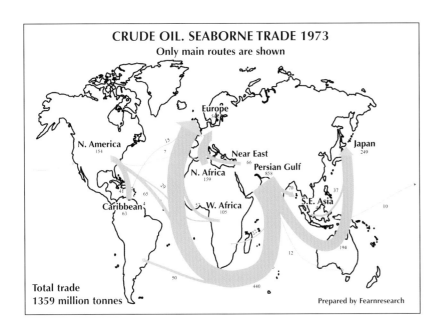

**CRUDE OIL. SEABORNE TRADE 1973**
Only main routes are shown

N. America 154
Europe
Near East 66
N. Africa 159
Persian Gulf 858
Caribbean 63
W. Africa 105
S.E. Asia
Japan 249

15
7
41
65
29
4
5
50
12
440
194
10
37

Total trade
1359 million tonnes

Prepared by Fearnresearch

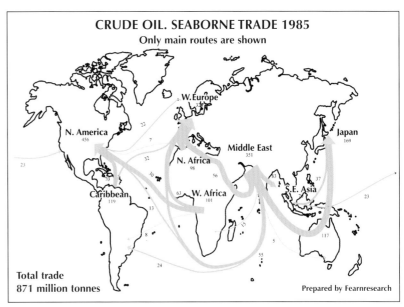

**CRUDE OIL. SEABORNE TRADE 1985**
Only main routes are shown

N. America 456
W.Europe
Middle East 351
N. Africa 98
W. Africa 101
Caribbean 119
S.E. Asia
Japan 169

22
7
23
32
30
70
63
56
13
15
24
55
5
117
23
37

Total trade
871 million tonnes

Prepared by Fearnresearch

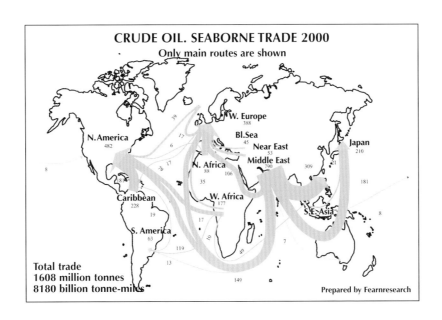

**CRUDE OIL. SEABORNE TRADE 2000**
Only main routes are shown

N.America 482
W. Europe 388
Bl.Sea 45
Near East 53
Middle East 790
N. Africa 88
W. Africa 177
Caribbean 228
S. America 63
S.E. Asia
Japan 210

39
17
6
17
78
21
106
35
8
18
19
17
10
119
49
7
13
149
309
181
8

Total trade
1608 million tonnes
8180 billion tonne-miles

Prepared by Fearnresearch

# Types of modern oil tanker

## Panamax tankers

Typical double hull ship of 60,000 dwt. 228.6 m length overall x 32.2 m breadth x 12.6 m draught - Lightship: 11,000 tons of steel

Ships in the 55-70,000 dwt size range, 70,000 dwt being the maximum size tanker able to transit the Panama Canal. The need to pass through a series of Canal locks dictates a maximum length of 274.3 metres and maximum breadth of 32.3 metres. In the Atlantic Basin trades Panamax vessels have a competitive advantage over larger tankers due to physical trading and local port depth restrictions. North American imports of crude and fuel oil comprise the bulk of Panamax tanker business.

## Aframax tankers

Typical double hull ship of 100,000 dwt. 253.0 m length overall x 44.2 m breadth x 11.6 m draught - Lightship: 14,850 tons of steel

Tankers in the 75,000-120,000 dwt size range. AFRA is Average Freight Rate Assessment. At one time Aframax was used to refer to ships up to 79,999 dwt, the upper limit of one of six dead-weight groups for which the the AFRA rate is assessed. Aframax has since become a general term for ships in this overall size range. Aframax ships are traditionally employed on a wide variety of short and medium-haul crude oil trades. The biggest tanker that can be accommodated fully laden in the ports of the US - the world's largest importer of oil - is 100,000 dwt, and this only at a limited number of ports. Many of the more modern ships in the Aframax size range are built as long-haul product tankers, with epoxy-coated tanks.

## Suezmax tankers

Typical double hull ship of 150,000 dwt. 274.0 m length overall x 50.0 m breadth x 14.5 m draught - Lightship: 20,000 tons of steel

Suezmax tankers are ships in the 120,000-200,000 dwt size range and are generally identified as those capable of lifting one million barrel cargoes. The name was originally bestowed on such ships because from 1980, when a development project which deepened the waterway to 16.1 metres was completed, the largest tankers able to transit the Suez Canal fully laden were those of 140,000-150,000 dwt. This association effectively became redundant in 2001 when a project to deepen the Canal to 18.9 metres was completed. The Canal may be further deepened to 20.1 metres by 2005 and 22.0 metres by 2010.

## Very large crude carriers (VLCCs)

Typical double hull ship of 280,000 dwt. 335.0 m length overall x 57.0 m breadth x 21.0 m draught - Lightship: 35,000 tons of steel

VLCCs are tankers in the 200,000-320,000 dwt size range. Ships of this size were prompted by the rapid growth in global oil consumption during the 1960s and, in 1967, closure of the Suez Canal, necessitating voyages around the Cape of Good Hope. Today, VLCCs are the most effective way of transporting large volumes of oil, including 2-million barrel cargoes, to customers over relatively long distances. Relatively simple ships, VLCCs are subdivided into a number of cargo tanks by two longitudinal and several transverse bulkheads.

## Ultra large crude carriers (ULCCs)

Typical double hull ship of 410,000 dwt. 377.0 m length overall x 68.0 m breadth x 23.0 m draught - Lightship: 45,000 tons of steel

Tankers in excess of 320,000 dwt. Most ships of this type were built in the mid to late 1970s and are now approaching 25 years of age. There are now under 40 of these ships remaining. Rather inflexible and limited to serving a few deep water ports, ULCCs never achieved their full potential. In early 2000 a tanker owner ordered two 440,000 dwt ULCCs, with 2 options, the first ULCC order in 20 years.

100m          200m          300m          400m          500m

# Tankers and other manmade structures

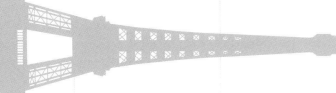

## Eiffel Tower
Tower is 318.7 metres high, including antenna, and has a gross weight of 10,100 tonnes

The 312-metre tall tower of open-lattice wrought iron took the world by storm when it was opened to the public in Paris to tie in with the Centennial Exposition of 1889 commemorating the French Revolution. Bridgebuilder Alexandre-Gustav Eiffel's masterwork was raised in a matter of 24 months by a small labour force at modest cost. Nothing remotely like it had ever been built. It was twice as high as St Peter's In Rome, and remained the tallest building in the world until the Chrysler Building in New York was completed in 1930. By the end of 1999 over 185 million people had visited the tower.

## Empire State Building
The 102-storey building is 381 metres high and has a gross weight of 365,000 tonnes

With a construction crew of 3,500, the Empire State Building in New York took an impressive 58 weeks from groundbreaking to handover in 1931.

Some 59,000 tonnes of riveted steel beams were used in the construction, along with 10 million bricks.

## Queen Elizabeth 2
The 70,327 grt QE2 is 294.0 m length overall x 32.0 m breadth

When she sailed from Southampton on her maiden voyage in 1969, Queen Elizabeth 2 was entering service at a time when jet aircraft had captured the transatlantic passenger market. The distinctive passenger ship was designed to complete five-day transatlantic crossings during the summer season and to serve the cruise market in the winter. She is able to carry 1,778 passengers and has a crew complement of 921. In 1987 QE2 was re-engined, her steam turbines being replaced with nine diesel electric motors. Developing 130,000 bhp, the propulsion plant remains the most powerful of any merchant ship and QE2 retains the title of fastest merchant ship in service.

## T-2 tankers
The 16,800 dwt T-2 tankers were 160.0 m length overall x 21.0 m breadth x 9.0 m draft.

Some 525 T-2 tankers were built at six American shipyards during the Second World War to replace, as quickly as possible, the vast amount of tanker tonnage sunk in action. Most of the parts were prefabricated using modular construction techniques and the hull and structural elements were entirely welded. Some T-2 tankers were completed, from keel-laying to delivery, in under six weeks. A few T-2 tankers, since fitted with new forebodies, are still in service.

## World's largest tanker
The Jahre Viking is 458.5 m length overall x 68.8 m breadth x 24.6 m draft.

The largest tanker, and the largest ship afloat, is the 564,763 dwt Jahre Viking (ex-Happy Giant, ex-Seawise Giant), built in 1979. Due to depth restrictions, she is unable to transit the English Channel with a full cargo. The ship was virtually rebuilt at a cost of US$60 million in 1991 after being extensively damaged in the Iran-Iraq War.

100m    200m    300m    400m    500m

ANTI - POLLUTION STATION
OIL SPILL EQUIPMENT
(AS PER O.P.A. '90 & S.O.P.E.P.)

1. ABSORBENT MATERIAL (HEAVY PETROLEUM)... 160 Pcs
2. ABSORBENT MATERIAL (LIGHT PETROLEUM)... 240 Pcs
3. OIL SPILL DISPERSANT................. 50 Ltr.
4. AIR PUMP WITH SPRAY GUN & HOSE....... 1 Set
5. WILDEN PUMPS...................... 2 Pcs
6. BROOMS........................... 12 Pcs
7. BUCKETS.......................... 6 Pcs
8. NON - SPARKING SHOVELS.............. 6 Pcs
9. PROTECTIVE CLOTH.................. 6 Set

Over the years the tanker industry has made tremendous efforts to provide safe transportation for commodities which are inherently dangerous. Yet the fact that the industry has an extremely good safety record tends to be overlooked whenever a serious spill occurs - particularly in the case of a grounding which usually attracts extensive media coverage of any environmental damage along coastlines.

But the reality is that tankers account for only a very small part of overall pollution of the seas by oil. Industrial waste is the biggest polluter, causing 62 per cent of all marine pollution, followed by non-tanker shipping at 15 per cent. By comparison, operational pollution from tankers is responsible for about 7 per cent and tanker accidents only 3 per cent.

## Non-tanker pollution on the rise

The relative amount of marine pollution caused by ships other than tankers rose in the last decade of the 20th century. According to the International Tanker Owners Pollution Federation (ITOPF), the loss of bunker fuel from non-tankers accounted for 38 per cent of the spills it attended in the period 1995-2000, while over the last two years of this period the figure rose to 50 per cent. Over the last three decades there have been significant reductions in oil spills from tanker accidents. For example, during the 1970s there were on average 24 spills a year of more than 700 tonnes. This dropped to 8.8 spills a year in the 1980s and to 7.3 in the 1990s.

Despite the substantially decreased quantity of oil that has spilled into the sea from high-profile tanker accidents, it has still had a profound effect on the way tankers are built and operated; on how liability for pollution is allotted; and on the relationship between the oil companies and independent tanker owners. For example, damage to the environment caused governments to introduce legislation but the industry itself often acted voluntarily in advance of political action.

## Early fears over oil transport

Since oil was first carried at sea in the 19th century, tanker cargoes have been viewed with caution, if not fear.

When oil began to be transported in bulk, first in wooden, then iron and steel ships, the much larger volumes obviously posed the risk of bigger explosions.

Two serious tanker explosions in 1892 led to a British Board of Trade inquiry. This revealed that the dangers of gas in tanks remained long after a cargo discharge had been completed and led to new rules requiring proper ventilation. In 1909 a three-masted steel barque, *Jules Henri*, blew up in Marseilles where it was due to undergo overhaul and repairs. A manhole had been opened to see if the tanks were empty and an explosion occurred, which killed several crew and workmen.

## Series of VLCC explosions

The development of VLCCs and ULCCs in the late 1960s posed a new set of problems for tanker operators. The huge dimensions of cargo tanks created an environment in which the risk of explosion increased, particularly when ships were performing tank cleaning operations during ballast voyages. In one of the blackest months for the tanker industry, December 1969, two VLCCs were lost and a third badly damaged while underway at sea. On 14 December a new Shell VLCC sank on its maiden voyage after suffering a massive explosion. On 29 December another of the oil major's VLCCs was ripped apart by an explosion which occurred while tank washing and the next day the 219,00 dwt *Kong Haakon VII*, owned by Hilmar Reksten of Norway, became the largest casualty when she suffered an explosion followed by an enormous fire. While the first two tankers were total losses the latter ship was subsequently salvaged and repaired.

It was later discovered that the explosions had been caused by a build-up of static electricity within the cargo tanks in what came to be known as the 'thunderstorm effect'. Gases within the tanks were ignited by the static electricity generated during high-pressure water washing of the tanks. The cavernous spaces of VLCC tanks enabled a cloud of electrically charged vapour to develop which then produced its own 'lightning' with devastating effect.

The disasters accelerated the adoption of inert gas systems (IGS) which filled the cargo tanks with a safe atmosphere, using the exhaust gases from the ship's own engines. The use of IGS had first been explored in the 1930s by several oil companies and tanker operators, including Chevron, BP, Shell, P&O and A P Møller. These companies were among the first to install IGS but the system had not yet been adopted as standard by the time of the 1969 explosions.

## Inert gas proves its worth

An intensive period of research by industry bodies took place in the first half of the 1970s and produced a series of recommendations and guides for both tanker and terminal operators. Installation of IGS became mandatory for most tankers in the 1980s and in particular when the method of tank cleaning known as crude oil washing (COW) was being used. COW uses the crude oil cargo as the washing medium. It is a practice which is both safer and more economical than water washing as it also enables more oil to be discharged to the shore and helps minimise the accumulation of oily water mixtures. Before IGS became compulsory, it had proved its worth in a notable incident involving a C Y Tung VLCC, *Energy Concentration*. The ship broke its back during discharge operations at a terminal in Rotterdam Europoort in 1980, but because it was fitted with IGS it did not suffer either fire or explosion. In contrast, a year earlier the Total-owned *Betelgeuse* had blown up while discharging cargo at the Bantry Bay terminal in Ireland, killing 50 people and destroying part of the Gulf Oil terminal. *Betelgeuse* was not fitted with IGS.

Fires and explosions in engine rooms, accommodation areas and cargo tanks have continued to be the major category of accidents to tankers over the last 30 years in terms of numbers of incidents. A study in 1998 by INTERTANKO 'A Systematic Approach to Tanker Accidents' found this category accounted for 240 out of 500 serious tanker casualties in the period 1963-96. Such incidents do not usually lead, however, to big oil spills. Another ITOPF study attributed only six per cent of large oil spills, i.e. those over 700 tonnes, to fires and explosions in the 1974-2000 period. In contrast, 35 per cent of such spills were attributed to groundings and 28 per cent to collisions.

The majority of oil spills occur during routine operations, such as cargo loading and discharging. According to ITOPF, on a numerical basis about 92 per cent of tanker spills have involved less than seven tonnes of oil. Spills resulting from collisions and groundings are much rarer events but they involve larger volumes of oil. ITOPF estimates that 20 per cent of spills stemming from tanker collision and grounding incidents result in losses of over 700 tonnes of oil.

## Discharges at sea

Oil can also enter the sea by a tanker discharging oily residues from tank washings or engine room waste. This was a common practice in the early days of the industry. One method adopted by the industry to minimise the amount of oil discharged deliberately in this way was the 'load-on-top' method. This was pioneered by Shell and came into use in the 1960s. Load-on-top relies on the fact that water and oil separate out. In practice, the oily water mixtures produced by tank cleaning operations are pumped into a slop tank where the water (being heavier than oil) settles out by gravity leaving the oil on top. The clean water can then be pumped into the sea and at the next load port new cargo can be loaded on top of the oil left in the slop tank. Load-on-top was adopted as an international measure in 1978, but the problem of retained slops onboard a tanker has not been helped by the failure of many ports to provide the necessary reception facilities. Such facilities were first advocated in the 1950s and proposed by an international convention in 1962 and later reinforced by the requirements of the 1973/78 Marine Pollution (MARPOL) Convention. During the tanker oversupply crisis of the 1970s, INTERTANKO even proposed that laid-up surplus tankers should be converted into reception facilities, so helping to solve two problems at one stroke. The idea was not taken up and the problem of the lack of adequate reception facilities for oily slops from tankers continued in varying degrees to the end of the century.

# LOAD ON TOP

*The first serious effort to deal with oil pollution caused by the operations of tankers was Load-on-top developed by Shell International Marine. Although now superseded by crude oil washing and segregated ballast requirements Load-on-top prevented several hundreds of thousands of tonnes of oil a year from being discharged into the sea*

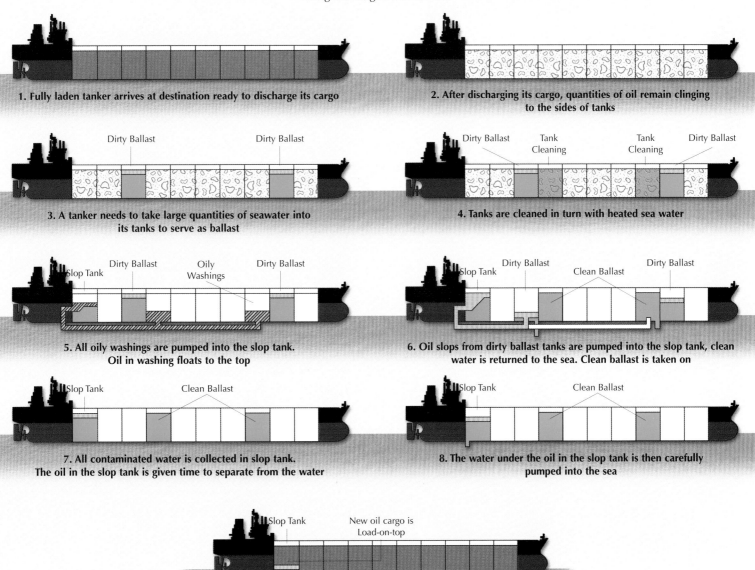

1. Fully laden tanker arrives at destination ready to discharge its cargo

2. After discharging its cargo, quantities of oil remain clinging to the sides of tanks

Dirty Ballast    Dirty Ballast

3. A tanker needs to take large quantities of seawater into its tanks to serve as ballast

Dirty Ballast    Tank Cleaning    Tank Cleaning    Dirty Ballast

4. Tanks are cleaned in turn with heated sea water

Slop Tank    Dirty Ballast    Oily Washings    Dirty Ballast

5. All oily washings are pumped into the slop tank. Oil in washing floats to the top

Slop Tank    Dirty Ballast    Clean Ballast    Dirty Ballast

6. Oil slops from dirty ballast tanks are pumped into the slop tank, clean water is returned to the sea. Clean ballast is taken on

Slop Tank    Clean Ballast

7. All contaminated water is collected in slop tank. The oil in the slop tank is given time to separate from the water

Slop Tank    Clean Ballast

8. The water under the oil in the slop tank is then carefully pumped into the sea

Slop Tank    New oil cargo is Load-on-top

9. Clean ballast has been discharged. New oil cargo is also Loaded-on-top of the slops

*Source: Sea Shell by Stephen Howarth, published in 1992*

*The giant oil tanker, Torrey Canyon, trapped on the rocks of Seven Stones. The ship was broken completely in two by the giant seas which pounded her*

In the meantime, mandatory restrictions on operational discharges into the sea from tankers increased, particularly with more areas being designated as "Special Areas" in which the practice was totally banned. Coastal states were also able to impose severe penalties against any tankers found guilty of breaching the rule governing the discharge of oil into the sea.

It was large, accidental oil spills, however, that made the headlines and resulted in most new regulations. The first of these infamous accidents involved the Liberian-flag *Torrey Canyon* which in 1967 ran aground off the Scilly Isles, southwest of the Cornish coast of Britain.
The accident occurred in fine weather and was later proved to have been the result of navigational error. Around 100,000 tonnes of crude oil was spilled into the sea, some of which was swept onto the shores of Cornwall and carried across the English Channel to the coast of Brittany. The British Royal Air Force was ordered to destroy the grounded tanker and burn off the remaining cargo.

## Argo Merchant outrages US

Another pollution incident occurred which led to further changes. In the winter of 1976 a series of 15 tanker casualties impacted the US East Coast. One of these was *Argo Merchant* which created headlines and outrage in America and led to a sustained ship inspection campaign by the US Coast Guard. The 23-year-old, Liberian-flag *Argo Merchant* had spilled a cargo of heavy fuel oil and, although most of the oil was carried out into the Atlantic and did not pollute the shoreline, the incident and the other tanker casualties focused US attention on old and foreign-flag ships. An inquiry into the *Argo Merchant* foundering revealed flaws in the ship's navigational equipment and officers' seamanship and qualifications.

At the international level, the US pressed for tighter regulations and presented IMO with a set of measures. In 1978 the Tanker Safety and Pollution Prevention diplomatic conference met in London and adopted two protocols to the 1973 MARPOL Convention and the 1974 Safety of Life at Sea (SOLAS) Convention.

It also became apparent that the mechanism by which international agreements on safety and pollution prevention came into force around the world was too slow and cumbersome. As a result, faster methods of ratifying international agreements adopted by IMO such as 'tacit acceptance' were introduced.

The 1973 MARPOL Convention, for example, was not in force by the time of the 1978 Tanker Safety Conference and the combined 1973/1978 MARPOL rules did not come into effect until 1983 or, in some cases, 1986.

## MARPOL Convention 1983 introduced

Barely a month after the 1978 conference in London, the laden Liberian-flag, 230,000 dwt *Amoco Cadiz* ran aground in heavy seas off Porsall on the French coast of Brittany, causing massive ecological damage due to the spillage of the entire cargo. The lessons from this disaster - the need for duplicate and independently operated steering gear controls and radars and improved towing facilities - were incorporated into the SOLAS Convention through the 1979 SOLAS amendments. Eventually, a complex package of anti-pollution measures came into force under the MARPOL Convention in 1983, with different timetables for existing and new tankers and different requirements for a range of tanker sizes.

The main provisions were that existing crude oil tankers had to be retrofitted with segregated ballast tanks (SBT) in protectively located spaces (PLS) and crude oil washing (COW) equipment had to be installed in combination with an inert gas system (IGS). Existing tankers were also required to adopt the load on top (LOT) procedure.
New tankers had to be equipped with duplicate steering systems and two independently operated radar systems.
Operational pollution was to be curbed by the installation of oily water separators and oil content measuring systems.

At the time of the *Amoco Cadiz* spill France had ratified CLC but not the Fund Convention. As a result, claimants unhappy with the limits on the shipowner's liability sued in the US, the country of domicile of the oil company which owned the ship. American courts allowed the claimants to use an archaic act from 1851 under which the owner could be found to have unlimited liability.
The case ran for 15 years and cost millions of dollars in legal expenses.

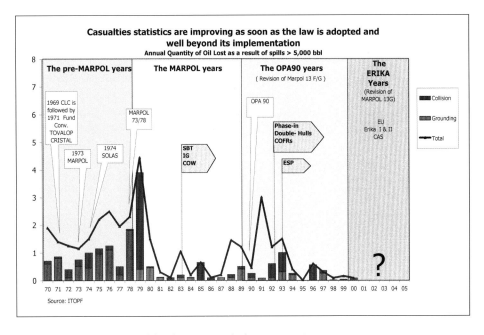

But it was the *Exxon Valdez* disaster in Alaskan waters in 1989 which caused the greatest repercussions for the tanker industry. This involved a relatively modern, oil company-owned 211,000 dwt tanker. Built in 1986, *Exxon Valdez* was a US-flagged and US-crewed ship. Despite these domestic connections, the *Exxon Valdez* spill did not take the pressure off foreign-owned, foreign-flag tankers in the US.

At 37,000 tonnes, the amount of oil spilled was considerable. However, it was the location that was the all-important factor in this case. The tanker had run aground in an environmentally important part of Alaska that was also an area of rich fishing grounds. The spill - which resulted in extensive media coverage - brought into focus environmentalists' concerns over pollution of a 'wilderness'.

## OPA 90 and double-hulls

The US Oil Pollution Act of 1990 (OPA 90), which was passed as a result of the *Exxon Valdez* spill, unilaterally imposed stringent requirements on tankers trading to the US. The most important requirements were that all tankers trading to ports in the US (other than the LOOP or designated lightering zones) be fitted with double hulls by 2010 in accordance with the phase out schedule.

*Greek owners were among the first to order double hull, double bottom tankers in the mid 1980s, in advance of OPA 90 requirements.*

*Pictured top is Arosa, a 291,381 dwt VLCC built in 1993 for Lykiardopulo & Co Ltd. This was one of the first of a line of double hull tankers built by Hitachi Zosen Corporation, Nagasu, Japan.*

*Eletson were also early to begin their double-hull newbuilding programme with Korea & Engineering Corporation. Four vessels were ordered in 1986 and delivered in 1989/90. For both environmental and operational reasons, Eletson ordered the vessels with ballast spaces segregated from cargo spaces. Pictured above is the 46,538 dwt Shinoussa, built 1990*

In addition owners needed to carry proof of their ability to meet the costs of a clean-up, i.e. the so-called Certificate of Financial Responsibility. The burden of liability for an oil spill was also placed solely on the shipowner, rather than being shared with the cargo owner as in the internationally agreed compensation schemes, while the threat of unlimited liability remained. Taken together, this package of measures sent shock waves through the industry.

OPA 90, also required ships to have oil spill response plans approved by the US Coast Guard; to carry oil spill containment equipment; and to have contracted with an approved, US-based clean-up organisation in the event of a spill.

In 1992, in the wake of OPA 90 in the US, IMO added new rules to its MARPOL Convention, stipulating that all new tankers above 5,000 dwt be built with double hulls from July 1993. Existing single-hull tankers over 20,000 dwt, on reaching the age of 25, would have to fit protectively located segregated ballast tanks or adopt the method of hydrostatically balanced loading.
This latter approach generally requires a slight reduction in the amount of oil loaded in the tanks to enable the pressure of oil in the bottom of the tanks to be equal to, or less than, the pressure of water outside the hull. In the event of a grounding which ruptures the tanks, the water pressure on the hull acts as a seal and prevents escape of oil from the tanks. However, under the new MARPOL requirements existing tankers would not be allowed to continue past the age of 30 unless fitted with a double hull.

Although tanker owners had failed to change the mind of the US government as regards implementation of OPA 90, they were determined to prevent individual US states from introducing their own anti-pollution legislation differing from the Federal regime. Conflicting safety regimes were viewed by the tanker owners to represent a significant threat to tanker safety and environmental protection.
An important legal battle was won by INTERTANKO in 2000 when the state of Washington was ordered by the US Supreme Court to desist from bringing in its own laws affecting the manning of tankers and their construction, design and operations.

## Erika and the age factor

The major pollution incidents with implications for the tanker industry had involved large crude tankers and subsequent crude oil tanker incidents such as *Braer* in 1993 and *Sea Empress* in 1996 had further tested the existing system. However, it was the 24-year-old, 37,000 dwt product tanker *Erika* sinking in heavy weather off the northwest coast of France in December 1999 that threatened to produce as big a response as that to *Exxon Valdez*. *Erika* sank after it had broken up in two while underway at sea, the structural failure being attributed to corrosion. The cargo of heavy fuel oil caused extensive pollution of beaches in France and, as a result, the European Union threatened to introduce its own rules on tanker safety and pollution in the manner of the US after *Exxon Valdez*. Many of the EU's proposed actions were directed to IMO which resulted in international consensus on a new timetable which calls for the accelerated phase-out of single-hull tankers.

The EU proposals also included a 'third-tier' pollution compensation regime (on top of the CLC and FC schemes) to cover oil spills in EU waters and to be financed by European oil receivers. Where claims exceed the existing schemes' maximum limits, the European regime would be activated. A similar proposal was considered and adopted by IMO in an international context.

The most immediate result of the *Erika* casualty, however, was a sudden and widespread move by a number of charterers to take only modern and 'quality' tankers, creating a two-tier market. Influenced by this and the planned and complex phase-out of single-hull tankers drawn up by IMO in April 2001, owners of tankers in the *Erika* size range began planning their scrapping and newbuilding strategies.

## Enhanced environmental standards

Tanker owners have had to accept that although the world still needs oil in great quantities and as cheap as possible, it has also become increasingly intolerant of pollution and its causes, whether deliberate or accidental. As a consequence of this the tanker industry is one of the most regulated and inspected in the world today.

The industry invests more on safety and pollution prevention than the industries that actually pump their waste into the rivers and seas. An inert gas system, so important to tanker safety, costs around $2 million per ship. Double hulled tankers designed to meet the requirements of OPA 90 add up to 15 per cent in the cost of a newbuilding compared to a single hull configuration.

In all some 20 per cent of the cost of a new tanker is spent on safety and anti-pollution measures.

The history of tanker incidents and pollution has been a painful combination of learning by experience and adapting to major regulatory changes occurring after politically sensitive incidents. The threat of unilateralism has also put great pressure on the system of international consensus and harmonisation.

While the industry is still making considerable efforts to further reduce pollution from tankers, it can also fairly claim that 99.998 per cent of all oil cargoes are delivered safely.

At the start of the 21st century tanker owners are hoping that the regulatory forces that have driven their industry for the past 20 years are spent. Many owners having built safe and environmentally friendly tankers, often well beyond the standard required by the regulations, charterers and public opinion, are now keen that they should, once again, be able to conduct their operations influenced only by the normal economic forces that apply to the commercial world. At the same time responsible owners want rigorous and uniform enforcement of the existing rules to ensure that substandard operators are prevented from plying their trade.

## Liability and compensation for oil pollution

*Torrey Canyon* exposed the shortcomings of the existing legal and insurance systems to provide compensation for damages arising from tanker spills. Under pressure from the British and French governments, an emergency meeting of the International Maritime Organization (IMO) began work on an international convention on tanker owners' liability. Pending the introduction of any mandatory compensation regimes, two voluntary schemes were set up by the industry. The 1969 Tanker Owners Voluntary Agreement concerning Liability for Oil Pollution (TOVALOP) created a special insurance scheme for shipowners, while the 1971 Contract Regarding an Interim Supplement to Tanker Liability (CRISTAL) did the same for cargo owners. CRISTAL supplemented the TOVALOP funds available for clean-up costs and third-party damage claims.

Mandatory international and compensation regimes came into effect in 1975 through the Civil Liability Convention (CLC) and in 1978 through the Fund Convention (FC). A basic compromise was reached whereby the shipowner accepted liability without regard to fault against the right to limit this liability. The liability was channelled to the registered owner of the vessel and the intention was to make litigation unnecessary for oil spill victims. CLC limited a shipowner's liability to the lesser of either $200 per ton of a tanker's gross tonnage or $19 million.

These limits were increased in 1996 when the limit for small tankers up to 5,000 grt was set at $4 million and gradually increased according to ship size to $81 million for tankers of 140,000 grt and above.

The Fund Convention established the International Oil Pollution Compensation Fund, financed by the receivers of crude oil and heavy fuel oil. The combined maximum compensation of CLC and FC was originally $81 million. It was increased to $182 million by the 1992 Fund Protocol which came into effect in 1996*. A further rise of 50 per cent has been proposed and is due to come into effect by late 2003. The industry-backed TOVALOP and CRISTAL agreements ran alongside the mandatory schemes until being phased out in 1997.

While the Americans had signed both CLC and FC, these international compensation regimes never came into force in the US. Instead, the US relied on domestic legislation such as the 1977 Clean Water Act which established strict liability and set clean-up costs at $150 per grt. Owners also faced the threat of unlimited liability if it could be proved that an incident was due to 'privity or knowledge' of the owner. Individual states were not pre-empted from enforcing their own oil spill liability regimes and by the end of the 1980s nearly 20 states had their own laws on liability. With the introduction of OPA 90, the US continued to rely on domestic oil spill legislation rather than taking part in the international system.

*CLC and FC figures are based on a rate of 1 SDR = $US 1.35*

*Globtik Tokyo, 476,000 dwt*
*ULCC, built 1973*

*The 89,004 gt ore oil carrier (OBO) Front Viewer, built 1992*

The technology of the tanker - from the early wooden sailing ships to modern steel-hulled giants - has been driven mainly by the forces of supply and demand which stimulated innovations in design as the industry developed ever larger and more efficient ships. However, regulatory pressures prompted by environmental concerns have also played their part.

Economics and safety dictated that oil be carried in bulk if the technology could deliver such a method. The use of iron, then steel, compartmentalised hulls driven by steam and diesel engines created the basic bulk tank ship design. Pumping technology was adapted and improved to give faster discharge times. Ship construction methods were devised to create stronger hulls that would prevent buckling and cracking and enable tanker sizes to increase.

## Making the hull oil-tight

The problems of cargo leakage in early tankers also called for construction methods which would make hulls oil-tight. In the late 19th century rivetted iron hulls improved on the performance of wooden hulls. Then, in 1886, caulking of the hull plates and boiler rivetting were used for the first time. The problem of cargo expansion was also acknowledged and separate regulating tanks or trunking were fitted to early tankers. All-welded ships began appearing in the 1930s and welding was used in the mass-production methods of ship construction during the Second World War. As well as creating a more oil-tight structure, welding helped to reduce hull drag by eliminating overlapping plates and protruding rivets.

Economics first prompted Marcus Samuel, the founder of Shell, to install a tank-washing system using steam cleaning in his first tankers in the 1890s. This enabled the ships to carry backhaul cargoes such as tea or rice in the tanks after delivering their cargoes of Caspian Sea oil to Far East destinations. The search for a way to eliminate or minimise non-earning ballast voyages continued through the 20th century, giving rise to ship hybrids such as the ore/oil carrier, the ore/bulk/oil carrier (OBO) and the petroleum product/ore/bulk/oil carrier (PROBO).

## Diesel chosen over steam

The choice of engine type and fuel economics was a major factor in ensuring the commercial success of tanker shipping. In the early days of the battle between steam and diesel, *Vulcanus*, built in 1910, gave a demonstration of the benefits of diesel engines. Powered by a six-cylinder Werkspoor engine giving her a speed of seven knots, she could run for 88 days without refuelling, and the diesel oil she carried weighed only one-fifth of the weight of coal carried by a similar-sized steam turbine ship on an equivalent voyage. Her engine room was also manned by five engineers only, compared with the usual 16 on steamships of the day.

Diesel eventually became the preferred choice of engine for tankers when the price of bunkers shot up after the 1973 oil shock. Before then, most large tankers had been built with steam turbines. Early turbines sometimes operated on more expensive but purer marine fuel. Eventually, however, steam turbines, like diesels, burned heavy fuel oil, albeit at a greater rate. The new post-1973 economics provided diesels with an important cost advantage but it meant that diesel engine manufacturers had to build a single engine powerful enough to drive a VLCC. They succeeded and during the 1980s several steam-driven VLCCs were re-equipped with diesel engines. More exotic, perhaps, have been the few gas turbine powered-tankers that were built, while Japan experimented in the 1980s with sail-assisted tankers in an attempt to reduce fuel costs.

## Advantages of size

The overriding feature of tanker design, however, has been the economy of scale factor. This had become evident before the First World War when Eagle Oil built the first 15,000 dwt tankers in 1913. These ships proved that a given volume of oil could be carried 10 per cent cheaper than in their 9,000 dwt tankers. The ships also incorporated steam heating coils in the tanks to speed up discharge if necessary.

Ship size did not increase greatly over the next 35 years, as evidenced by the American T-2 tanker of World War Two - a ship of 16,600 dwt. After the war, however, as the demand for tanker tonnage soared, growth in ship size began to accelerate. It took only a decade to leap from the 30,011 dwt *Bulkpetrol* in 1948 to the 104,520 dwt *Universe Apollo* in 1959. By the time of the crash of the tanker market in the 1970s tankers of over 550,000 dwt had been built and there had been serious plans to construct a one million tonner. Such a giant ship appeared technically feasible but the plans fell victim to market sentiment after the 1973 oil shock. *Jahre Viking*, built in 1976 and subsequently enlarged to 565,000 dwt, the present size, has remained the largest tanker ever to sail the world's oceans.

## The drive for cheaper transport

The oil companies' need to reduce their transport costs had fuelled the tremendous growth in ship size. In the post-World War Two years the Middle East had become the main source of oil for the global market and long voyages became the norm. When smaller tankers were used, transport represented 10-20 per cent of the total cost of the oil to the consumer. With the use of larger tankers, transport costs, as a percentage of the delivered price, were much reduced.

Larger tankers proved economical to operate because the power requirement did not increase in direct proportion but rather by a ratio of two-thirds to the increase in displacement. A laden 60,000 dwt steam-powered tanker could be driven at 15 knots by 16,000 hp, while a 260,000 dwt ship needed 42,500 hp, an increase in power of less than three times, but for more than four times the cargo-carrying capacity.

There were also savings in fuel consumption, as a 60,000 dwt tanker needed 53 tonnes of fuel a day, compared with 140 tonnes for the 260,000 dwt ship. Other savings could be made in crewing costs. As the century progressed and tanker size increased, sophisticated shipboard systems were introduced in the drive to reduce crew numbers.

Automation of the engine room, in particular, helped reduce crew complements. A further contribution to economy was the bulbous bow introduced in the early 1960s. This counteracted the normal bow wave effect and brought speed gains of around 0.5 knot on average, with reduced power requirements.

*Close up of the bulbous bow of a tanker in ballast (foreground)*

Another significant change was the ratio of LCT (length of the cargo tank space) to LBP (ship length between perpendiculars). This ratio was under 60 per cent in *Glückauf* but increased through the T-2s to well over 70 per cent and almost 80 per cent in ULCCs. In the early days engines and bunkers required a great deal of space. To encourage designers to make engine rooms big enough and more habitable for engineering crew, the tonnage rules stipulated that the deduction from gross tonnage (grt) for net tonnage (nrt) would be 13 per cent, provided that engine rooms were at least 7.01 per cent of grt.

To achieve this lower nrt allowance, tankers continued to be built with long engine rooms aft, even after machinery and bunker space requirements had become much smaller.

The result was lost cargo cubic capacity and heavy sag bending moments requiring more steel in the hull.

In the 1950s it was realised that the tonnage deduction would not be as valuable as the increase in cargo capacity and savings in steel if engine rooms became shorter and smaller. This allowed LCT / LBP ratios to increase, giving more cargo space. Also, bending moments in load and ballast conditions became more favourable. The result was major savings in the cost of tankers.

During the 1960s and 1970s new types of hull paints were developed with effective anti-fouling agents to inhibit weed growth and barnacles on the hull to reduce the onset of drag. This enabled ships to maintain optimum speed for minimal additional power requirement and widened the intervals between drydocking from one year to over two years or longer. However, the toxic aspects of these paints later became the subject of debate.

It also became the trend in the 1960s and 1970s to reduce the number of tanks as ship sizes increased. This was not only a cost-saving device, it also reflected the diminished need for segregated parcels as the longhaul trades became more defined. Larger size ships were allocated to crude oil shipping while the smaller vessels were devoted more to the distributive trades involving parcels of different cargoes.

## Size brings its own problems

Increasing ship size, particularly as regards the larger VLCCs and ULCCs, did, however, bring some difficulties. It was difficult to quantify precisely the dynamic and static forces at work on a tanker's structure over the ship's working life until computer-based design technology first became available in the late 1960s. During the early days of rapidly increasing tanker size classification societies and shipyards were cautious in their approach to the design and construction of this new generation of large tanker and conservative in their rules for the steel dimensions. This meant that in the early 1970s tankers were built with relatively high margins against fatigue and corrosion. By the mid-1970s, experience and improved design techniques led to these margins being reduced, enabling large tankers to be built with less steel and at

reduced cost. Increasing amounts of high-tensile steel (HTS) were used in the construction of the larger ships, allowing the dimensions of plating and structural members to be reduced without sacrificing strength. However, subsequent problems with cracking raised questions about the use of such high percentages of HTS.

Other problems of ship size were the limited access of VLCCs and ULCCs to ports and waterways, not least the Suez Canal when it was re-opened in 1975. As the largest tankers had draughts of over 28 metres, only a limited number of ports and terminals could take the laden giants. Deepwater terminals such as Bantry Bay in Ireland or offshore discharging facilities such as the Louisiana Offshore Oil Port in the US Gulf had to be purpose-built.

## Challenge to surveyors

The huge size of ships also imposed limitations on technical inspections. Internally, the huge spaces of the cargo tanks presented new challenges to classification society inspectors as they checked for signs of corrosion and fatigue during scheduled surveys. These checks were

regularly carried out at sea during ballast voyages by torchlight by a surveyor in a small inflatable boat which was raised or lowered by varying the amount of water in a tank.

Externally, the typical VLCC also presented a challenge to surveyors. The total area of the exterior plating was typically 50,000 square metres, while the total length of the main welding 100,000 metres. It was estimated by the Salvage Association in 1992 that ultrasonic testing of a VLCC's plating would take 50,000 man-hours, while visual examination of the welding would take another 20,000 hours or 100,000 hours using magnetic particle inspection. Instead, sampling of areas known to be the most vulnerable to corrosion and other damages became the standard practice.

## Impact of regulation

After the tremendous growth in fleet size and the rapid escalation of tanker sizes in the post-war period, the primary focus in tanker technology from the mid-1970s onwards tended to be on regulatory developments, as the industry sought to ensure the safe design and operation of these new behemoths. Even so, other innovations came about for commercial and technical reasons - for example, the development of shuttle tankers for North Sea oil and tankers for use as floating storage units (FSUs) and floating production, storage and offtake (FPSO) vessels. The latter two options also provided tanker owners with a chance to convert existing ships and ensure profitable employment for what might otherwise have been wasting assets.

The technical challenge of reducing the risk of pollution arising out of tanker accidents in recent years has been sidetracked, to a certain extent, by expedient rulemaking. Double hulls appear to have won the debate by providing an acceptable level of pollution protection.

## Basic design unchanged

During the 20th century the most dramatic tanker technology change came with the post - World War II boom. With the basic hull structural design parameters established, in which finite element analysis and three dimensional frame analysis played an important part, economies of scale and larger and larger ships became the dominating factor.

With the advent of the new millennium the industry's goal is to build state-of-the-art tankers with extremely high levels of safety which can provide at least 20 years of reliable service.

This means built-in quality standards to reduce maintenance costs and unplanned repairs. These vessels will offer greater operating efficiency and flexibility of service and have better environmental protection than ships of 10 and 20 years ago. Improved navigational, communications and IT systems will minimise the scope for human error. Some of the new generation of tankers are already embodying such features.

Looking further ahead, current research into tanker technology and design aimed at minimising harmful air emissions is investigating such equipment as main engine exhaust scrubber systems, gas separators/splitter, hydrocarbon gas absorption columns, cooling/heat exchanger systems and various compressor plants. Such equipment could, if fitted, dramatically change the appearance of the future tanker into something more like a floating refinery.

*Futura, 95,200 dwt, built 1997*

# Marine engine developments

When steam engines were first used in ships they were harnessed to drive paddle wheels. This drive system was superseded by the development of the screw propeller which provided an infinitely more efficient and versatile means of propulsion.

Early marine engines were relatively simple machines in which steam pressure forced a piston up and down within a cylinder and a crank converted this reciprocating movement into a rotary action. The performance was later improved by the 'double-acting' method which enabled steam to be admitted alternately to each side of the piston.

Next, in the 1850s, came the compound engine with two or more cylinders of increasing size which provided for greater expansion of the steam and higher efficiency.
The first and smallest piston was activated by the initial high pressure steam which was then exhausted at lower pressure to power the second, larger, piston, hence the term double expansion engine.

This method was extended by adding more cylinders to give triple and quadruple expansion engines. The triple expansion type was widely adopted during the 1880s and was an important factor in the increasing application of steam power in ships. Another breakthrough in efficiency was the switch from coal-fired to oil-fired boilers which brought useful savings in bunker space and weight, as well as reductions in engine room personnel and cheaper running costs. There were also progressive developments in boiler design which allowed higher steam temperatures and greater operating pressures to be used, giving better thermal efficiency and improved power delivery.

A major advance in steam propulsion came with the introduction of the steam turbine in 1894 by the British marine engineer Sir Charles Parsons. This system utilised high pressure steam jets discharged through a series of stationary and moving vanes which revolved a rotor at high speed. This process raised steam power to new levels of efficiency and, with suitable gearing, provided a smooth and reliable power source.

*Sir Charles Parsons demonstrates the superior performance of his new steam turbine engine as Turbinia speeds away from pursuing torpedo-boat destroyers at over 34 knots*

Parsons demonstrated the superiority of his engine in a particularly audacious manner on the occasion of the Diamond Jubilee Fleet Review which took place at Spithead off the south coast of Britain in 1897.

In his small turbine-powered vessel *Turbinia* he daringly overtook the Royal Squadron of Queen Victoria and her entourage as it steamed through the 30-mile lane of anchored warships of the British Navy. The Navy's latest and fastest torpedo-boat destroyers immediately gave chase but the rakish looking *Turbinia*, with Parsons himself on the bridge, easily outdistanced them as it accelerated away at over 34 knots - a staggering speed at that time. This performance was achieved by an engine that produced 2,000 hp, greatly surpassing the output of the triple-expansion steam engines in the pursuing destroyers.

The Admiralty's previous doubts about the merits of the steam turbine were swept away by *Turbinia's* convincing demonstration and within a few years many British Navy ships were powered by steam turbines, including over 200 new destroyers whose 24,000 hp Parsons turbines gave them a speed of almost 30 knots.

Meanwhile, in 1882 Rudolph Diesel had delivered a paper on 'The theory and design of an economical heat engine' and in 1893 patented his 'rational heat' engine.
He later awarded patents to MAN of Germany, Sulzer of Switerland and Burmeister Wain of Copenhagen to make industrial diesel engines and his first engine, built by MAN, was demonstrated in 1897.

Prior to this two British engineers, Herbert Ackroyd Stuart and Charles Richard Binney, had patented a new oil engine in 1890. Soon afterwards, in 1892, Richard Hornsby & Sons, another British firm, built the world's first commercially successful oil engine and then produced a 9.5 hp vertical twin four stroke oil engine to power a Glasgow-built launch. This was followed by a four cylinder marine engine supplied to the British Admiralty in 1903.

Another interesting development was diesel electric propulsion which was first fitted to the 800 dwt oil barge *Vandal* in 1903/4. This vessel incorporated three 120 hp engines by A/B Diesel Motoren of Sweden which were fitted amidships and coupled to electric transmission motors located aft, driving triple propellers, thus obviating the need to run propeller shafts through the intervening cargo tanks. The electric motors also provided astern propulsion as, until 1906, diesel engines were not reversible.

*Following the 1973 oil shock, which escalated oil prices the shipping world sought ways to reduce fuel costs, including by slow steaming. The development of sail assisted motor ships was also considered and Japan put the idea into practice.*

*Cooperation between the Japanese government and civilian shipyards led in 1980 to the building of the world's first 'commercial and energy-saving' ship, Shin-Aitoku Maru. A petroleum product carrier, 699 grt, classified by NK as 'equipped with computer-controlled auxiliary sailing system'. The system consisted of two sets of sails utilising rectangular flow-type sail canvas on steel frames, computer controlled for optimum sail setting relative to the wind. Reputedly capable of cutting costs by 10 per cent or more, including savings on fuel, she became a focus of attention from the shipping and shipbuilding industries worldwide. With the subsequent drop in oil prices, the fuel savings from sail assisted ships became less important. For this reason, as well as the burden of maintaining the sailing equipment, the development of sail power was largely abandoned.*

The first ocean-going vessel to be equipped with diesel power was the 1, 210 dwt Shell tanker *Vulcanus* built by the Netherlands Shipbuilding Company in 1910 and fitted with a Werkspoor 490 hp engine. *Vulcanus* logged over a million miles before being sold in 1932.

The diesel engine proved its reliability under extreme conditions for the Norwegian explorer Roald Amundsen when he became the first man to reach the South Pole. His vessel *Fran* sailed as far as the Great Ice Barrier within the Antarctic Circle, from where the expedition was able to reach the South Pole by December 1911, some 35

days ahead of the arrival of the British attempt by Captain Scott. *Fran* was powered by a 180 hp engine of A/B Diesels Motoren which performed so well that the term 'Polar' was then used by the company for certain of its engine models.

Among the diesel engine developments in that period were the opposed piston design built by William Doxford & Sons in 1919, the Werkspoor double-acting two stroke engines of 4,000 hp fitted to some Shell tankers in 1924, and the Scott-Still diesel/steam engines with pistons that were driven by fuel combustion from the top and steam pressure from below. The engines had several unique features, including a supercharging valve in each exhaust gas outlet from the combustion cylinders, and starting by steam only.

During the 1920s MAN, Burmeister & Wain, Krupp and Sulzer developed larger 'cathedral engines' which were double-acting two stroke designs giving higher outputs without greatly increasing their size.

The search for greater power continued and in 1933 one of the most powerful marine diesel units of the time was installed in the passenger liner *Oceanus* which was equipped with four eight cylinder two stroke engines developing 22,000 hp. During the Second World War some 2,700 Liberty ships, of which 62 were tankers, were fitted with triple-expansion steam engines while the 481 T-2 SEA1 tankers used turbo-electric main engines. This was because the US did not have the facilities to build large, slow-revving diesel engines suitable for marine use. Also, limitations on the production of reduction gears needed for steam turbines meant that most of these units were reserved for US Navy vessels.

The high cost of diesel fuel led to a search for alternatives and in 1946 Shell adapted the Werkspoor four stroke engine in its 12,000 dwt tanker *Auricula* to run on high viscosity fuel (HVF). One of the higher fractions of crude oil, this fuel was so dense that it was generally used as boiler fuel in steamships and power stations. The maiden voyage of *Auricula* to Curacao was the first time any motorship had operated on HVF alone, although it was sometimes used in conjunction with lighter fractions.

The experiment proved successful, as her fuel consumption was exactly the same as if she had run on diesel. But HVF was significantly cheaper and the company calculated that its use would save about half a million pounds sterling a year. Within a decade every motor ship in Shell's fleet had been modified to run on HVF and so had many others. By the mid 1950s about 500 vessels were also using HVF.

In another experiment with new types of propulsion Shell fitted a large gas turbine to replace the four diesel engines in its 12,290 dwt tanker *Auris* in 1951. Although the unit was lighter in weight and simpler to operate and maintain than a traditional diesel engine, it was no cheaper per unit of power produced. It was also very expensive to install so the idea was dropped. The technology was taken up by navies for use in warships, for example in Rolls Royce 'Olympus' engines which are used to power naval frigates and other vessels.

During the 1960s and early 1970s diesel and steam turbine engines became the preferred choice of tanker operators because they were reliable, efficient and could be developed to drive bigger and bigger ships.

## Diesel engine developments and diesel-electric propulsion

Initially, the use of slow-speed diesel engines was restricted due to the difficulty of matching engine power output with the rapidly escalating size of tankers. By the mid-1960s, however, diesels with outputs of 2,000 hp per cylinder were being built and this type of engine began to come into the reckoning for owners of larger tankers.

Over the past three decades, thanks to improvements in fuel injection techniques and higher levels of cylinder pressure charging, the per cylinder power and torque ratings of diesels have been steadily increased, to the extent that fuel-hungry steam turbines are no longer an economically viable option for tanker propulsion. Today, steam turbines are utilised on liquefied natural gas (LNG) carriers, where natural gas which boils off from the cargo during the course of the voyage is fed into the boilers for use as supplementary fuel.

## Diesel-electric potential

A more recent notable development in propulsion systems is the greater use of diesel-electric machinery by certain types of tanker. By linking a number of medium-speed diesel engines up to an electric motor, the ship can be provided with a considerable degree of redundancy to guard against possible engine failure. Diesel-electric propulsion is utilised onboard many modern shuttle tankers to enable them to provide uninterrupted service on a year-round basis, carrying oil from offshore fields to shore terminals and refineries according to a tight schedule aligned to the field's production capability.

The ability of diesel-electric systems to handle variable load requirements also suits shuttle tanker operations which entail careful manoeuvring and dynamic positioning in open seas at offshore loading locations, rapid cargo discharge sequences and quick port turnarounds.

In the mid-1990s a leading chemical tanker operator specified diesel-electric propulsion for the range of chemical parcel tankers of different sizes that comprise its latest newbuilding programme. This was the first time that such propulsion had been specified for parcel carriers, a type of ship which - like shuttle tankers - experiences widely varying load requirements during the course of a voyage. Chemical parcel carriers carry up to 50 different bulk liquid cargoes simultaneously and cargo-handling operations at the main petrochemical hub ports can be intense, with several cargoes being loaded and several more being discharged at the same time. The flexibility of diesel-electric systems, particularly as regards matching fuel consumption to power requirements, has proved to be well-suited to parcel carrier operations.

Diesel-electric propulsion systems also reduce air pollution, noise and vibration compared with slow-speed diesels - important considerations at a time when atmospheric pollution and crew comfort are becoming increasingly important considerations.

# Tackling the hazards of ice

In August 1969 the 115,000 dwt American tanker *Manhattan* left Delaware Bay on the US East Coast for an epic experimental voyage to gather data on whether purpose built new tankers could deliver cargo safely through Arctic ice fields to the American east or west coasts. The specially modified *Manhattan* was on bareboat charter to Exxon and had also received financial support from BP and ARCO

The experiment was set up to help decide whether new icebreaking tankers would be a better option than pipelines to deliver crude oil from Prudhoe Bay on Alaska's northern coast to refineries on the east or west coasts of America. By sea this would involve a 4,400 mile voyage to the East Coast or 2,900 miles to the west coast. Easterly passage through the Arctic would be in latitudes as high as 76 degrees north via the Northwest Passage, or westerly through the Bering Strait. Nearly half of the distance of either route would be through ice cover.

At that time *Manhattan* was the most heavily built and powerful twin-screw tanker in the world, and her short cargo tank lengths and steel deck and upper hull plating made her especially suitable for the experiment.
The preparation of the vessel for Arctic testing involved reinforcement of the hull and installing an icebreaker bow. New propellers and shafting were fitted and major modifications to propulsion machinery and rudders were included.

The conversion took seven months by five shipyards and was co-ordinated by Sun Shipbuilding of Chester, Pennsylvania with Exxon serving as project leader, with "ice knowhow" from Wartsila Shipyard (now Kvaener MASA) of Finland, the world's leading icebreaker builder. The hull reinforcement utilised 10,000 tonnes of steel and included provision for an ice belt around the ship's waterline and a double hull structure to protect the engines, boiler room and steering gear areas.

For the experiment the *Manhattan's cargo* tanks were filled with water to simulate a laden voyage and the ship was accompanied by two icebreakers. Initially, the ship encountered some new and not very substantial ice but the ship then came up against hard-set floes of second year ice with the salt leached out and re-frozen after the summer melt. *Manhattan* was able to maintain speed in ice up to four feet thick, but consistent thickness was rare and mostly the ship had to contend with ice in ridges and blocks extending sometimes as much as 50 feet below the waterline, for which ramming was necessary.

A return voyage was made in spring 1970 to further study the ship's capabilities in harder winter ice. Because *Manhattan* was clearly not powerful enough, or made of suitable steel for an Arctic winter, her voyages were in essence a gigantic model test. Results of both voyages were utilised in a new ice model basin testing programme which showed that icebreaking tankers of up to 300,000 dwt needed propulsive power four to five times greater than that required for conventional tankers. In addition they needed to be constructed of low-temperature steels able to withstand Arctic winters without becoming brittle.

The experiment cost around $54 million and was highly successful in demonstrating that the operation of icebreaking tankers was technically and commercially feasible. In fact the *Manhattan* experiment is still the leading source of large ship powering and structural data used by ice model basins and icebreaker builders of the world.

The tanker studies were suspended in 1970 when the oil companies decided that the pipeline alternatives represented the optimum route for Alaskan North Slope oil. However, those who participated in these tests were convinced that icebreaking tankers are feasible in many parts of the Arctic. In fact, two newbuilding icebreaking tankers of improved Finnish design are currently under construction for service in the Russian arctic commencing in August 2002.

*Ice party working alongside Manhattan in latitude 76 degrees north*

# Training with models and simulators

In the mid 1960s when tankers increased hugely in size from some 90,000 dwt to 190,000 dwt their manoeuvrability came into question.

To provide some answers Exxon, in 1968, carried out numerous model tests followed by full scale manoeuvring trials with 190,000 and 250,000 dwt VLCCs to verify the results. Similar tests were conducted for their first 400,000 dwt prior to delivery in 1976. The following year Exxon, together with other tanker operators and the US government, sponsored a project to provide information about VLCC manoeuvrability in shallow waters for incorporation in training simulators.

Prior to this tanker masters had been given advance experience in the ship handling characteristics of larger vessels at a special training unit in Grenoble, France.
Set up in 1966/7 by Exxon and the French hydraulics company Sogreah, this unique facility was created in a remodelled lake which reproduced major tanker waterways and terminals through the world on a 1/25 scale.
Similarly scaled model tankers gave officers the equivalent of years of experience in the behaviour of vessels under varied operating conditions within the space of a few days.

In 1971 tanker officers were able to use a ship handling simulator at Institute TNO in Delft, Netherlands which provided methods similar to those of the airline industry for training pilots. This enabled the officers to perform various manoeuvres - like entering harbour or negotiating a narrow channel - from a simulated 'bridge'.
The horizon, sky and forward section of the ship were projected onto a large screen facing the officer and, as the 'bridge' controls were operated, a computer instantly registered the changes and converted them into corresponding visual movements on the screen. The immediate feed-back gave the officers a 'feel' for the vessel before they took command of a real ship. The simulator was also used to provide refresher courses for experienced mariners.

One of the main benefits of the system was that it also provided training for the 'bridge team' of captain, officers and pilot.

*Picture shows the training facility at Port Revel near Grenoble, France with a scaled tanker model approaching an offshore mooring buoy*

# Features of a modern product tanker

(Tanker of 45,000 dwt)

Tanker design has continued to evolve over the past 30 years, to the extent that the modern product tanker has achieved a level of sophistication unknown to its predecessors. Double hull construction ensures that all the structural members are located on the outside of the cargo tanks, leaving flush, epoxy-lined tank walls which, following discharge operations, are easy to drain of cargo and easy to clean. Each tank is equipped with its own stainless steel deepwell cargo pump and is connected to the cargo manifold via its own individual pipework to provide a high degree of cargo segregation. Tank levels are measured using radar-based gauges and cargo operations are controlled and monitored via remote computers. An increasingly popular cargo heating system is that provided by deck-mounted stainless steel heat exchangers - an arrangement which also makes a tank easier to clean than if it were fitted with the more traditional heating coils.

A variety of product tanker types have evolved to handle the deepsea balancing movements of refined petroleum. So-called Handysize ships of up to 35,000 dwt and Handymax vessels of 45,000 dwt remain the workhorses of the product tanker fleet. In more recent years, however, larger ships have come to the fore on certain routes and in certain trades, as owners seek to take advantage of the economies of scale opportunities opening up in the refined product sector. Large range 1 (LR 1) ships, in the 55-80,000 dwt size range, and LR 2 ships of 80-110,000 dwt carry large-volume cargoes such as condensate, naphtha, residual fuel oil and some middle distillates on longhaul routes. For example, considerable tonnages of naphtha, a light product used as a petrochemical feedstock, are currently being transported from Middle East refineries to Japan, Korea and Taiwan in LR 2 ships.

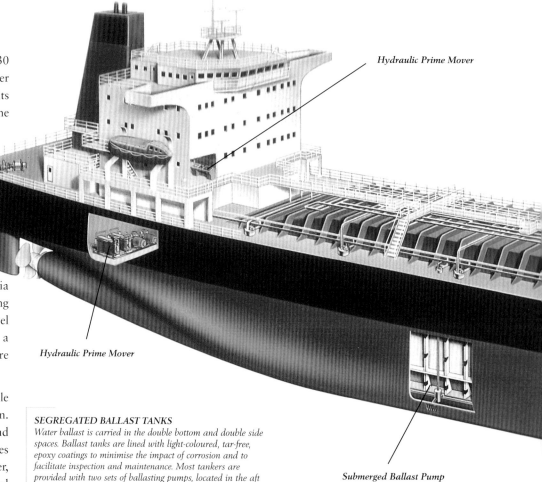

*Hydraulic Prime Mover*

*Hydraulic Prime Mover*

*Submerged Ballast Pump*

**SEGREGATED BALLAST TANKS**
*Water ballast is carried in the double bottom and double side spaces. Ballast tanks are lined with light-coloured, tar-free, epoxy coatings to minimise the impact of corrosion and to facilitate inspection and maintenance. Most tankers are provided with two sets of ballasting pumps, located in the aft cofferdam or pumproom, for ballasting/deballasting. An alternative arrangement has been developed in which ballast pumps are installed submerged in one of the segregated ballast tanks. This approach, in combination with a submerged pump in each cargo tank, enables the traditional pumproom to be eliminated.*

**PIPING AND CARGO SEGREGATION**
*Cargo piping systems are designed with optimal loading, discharge, draining and cleaning characteristics in mind. Dedicated product tankers usually have four to six segregations, with two or more submerged cargo pumps connected to each cargo line and crossover. Combined product/chemical tankers are designed with one pump, line and manifold crossover per tank to ensure that each tank can carry a different cargo in a fully segregated manner.*

## PROPULSION SYSTEM

Driving a fixed-pitch propeller, the slow-speed diesel engine develops 15,000 bhp at 80 rpm to provide a ship service speed of 15 knots. Three auxiliary engines provide electrical power while steam requirements are met by a marine boiler. The tanker is provided with a software package which uses artificial intelligence and data acquisition techniques to monitor and control machinery performance, and offers a diagnostics capability. An electrically driven bow thruster is fitted for increased manoeuvrability.

## OTHER CARGO-HANDLING AND SAFETY FEATURES

Modern product tankers incorporate many other distinctive cargo-handling and safety features as standard, some of which are itemised below:
- Stainless steel heat exchangers on deck, through which the cargo is circulated using the submerged cargo pumps. The absence of heating coils in the tank facilitates tank cleaning
- Fully automatic vapour emission control system features an independent high-high level alarm for the cargo and slop tanks, and a fixed oxygen analyser for the vapour manifolds
- Tank levels are monitored by means of radar devices fitted in each tank. Cargo operations controlled and monitored remotely via loading computer in bridge cargo control room
- The ship is fitted with an inert gas generator and emergency towing equipment. Ballast tanks are inerted and crude oil washing can be carried out.

Salamina, 45,425 dwt, built 1991

**Cargo Heater**

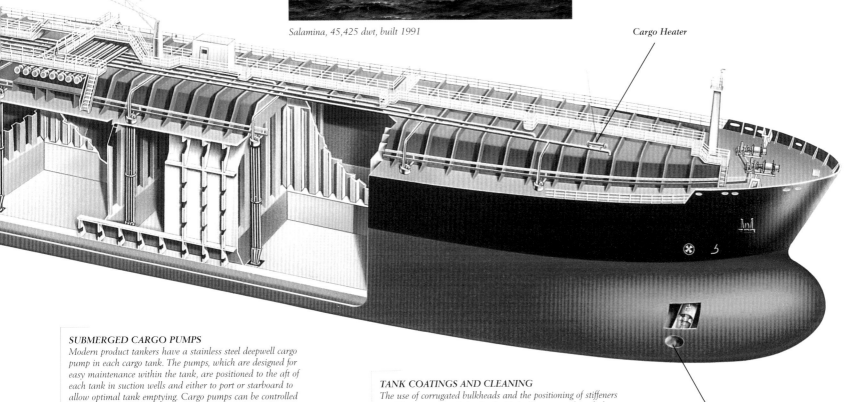

**Bow Thruster**

## SUBMERGED CARGO PUMPS

Modern product tankers have a stainless steel deepwell cargo pump in each cargo tank. The pumps, which are designed for easy maintenance within the tank, are positioned to the aft of each tank in suction wells and either to port or starboard to allow optimal tank emptying. Cargo pumps can be controlled either remotely from the cargo control room or locally by means of their capacity control valves. During cargo discharge, when the tank is empty the pump can be switched to the "dry running" mode to permit final stripping of the remaining cargo residues. A typical discharge rate for a cargo pump on a ship of this size is 450 m≥/hour, and the hydraulic power pack enables the use of up to six pumps simultaneously.

## TANK COATINGS AND CLEANING

The use of corrugated bulkheads and the positioning of stiffeners outside the cargo tank, in the double hull spaces and on deck, enables cargo tanks to be designed with flush walls to facilitate cleaning. The arrangement is also conducive to the application of cargo tank linings. Typical product tankers have three-coat epoxy tank lining systems, although if it is a product/chemical tanker which will be engaged in the methanol trades, then a zinc silicate lining system will be specified.

# Features of a typical, modern VLCC

(Tanker of 290,000 dwt - 2 million barrel capacity)

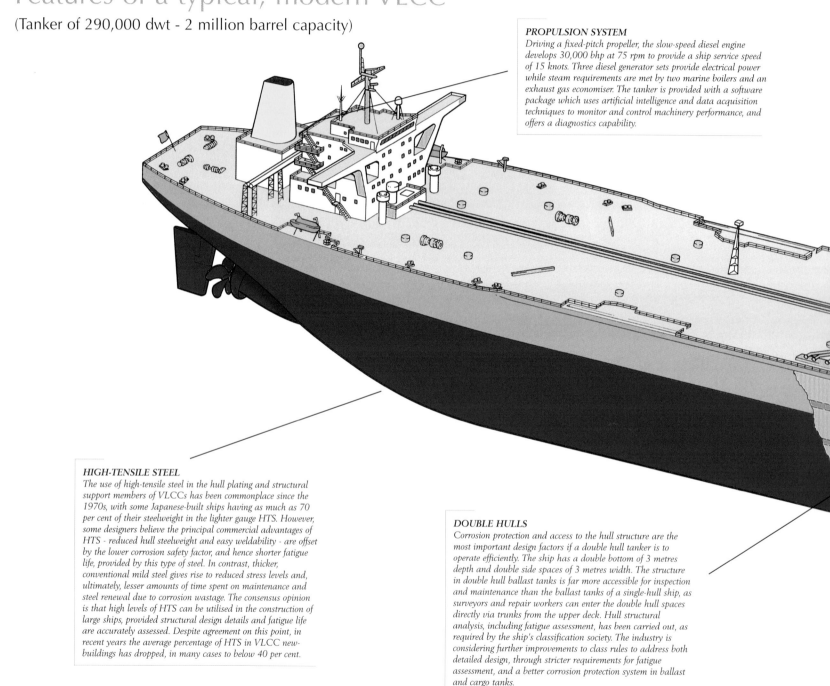

**PROPULSION SYSTEM**

*Driving a fixed-pitch propeller, the slow-speed diesel engine develops 30,000 bhp at 75 rpm to provide a ship service speed of 15 knots. Three diesel generator sets provide electrical power while steam requirements are met by two marine boilers and an exhaust gas economiser. The tanker is provided with a software package which uses artificial intelligence and data acquisition techniques to monitor and control machinery performance, and offers a diagnostics capability.*

**HIGH-TENSILE STEEL**

*The use of high-tensile steel in the hull plating and structural support members of VLCCs has been commonplace since the 1970s, with some Japanese-built ships having as much as 70 per cent of their steelweight in the lighter gauge HTS. However, some designers believe the principal commercial advantages of HTS - reduced hull steelweight and easy weldability - are offset by the lower corrosion safety factor, and hence shorter fatigue life, provided by this type of steel. In contrast, thicker, conventional mild steel gives rise to reduced stress levels and, ultimately, lesser amounts of time spent on maintenance and steel renewal due to corrosion wastage. The consensus opinion is that high levels of HTS can be utilised in the construction of large ships, provided structural design details and fatigue life are accurately assessed. Despite agreement on this point, in recent years the average percentage of HTS in VLCC new-buildings has dropped, in many cases to below 40 per cent.*

**DOUBLE HULLS**

*Corrosion protection and access to the hull structure are the most important design factors if a double hull tanker is to operate efficiently. The ship has a double bottom of 3 metres depth and double side spaces of 3 metres width. The structure in double hull ballast tanks is far more accessible for inspection and maintenance than the ballast tanks of a single-hull ship, as surveyors and repair workers can enter the double hull spaces directly via trunks from the upper deck. Hull structural analysis, including fatigue assessment, has been carried out, as required by the ship's classification society. The industry is considering further improvements to class rules to address both detailed design, through stricter requirements for fatigue assessment, and a better corrosion protection system in ballast and cargo tanks.*

## FLEXIBLE CARGO HANDLING

If required, the VLCC can handle three grades of cargo simultaneously with double valve segregation. Three steam-driven 5,300 m³/hour cargo pumps are located in the pumproom and cargo discharge operations can be run automatically. Cargo loading rates of up to 20,000 m³/h can be accommodated through the central manifold. The risk of cargo vapour explosion is minimised through the main inert gas plant which uses boiler flue gas and incorporates a topping up generator. The ship has been designed to enable partial filling of any cargo tank, and fill levels are monitored by means of a radar-based level gauge.

*Ryuohsan, built 2000*

## OTHER SAFETY/ENVIRONMENT - FRIENDLY FEATURES

Modern VLCCs incorporate many other safety features as standard, some of which are itemised below:

- Carbon dioxide ($CO_2$) is used instead of Halon as the fire-extinguishing agent for the engine and pumprooms
- Gas detectors are installed in the ballast tanks, which also have a clean air purging system and emergency inert gas connections
- The ship has a cargo vapour control system which features an independent high level alarm for the cargo and slop tanks, a fixed oxygen analyser for the vapour manifolds and a means of transferring ashore volatile organic compounds (VOCs) generated during loading operations
- In the cargo spaces the tank bottoms and 1.0 metre up from the bottoms, as well as the deckheads and 1.0 metre down from the deckheads, have been coated with tar epoxy to minimise damage caused by microbial corrosion
- As is now mandatory, the tanker is fitted with emergency towing equipment
- To comply with 1996 amendments to the Safety of Life at Sea (SOLAS) Convention, "safe access to the tanker bow" is arranged on the upper deck
- The mooring system accords with OCIMF Mooring Equipment Guidelines
- Like all new tankers, this ship is fitted with gauging and alarm systems in the cargo pumproom. Switching on the lighting activates the pumproom ventilation system. Two alarms are provided, the first activating when hydrocarbon concentrations in the pumproom reach 10 per cent of the lower explosive limit (LEL) and the second at 30 per cent LEL. Many of these features are to be fitted retroactively in all tankers.

## SEGREGATED BALLAST TANKS

Water ballast is carried in the double bottom and double side spaces. The tanker has been provided with ballast tank capacity in excess of that required by the rules to reduce hull stresses in the ballast condition and, hence, improve cargo loading and ship structural integrity. Ballast tanks are lined with light-coloured, tar-free, epoxy coatings to minimise the impact of corrosion and to facilitate inspection and maintenance. Two sets of ballasting pumps driven by electric motors are provided for ballasting/deballasting.

# Features of a typical Liquified Natural Gas Tanker

(Tanker of 125,000 cu.m.)

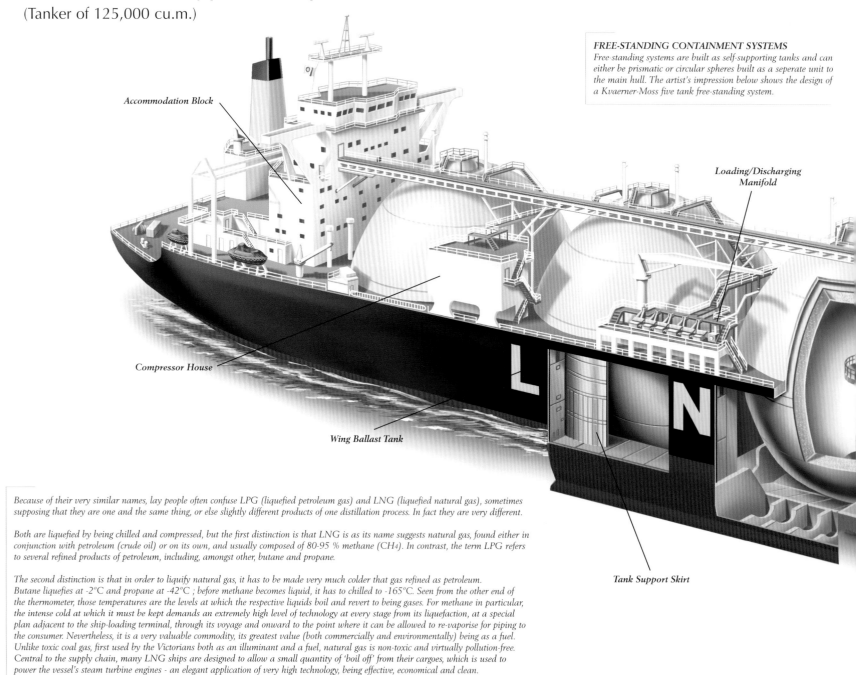

**Accommodation Block**

**Compressor House**

**Wing Ballast Tank**

**Tank Support Skirt**

**Loading/Discharging Manifold**

**FREE-STANDING CONTAINMENT SYSTEMS**
*Free-standing systems are built as self-supporting tanks and can either be prismatic or circular spheres built as a seperate unit to the main hull. The artist's impression below shows the design of a Kvaerner-Moss five tank free-standing system.*

*Because of their very similar names, lay people often confuse LPG (liquefied petroleum gas) and LNG (liquefied natural gas), sometimes supposing that they are one and the same thing, or else slightly different products of one distillation process. In fact they are very different.*

*Both are liquefied by being chilled and compressed, but the first distinction is that LNG is as its name suggests natural gas, found either in conjunction with petroleum (crude oil) or on its own, and usually composed of 80-95 % methane ($CH_4$). In contrast, the term LPG refers to several refined products of petroleum, including, amongst other, butane and propane.*

*The second distinction is that in order to liquify natural gas, it has to be made very much colder that gas refined as petroleum. Butane liquefies at -2°C and propane at -42°C ; before methane becomes liquid, it has to chilled to -165°C. Seen from the other end of the thermometer, those temperatures are the levels at which the respective liquids boil and revert to being gases. For methane in particular, the intense cold at which it must be kept demands an extremely high level of technology at every stage from its liquefaction, at a special plan adjacent to the ship-loading terminal, through its voyage and onward to the point where it can be allowed to re-vaporise for piping to the consumer. Nevertheless, it is a very valuable commodity, its greatest value (both commercially and environmentally) being as a fuel. Unlike toxic coal gas, first used by the Victorians both as an illuminant and a fuel, natural gas is non-toxic and virtually pollution-free. Central to the supply chain, many LNG ships are designed to allow a small quantity of 'boil off' from their cargoes, which is used to power the vessel's steam turbine engines - an elegant application of very high technology, being effective, economical and clean.*

## PROPULSION SYSTEMS

LNG vessels have traditionally employed steam turbine propulsion systems. These systems have given a high degree of reliability and this, coupled with the ease with which they can handle the use of boil off gas as fuel, has resulted in steam turbines being the first choice for all large LNG ships to date. It is acknowledged however, that the steam turbine has almost entirely been replaced in other merchant shipping sectors by the diesel engine. The diesel engine offers significantly better fuel consumption but technical considerations arise with the use of gas as fuel in large diesel engines. These have not been resolved in LNG vessels to date, hence the continuing dominance of the steam turbine in LNG ships.

## LNG SHIP DESIGN AND CONTAINMENT SYSTEMS

Several types of ship have been developed over the years to carry butane, propane, ethane, ethylene and natural gas in liquid form. These vessels have ranged from fully pressurised, through semi-pressurised to fully refrigerated systems. Natural gas however, has only ever been shipped commercially in a fully refrigerated, liquefied form at low (essentially atmospheric) pressure.

All LNG hulls require specially designed insulation to carry LNG at –160 C. As the cargo is at its boiling point, any heat flow from the outside into the containment system will cause evaporation, or 'boil off'. Insulated tanks therefore minimise heat transfer and development in this field has reduced boil off significantly in recent years. In addition, the insulation protects the integrity of the outer mild steel hull.

Since the mid 1960s, two main designs for the transport of LNG have emerged and remain predominant - the single barrier, self-supporting Moss system and two membrane systems, Technigaz and Gaz Transport.

*Insulated Aluminium Cargo Tank*

# Historical Development in Tanker Size and Dimensions

(Courtesy of Lloyds Register of Shipping)

| | Dimensions (feet) | | | | Length overall (feet) |
|---|---|---|---|---|---|
| Year | Deadweight tonnage | Length overall | Extreme breadth | Summer draught | |
| 1886 | 3,000 | 301 | 37 | 23 | |
| 1902 | 10,000 | 471 | 55 | 33 | |
| 1914 | 17,900 | 530 | 67 | 34 | |
| 1921 | 22,600 | 570 | 75 | 43 | |
| 1948 | 26,600 | 602 | 83 | 43 | |
| 1953 | 46,000 | 775 | 95 | 40 | |
| 1956 | 85,500 | 854 | 125 | 47 | |
| 1958 | 114,3000 | 949 | 135 | 50 | |
| 1962 | 130,200 | 954 | 141 | 54 | |
| 1965 | 151,200 | 1005 | 156 | 52 | |
| 1966 | 206,000 | 1122 | 163 | 58 | |
| 1968 | 326,600 | 1135 | 175 | 79 | |
| 1971 | 366,800 | 1135 | 178 | 88 | |
| 1976 | 544,900 | 1312 | 206 | 93 | |
| 1980 | 555,800 | 1504 | 225 | 80 | Jumboized |

Length overall (feet)

# Tanker Types

## Crude oil tankers

Crude oil tankers are designed to carry crude oil from oilfields to refineries around the world – usually making the return journeys in ballast. The size of these ships increased steadily, peaking in the 1970s in order to bring economies of scale and the cost of oil transportation to the absolute minimum. The era of the 'supertanker', which commenced in the 1960s, quickly led to the construction of a very large and ultra-large crude carriers (VLCCs and ULCCs) which are the biggest ships ever built.

As cargo-handling technology progressed, many tankers were generally fitted with steam coil heating in the cargo tanks to keep heavier grades of oil viscous and speed up the discharge of cargo. They were also equipped with crude oil washing equipment for tank cleaning and inert gas systems to reduce the risks of fire and explosion.
Some of the latest tanker newbuildings, incorporate other extensive safety features from double hulls, double engine rooms, propulsion and steering equipment. Ship navigational and communications systems have also become increasingly sophisticated in recent years.

## Product tankers

Product tankers are highly versatile ships which can carry a number of different refined oil products without the risk of contamination of one by another. These tankers have sophisticated cargo-handling arrangements to enable the carriage of several different products grades simultaneously in a fully segregated manner. The tanks are also coated to protect against corrosion, ensure cargo purity and facilitate tank cleaning.

There are two main types of cargo. White or 'clean' products are light distillates such as petroleum (petrol), kerosene, naphtha, gas oils, and clear lubricating oils. Black or 'dirty' products include fuel oils, crude and bitumen. Dirty product tankers require heating coils to increase the flow, and hence cargo-handling characteristics of the products.

Product tankers generally concentrate on one type of cargo to minimise tank cleaning as the transition from 'dirty' to 'clean' cargo involves extremely thorough and time-consuming procedures.

Product tankers are also occasionally used for the transportation of molasses which must be carried in heated tanks to prevent the cargo from solidifying.

## Chemical Tankers

These are a specialized variation of the products tanker which can contain up to 50 tanks, each with its own pumps, pipelines and inert gas system.

Designed to carry four main product groups, these comprise petrochemicals - such as paraffin's, naphtha and benzenes; organic chemicals - such as solvents, alcohols and methanol's; inorganic chemicals - such as sulphuric acid, nitric acid and caustic soda; and vegetable and animal oils - such as esters fats, palm oil, soya bean oil and animal oils.

Depending on the types of cargo carried the vessels can incorporate cargo heating and temperature control systems, anti-corrosive stainless steel tanks and special tank coatings.

Safety is a major priority and to reduce any risk of pollution from grounding or collision the cargo tanks are positioned independently of the hull structure to isolate them from possible impact damage.

## Parcel Tankers

These specialised ships are a development of the chemical tanker and are able to carry oil as well as chemicals. They range in size from about 6,000 tons up to 40,000 tons. The larger types can be fitted with up to 50 separate tanks and pumping systems which gives them the flexibility to carry a variety of different products at the same time.
Their cargoes include organic and inorganic chemicals, speciality oils and animal and vegetable oils.

## Chemical parcel tankers

Many petroleum product tankers are built with additional cargo-handling attributes and safety features to enable them also to carry 'easy' chemicals such as benzene, xylene, toluene and caustic soda solution. Such chemicals are carried in large volumes and present a relatively low hazard risk. Chemical/product tankers move easily between the oil and chemical trades, according to market demand.

The pinnacle of chemical tanker design is the sophisticated chemical parcel tanker whose cargo space is subdivided into a large number of tanks. On many ships the underdeck tanks are augmented by cylindrical deck tanks. Modern versions of chemical parcel tankers can carry upwards of 50 different 'parcels', or cargoes, simultaneously in a fully segregated manner, each in its own tank.

These cargoes range from chemicals, vegetable oils and lube oil additives to acids and other speciality liquids. Most parcel tanker cargoes are premium-quality, high-value products which require careful handling.
The predominant type of cargo - speciality chemicals often pose a range of hazards to personal health and the environment. Such hazards include toxicity, corrosivity, flammability and reactivity, while many cargoes are also classified as marine pollutants.

Although tank coatings were extensively used on earlier generations of ships, modern chemical parcel tankers have stainless steel cargo tanks throughout to ensure compatibility with a full range of cargoes and to facilitate tank cleaning. Stainless steel also helps minimise the risk of off-specification cargoes due to contamination by residues of previous cargoes or rust from tank walls.
Tank stiffeners and other structural elements are placed on the outside of the tank, creating flush tank walls and increasing the efficiency of cleaning operations and improving cargo outturns.

The optimum level of cargo segregation is ensured by equipping each tank with its own stainless steel deepwell cargo pump, cargo line and manifold crossover.

Many cargoes require special attention, including close temperature control. A dedicated nitrogen generator provides a high-purity product for use in blanketing and purging cargoes, thus reducing atmospheric pollution and increasing the level of cargo care. Cargo can be heated using hot water, steam, thermal oil or a combination of these. Also, cargo cooling systems can be provided to permit the carriage of semi-gaseous chemicals. Modern ships are provided with fully automatic vapour emission control systems to prevent atmospheric pollution during cargo loading and discharge.

Deepsea parcel tankers serving intercontinental routes tend to be in the size range 35,000- 40,000 dwt.
The shortsea trades are covered by coastal parcel tankers in the 3,000-6,000 dwt range. There are many parcel tankers of various intermediate sizes, designed for intra-regional trading or specific longhaul routes.

## Oil/bulk/ore (OBO or combination) carriers

The idea of combination carriers was first tried in the 1950s with vessels which carried iron ore on one leg of the voyage and crude oil on another. Later, the concept was extended to include other bulk cargoes such as bauxite, coal or grain and in 1965 the first real OBO was launched.

The versatility of these ships, which handled multiple cargoes and reduced the time which conventional tankers spent steaming in ballast, led to their initial success and within a decade OBOs of 200,000 dwt were in service.

OBOs typically have a number of large holds which can carry dry bulk cargoes such as grain and ore. These holds can also serve as oil cargo tanks if they are fitted with gas and oil-tight hatch covers and incorporate steam heating facilities. They are also built with double bottoms.

On OBOs, ore is dispersed in alternate holds to spread the weight evenly and tank cleaning systems are used to clean the cargo spaces, for example after carrying crude oil and before loading grain.

In spite of their early promise, oil/bulk/ore combination carriers did not prove an enduring success. This was primarily because their complexity and multi-cargo role did not fully compensate for the greater efficiency of dedicated ore carriers and crude oil tankers.

## LNG Carriers

The first liquefied natural gas (LNG) tanker was the appropriately named Methane Pioneer, a CI-M type standard cargo ship built in the US during World War Two and converted in Mobile, Alabama on the US Gulf Coast in 1958 to enable trial shipments of LNG in insulated tanks made of low temperature steel. This vessel delivered the first cargo of methane, which is the principal constituent of natural gas, from the US Gulf to a specially built British Gas terminal at Canvey Island in the Thames estuary in 1959. Following the success of this prototype ship, two purpose-built tankers, Methane Progress and Methane Princess, were delivered in 1964 to launch the full-scale commercial trade in LNG. Each of the 21,800 dwt tankers was able to carry up to 27,400 cubic metres of LNG and the pair were used to shuttle gas from Algeria to Canvey Island for almost three decades.

Seaborne LNG trade developed quickly as new sources of natural gas were found in Indonesia, Malaysia, Brunei, Alaska, Libya, Australia and Abu Dhabi, and gas buyers in Japan, South Korea, Taiwan, the US and Europe agreed long-term contracts for the supply of steady volumes of this clean-burning fuel. Once the LNG cargoes are regasified at the import terminals, the natural gas is used primarily as a domestic fuel and in power generation.

The third most important market for LNG is as a petro-chemical feedstock. Also, technological developments aimed at making more use of natural gas as a transport and vehicle fuel are opening up the potential of a new market sector. In more recent years Nigeria, Trinidad, Qatar and Oman have joined the ranks of LNG exporters, while several established LNG production facilities have had their capacities increased.

LNG carriers are built with a high degree of inherent safety to safeguard their flammable cargo, and the ships are amongst the most expensive afloat.

Tanks are insulated with special materials to maintain the cargo in liquid form at a temperature of -162°C, i.e. the boiling of natural gas.

Transporting natural gas as a liquid enables 600 times as much cargo to be carried in a given tank than if it was in gaseous form. In addition, cargo containment systems must be able to retain LNG under specific damage conditions. The most popular type of LNG containment systems in use today are large spherical tanks made of aluminium and membrane tanks made of either stainless steel or a special nickel alloy steel. During the loaded passage some of the gas cargo boils off. This is piped to the boilers for use as a supplementary fuel in order to power the steam turbine. LNG carriers are the last type of commercial ship to use steam turbines as the means of propulsion.

In the year 2000 some 100 million tonnes of LNG was shipped by sea, equivalent to 21 per cent of the international trade in gas. The current LNG carrier fleet stands at 130 ships and the average capacity of a newbuilding is 137,000 cubic metres. The industry has made great efforts over the years to ensure the safe design and operation of LNG carriers, and this commitment has paid dividends. In the four decades since Methane Pioneer made its groundbreaking voyage, there has never been a major release of an LNG cargo.

## LPG Carriers

The original liquefied petroleum gas (LPG) carriers carried propane, butane or mixtures of the two. Propane and butane are the primary constituents of LPG which is a very light hydrocarbon produced from either the fractionation of crude oil at petroleum refineries or certain grades of natural gas. Modern LPG ships are designed to carry many additional liquefied gas cargoes, including chemical gases. Cargo-handling capabilities usually encompass several of the following products: ammonia, butadiene, ethylene, propylene, vinyl chloride monomer (VCM) and ethane. LPG has a wide range of uses, including as a domestic and commercial fuel, motor fuel, petrochemical feedstock, in town gas production and in manufacturing processes.

LPG carrier cargoes have boiling points below commonly encountered ambient temperatures. Thus, to enable cargoes to be carried in a liquid form, it is necessary to transport them either at pressures greater than atmospheric; in refrigerated form at their boiling point; or a using a combination of the two. LPG carriers are subdivided into the following vessel types:

(a) fully pressurised (FP) ships (usually up to 3,000 cubic metres in capacity);
(b) semi-pressurised/fully refrigerated (semi-ref) ships (from 3,000 up to 22,000 cubic metres in size); and
(c) fully refrigerated (FR) ships (15,000 cubic metres and above).

The International Maritime Organization (IMO) lays down provisions governing the types of cargo tanks which can be used on liquefied gas carriers, including the relevant design pressures and whether or not there is a need for a secondary containment system. Fully pressurised (FP) LPG carriers have heavy spherical or cylindrical tanks - configurations which do not make optimum use of the cargo-carrying space available. However, there are advantages to this method of carrying LPG, not least the simple, low-cost mode of operation. There is no need to build cargo tanks with special low temperature steel; to insulate the cargo tanks; or to provide a shipboard reliquefaction plant to reliquefy cargo-boil-off and redirect it to the tanks.

All these features are required on semi-ref and fully refrigerated LPG carriers. Semi-ref ships are the most flexible of the LPG carriers. They have pressure vessel tanks which do not need to be as heavy or robust as those on FP ships. Semi-ref LPG carriers are designed to carry a number of different cargoes simultaneously, and to heat or cool cargoes during the voyage or cargo-handling operations. Fully refrigerated LPG carriers have insulated, prismatic cargo tanks which are designed for a minimum service temperature of about -50°C and a maximum working pressure of 0.28 kg/cm². FR ships require a full secondary barrier to retain leaking cargo should the primary barrier fail.

Approximately 50 million tonnes of LPG is carried by sea in ships each year. The Middle East region has traditionally been the major loading point for LPG. This will continue to be the case but in recent years the North Sea, West Africa and the Caribbean have emerged as more important export centers in their own right.

## FPSOs

Floating Production, Storage and Offloading (FPSO) vessels are floating oil processing installations moored in offshore oilfields. They are equipped with gas flaring systems to burn off unwanted fractions and can also partly process crude oil. Most FPSOs are converted tankers of about 100,000 dwt although some shipyards offer standard design FPSOs.

## Shuttle Tankers

As offshore oilfields were developed in ever greater depths in the North Sea and parts of the world using single point mooring systems (SPM) and FPSOs for transhipment, this created the need for a new type of tanker. Shuttle tankers are specially designed with bow loading facilities to load crude oil from SPMs, FPSOs or similar offshore loading installation for delivery to onshore refineries. To minimise any risk of pollution in coastal waters, shuttle tankers were usually built with double hulls even before this arrangement was mandated by legislation.

## Tanker classification by tonnage

As well as being grouped by type, tankers are also defined by their size, as follows:
Coastal tanker – up to 16,500 dwt
*(mainly short haul, products carrier)*
General purpose tanker – 16,500-25,000 dwt
*(crude oil or product carrier)*
Handy size tanker – 30,000 dwt
*(crude oil or products carrier)*
Aframax – specifically 79,990 dwt as defined by the London Tanker Broker Panel but generally accepted in the range of 75-120,000 dwt
*(crude oil or products carrier)*
Panamax – 55-70,000 dwt
*(crude oil or products carrier)*
Suezmax – 120,000-200,000 dwt
*(crude oil or products carrier)*
VLCC – 200,000-320,000 dwt *(crude oil carrier)*
ULCC – in excess of 320,000 dwt *(crude oil carrier)*

*Inca, 68,900 dwt, built 2000*

Voyage of a modern tanker

# Voyage of a modern tanker

## Action before departure

The sequence of events usually begins by giving notification to the terminal and local agent in advance of completing cargo operations. The cargo surveyor will then be called to the vessel to complete and verify that the vessel has discharged all her cargo as appropriate. The pilot and tugs are also ordered to attend the vessel in readiness for her departure. The ship's bridge and engine room gear will be tested to ensure that they are in good working order, in much the same way as an aeroplane will test its equipment before take off.

The tests include all modes of steering gear, the communication systems, the engine telegraph, radars and the Gyro and Magnetic compasses. Also that compass repeaters are aligned correctly and all navigational equipment, helm indicators and navigation lights are properly functioning. The engineers ensure that the main engine is warmed and there is sufficient air in the main engine starting bottle, and the engine turned over on air to ensure that it is free to move. All these tests are recorded in the deck and engine room log books.

During the cargo discharge operation a modern tanker takes onboard ballast into her Segregated Ballast Tanks (SBT). This is to ensure that there is sufficient weight in the vessel to immerse the hull deep enough in the water for the propeller and rudder to function efficiently, also to ensure that the vessel's stability is safe for the voyage. This helps the vessel to "ride" the waves correctly without undue pitching and rolling.

On very rare occasions a modern tanker may also take "heavy weather ballast" into designated cargo tanks in extreme weather and sea conditions.

Once the terminal and the vessel have agreed the cargo figures and the agent has delivered his port clearance certificate to the master, allowing him to sail, the unberthing procedure and outbound passage are discussed with the pilot in detail. After this the crew are called to "stations" and the vessel commences to "single up", this is usually to one head line and one spring line fore and aft. The tugs will be made fast and the vessel will let go from the terminal to commence her outbound voyage.

20:00 to 00:00
3rd Officer

00:00 to 04:00
2nd Officer

04:00 to 08:00
chief Officer

## Leaving port

During this time the vessel completes making ready for sea, i.e the mooring ropes are stowed below decks, any loose equipment secured and cargo tanks double checked as secure.

After the pilot disembarks and the vessel is clear of any dangers, the anchors are fully secured for the passage by the application of mechanisms such as "guillotines" or "devils claws" The pipe where the anchor chain enters the deck to the cable locker, called the spurling pipe, is covered with tarpaulin and cement to ensure that there can be no water ingress during bad weather encountered on the voyage.

A modern tanker is usually equipped with fixed automatic tank washing machines that are utilised for Crude Oil Washing (COW) during discharge, although manual COW machines can still be found on a modern tanker. The COW system reduces the sediment in the vessel's tanks which also increases the cargo out-turn.

After the COW procedure the machines can also be used during the ballast passage to water wash the tanks when tank entry is required or in preparation for the next cargo. The tank washings are then retained in designated slop tanks onboard.

These slops are "decanted" i.e. they are allowed to settle out so that the oil floats on top of the water.

The decanted water can then be discharged into the sea in strict accordance with MARPOL regulations through the Overboard Discharge Monitoring Equipment (ODME) which reduces the quantity of slops remaining onboard on arrival at the next load port. The next cargo, if compatible, can then be loaded on top of these slops. This procedure is known as the "load-on-top" (LOT) system. Under the command of the master the vessel will follow its pre-planned course to the next port, with the assistance of the navigating officers who are collectively known as the Officer of the Watch (OOW). Each officer takes charge of two navigational watches a day, assisted by ratings who act as lookout and helmsman when required.

08:00 to 12:00
3rd Officer

12:00 to 16:00
2nd Officer

16:00 to 20:00
chief Officer

The route the vessel follows is the shortest distance after taking into account the effects of global weather patterns, weather routing advice, strength and direction of currents, traffic density, depth of water under the keel, available navigational aids and allowances for contingency plans in emergencies.

Although a modern tanker is equipped with a large number of electronic aids to navigation, the master, chief engineer, deck and engine room officers and ratings must all be fully qualified in accordance with international regulations for certification. In addition the senior officers on tankers must hold a recognised Dangerous Cargo Endorsement to their certificates of competency.

Like all vessels today, tankers are equipped with radar equipment. This usually comprises two sets, a 3cm and 10cm wavelength radar, of which at least one will also be an ARPA (automatic radar plotting aid) which is a computer-controlled aid for collision-avoidance.

This will automatically calculate and plot acquired vessels or targets and graphically represent their course projection on the radar screen, indicating a risk of collision should this arise.

Other navigational aids and electronic equipment on the bridge of a modern tanker include DGPS, echo-sounders, electronic Doppler logs, helm and rate of turn indicators, autopilot, weather and safety equipment, and radio and satellite communication systems. The latter are not only aids to the navigators, but also provide a reliable and safe means of communication to the shore and other vessels. On many ships, a number of these electronic aids are linked into an Integrated Bridge System. There are also course recorders, bridge control systems to control the main engine when the engine room is unattended, and back-up gyro and magnetic compasses.

These are complemented by fire detection systems and fire extinguishing activation systems as well as a wealth of back-up systems and power supplies in the event of a system failure.

### The ballast voyage

Once the vessel is clear of the port the main engines will be rung "Full away". The engineers will then slowly build up the revolutions of the main engine from full ahead manoeuvring to full sea speed.

The intensive work by the tanker's officers continues whilst at sea. This is the time when much of the vessel's maintenance is carried out relating to operational capability.

For example, fire fighting and life saving equipment, safety routines, onboard training and navigational and engineering duties. It must be remembered that all the services usually supplied ashore have to be provided by the engineering department while at sea. These include hot and cold fresh water; sewage treatment plant; heating and/or air conditioning; cooling services for the ship's storerooms and fridges; electrical supplies for lighting, navigational equipment, deck, engine and galley machinery; heating supplies for the fuel oil and/or cargo; and deck service supplies such as sea water, air, hydraulic oil, fresh water and steam. Whilst the bridge is often referred to as the brain of the vessel it is clear that the engine room is its heart.

All seafarers are trained in sea survival, fire fighting and life saving appliances and there is an onboard safety training programme that takes place weekly (weather permitting) consisting of pollution response drills, lifeboat launching drills, fire drills, (at the manifold, in the accommodation and in the engine room). Also cargo release drills, man overboard drills, emergency steering drills, responses to catastrophic accidents such as collision, grounding etc. and pump room rescue drills.

When the weather prevents such drills taking place these are replaced with training lectures by the ship's officers in the use of distress signals, self contained breathing apparatus equipment, escape equipment, and safety training videos. All such drills are entered in the ship's log book for inspection by Port State Control and the company's ISM auditing officer.

On a modern tanker the engine is usually unmanned at night while at sea. This period is called UMS (unmanned machinery space) and is only permitted if the engine room meets stringent requirements, including the provision of alarm systems in the event of any problems occurring during the UMS period. One engineer will be assigned the Duty Engineer each night to attend the engine room in case of any alarms, otherwise all the engineers work in the engine room during the day and are responsible for the maintenance and operation of different engine room equipment in accordance with the planned maintenance system.

08:00 to 12:00
3rd Officer

12:00 to 16:00
2nd Officer

16:00 to 20:00
chief Officer

A modern tanker tends to carry a fairly small crew, the total complement usually being in the region of 24 souls. As a result there is not the same social fabric onboard as there was a number of years ago. A modern vessel, however is well equipped with facilities for the crew when off duty, including satellite television and video, stereos, table tennis, swimming pool (in good weather), library and various board games and other such activities. Nevertheless the usual working day for watch keepers and day workers is 10-12 hours at sea. The watch keepers spend 8 hours a day on watch, split into 4 hour watches. During these periods of watch-keeping the OOW (Officer of the Watch) is confined to the bridge at all times and cannot leave his post unless relieved by another qualified bridge watchkeeping officer. Therefore the maintenance work for which that OOW is responsible must be performed outside his watch keeping duties.

The recognised daily watch keeping pattern is as follows

08:00 to 12:00 3rd officer
12:00 to 16:00 2nd officer
16:00 to 20:00 chief officer

20:00 to 00:00 3rd officer
00:00 to 04:00 2nd officer
04:00 to 08:00 chief officer.

The crew quarters on modern tankers have improved greatly over recent years and each crew member, from the master to the galley boy, is likely to have his own en-suite cabin. Today it is quite normal to have mixed nationality crews onboard, however it is compulsory for the crew to share a common language (usually English) not only to communicate in the routine running of the ship, but more importantly, to respond effectively in an emergency.

## Arriving at the loadport

Before the ship sailed the master and deck officers carefully conducted a passage planning exercise which covered the entire voyage safely from berth to berth. All the required charts, light lists, and radio signals were checked onboard and corrected up to date from the latest weekly notices to mariners and navigational warnings. On arrival at the loadport this passage plan will be carefully followed as the vessel is safely

navigated to the loading berth. A pilot (who will have boarded earlier) will advise the master, and tugs will assist in manoeuvring.

## Loading cargo

Once the tanker is in port the cargo must be loaded as safely and quickly as possible within the capabilities of the vessel. Any delays during loading attributable to the vessel will be for the owner's account, whereas any delays attributable to the shore will be for the charterer, and consequently the terminal's account. The ship's loading plan will have been agreed between the master and the chief officer before the vessel arrives in port. This will be based upon the charterer's requirements regarding how much cargo is required to be lifted by the vessel, of what grade(s) and within what options.

The plan will ensure that the vessel is not over stressed with regard to shear force and/or bending moments due to incorrect weight distribution on the vessel.

This will allow for the various load line zones that may be transitted, as each zone has different limits regarding how much freeboard the vessel must retain, depending on the density of the sea water and expected weather to be encountered.

The loading plan will be discussed with the terminal before commencing the operation and the chief officer and the 3rd and 2nd officers will take charge of the loading operation whilst in port.

The usual practice in port is for the bridge watch keeping teams to "break watches" and enter into port watches. The chief officer monitors the operation throughout and must be available at all times, but will try to take rest periods around critical moments of the cargo operation. The 3rd and 2nd officers enter into six hour watches as follows.

06:00 to 12:00 3rd officer
12:00 to 18:00 2nd officer
18:00 to 00:00 3rd officer
00:00 to 06:00 2nd officer

The master will be dealing with the various inspections from PSC, Class, ISM Audits, terminal inspections, ship's agents, customs, immigration, ship's chandlers and stores supplies, as well as monitoring the vessel safety and crew welfare and management from a command perspective.

08:00 to 12:00
3rd Officer

12:00 to 16:00
2nd Officer

16:00 to 20:00
chief Officer

## Loading in safety

The cargo is loaded through cargo hoses and/or chicksan arms. The chicksans are bolted to the vessel's manifold and are adjustable at the quayside to compensate for the change in freeboard of the vessel or any tidal effects.

A VLCC can accept cargo at around 15,000 cubic metres per hour. During loading the cargo is pumped onboard by the shore, at agreed rates, and distributed to the cargo tanks under the supervision of the chief officer. During loading operations the vessel simultaneously discharges her segregated ballast water.

Safety is very stringent on tankers and this is especially true during cargo operations. The vessel and terminal follow the guidelines contained in ISGOTT (International Safety Guide for Oil Tankers and Terminals), which includes a detailed checklist covering many items such as smoking regulations, safe access, emergency procedures, ship/shore communications etc.

A vessel is usually loaded to 98 per cent capacity in each cargo tank. The empty space left in the tank is called the "ullage" space and provides a built-in safety factor during "topping off" the tanks at the end of loading.

The chief officer must also carefully calculate additional ullage space if the cargo is expected to heat up and expand during the laden passage. For example, loading in the North Sea in winter and discharging in Singapore, when the ambient conditions would lead to the cargo heating up.

## Laden voyage

When the ship is ready to sail, the pilot comes onboard and discusses the unberthing plan and outbound passage with the master on the navigation bridge.

Many pre-departure tests are conducted onboard to ensure that all the ship's equipment is in proper working order before departure. Tug boats assist the vessel during her unberthing manoeuvres and the pilot remains on board until the vessel has safely cleared port waters. He is then disembarked into a pilot boat or helicopter.

Before heading out to open sea the vessel will again be secured for sea as described earlier. A new passage plan will be produced to the next port, this is normally the responsibility of one of the navigating deck officers for final approval by the master.

## Arrival at the discharge port

Preparations for the vessel's arrival at the discharge port are usually made well in advance by the charterers, owners, cargo receivers, agents and master. In some cases the vessel may be delayed in berthing and could be required to anchor offshore. The berthing operations, which are undertaken under the advice of a pilot, can be very delicate and require a high degree of skill on the part of all involved. Sometimes a number of tugs are utilised to assist with berthing a large tanker alongside a jetty.

The discharging procedure is different to that of loading, in that the vessel's own pumping equipment is utilised. A large modern tanker may be fitted with three or four large pumps, each capable of pumping at around 4,000 to 5,000 cubic metres per hour.

Where the final discharge port is not deep enough to accept a fully laden tanker man-made deepwater oil-discharging facilities have been developed and single point mooring systems, known as monobuoys, are common. One of the first true deepwater oil-discharging facilities in the US is the Louisiana Offshore Oil Port (LOOP). Alternatively, a large vessel can discharge part of it's cargo into a smaller tanker alongside. This technique is called lightering.

During discharge, the vessel's inert gas system (IGS) supplies gas to fill the tank space that has been vacated by the cargo. On large tankers exhaust gas from the vessel's boiler is used, this contains less than 5% oxygen at source and prevents the possibility of fire or explosion in the cargo spaces.

Nowadays the length of trips at sea is normally in the region of 3-4 months and every day is a working day. However, at the end of such a trip the seafarer will normally have about 6-8 weeks leave before returning to the ship.

# At the start of the new millennium, still only one product feeds the powerhouse of growth - oil

*Despite price shocks, efficiency gains and a vociferous environmental debate, the consumption of fossil fuel continues to grow and oil remains pre-eminent, meeting more than 40% of global energy demand.*

*Oil is the lifeblood of our civilisation.*
*It gives us heat and light. It powers our industries,*
*fuels our cars, our trucks, our planes and our ships.*
*It also provides an essential ingredient in our medicines, chemicals,*
*fertilisers and paints and in the manufacture of plastics,*
*electronic components and so much more.*

*With all the advances of modern society still only
one mode of transportation delivers all the benefits of
oil to the farthest corners the world - the Tanker.
In fact, some 6500 large tankers working day in, day out,
carry 60% of all the world's crude oil, while other
specialised tankers deliver refined products, chemicals,
liquefied petroleum gas and liquefied natural gas.
Tankers carrying the cargoes on which hundreds of millions
of jobs, directly or indirectly depend.
On which our very standard of living relies.*

# For as long as the world needs oil
# it will also need tankers

# INTERTANKO

wishes to thank

## Members and Associate Members
## for Supporting
## A Century of Tankers

Alliance Marine Services L.P.
www.alliancemarine.com

Allseas Marine S.A.
www.allseas.gr

American Eagle Tankers Inc Ltd
www.aetweb.com

Anders Wilhelmsen & Co AS
shipping@awilco.no

These companies are now divided
between the three sons

Aeolos Management S.A.
London Agents
Andros Maritime Agencies Ltd.
andros@commonwealth-house.com

Anglo-Eastern Ship Management Ltd
www.angloeasterngroup.com

Antares Naviera S.A.
info@antaresnav.com.ar

Arcadia Shipmanagement Co Ltd
info@arcadiasm.gr

Athenian Sea Carriers Ltd
www.atheniangroup.com

www.aims.it

Aurora Tankers Sdn Bhd
www.imcshipping.com

Avin International S.A.
www.avin.gr

B+H Shipping Group
www.bhocean.com

Bergesen d.y. ASA
www.bergesen.no

mail@bergshav.com

Bluewater Energy Services B.V.
www.bluewater.nl

Blystad Shipping (USA) Inc
www.blystad.com

Broström Tankers S.A.
www.brostrom.se

Centrofin Management Inc
centrofin@centrofin.gr

Ceres Hellenic Shipping Enterprises Ltd
chse@ceres.gr / www.ceres.gr

Chandris Hellas Inc
chandris-hellas@chandris-group.gr

Chemikalien Seetransport GmbH
www.chemikalien-seetransport.de

Concordia Maritime AB
www.concordia-maritime.se

d'Amico Societá di Navigazione SpA

Dampskibsselskabet "NORDEN" A/S
www.ds-norden.com

A/S Dampskibsselskabet Torm
www.torm.dk

Dannebrog Rederi AS
www.dannebrog.com

Dorian (Hellas) S.A.
www.eagleocean.com

DS-Schiffahrt GmbH
info@ds-schiffahrt.de

Einar Lange Management A/S
einarlma@online.no

Eletson Corporation
www.eletson.com

EMPRESA NAVIERA ELCANO, S.A.
www.elcano-sa.es

Ernst Jacob (GmbH & Co KG)
www.ernstjacob.de

John T. Essberger GmbH & Co
www.essberger.de

Eurasia Group of Companies
www.eurasiagroup.com

Eurotankers Inc
eurotank@hol.gr

First International Corp
firstinternational@msn.com

First Olsen Tankers Ltd AS
first@fredolsen.no

Fratelli d'Amico Armatori S.p.A.
www.damicofratelli.it

General Maritime Corporation

German Tanker Shipping GmbH & Co. KG
www.german-tanker.de

Gestioni Armatoriali S.p.A.
gesarmra@tin.it

Groton Pacific Carriers Inc.
www.grotonpacific.com

Halkidon Shipping Corporation
halkship@otenet.gr

Heidenreich Marine Inc
www.heidmar.com

Histria Shipmanagement SRL
www.histria.ro

Interorient Navigation Co Ltd
www.interorient.com

Iver Ships AS
www.iverships.no

Jahre Dahl Bergesen AS
www.jdb.no

Jahre-Wallem AS
jawa@jawa.no

Kawasaki Kisen Kaisha, Ltd.
www.kline.co.jp

Kristen Navigation Inc
kristen@internet.gr

Kyklades Maritime Corporation
admin@kykmar.gr

Latvian Shipping Company
www.latshipcom.lv

Laurin Maritime
www.laurinmar.com

Leif Höegh & Co ASA
www.hoegh.no

Liquimar Tanker Management Inc
lqmr@hol.gr

Lundquist Shipping Company
administration@lundqvist.aland.fi

Lyras Shipping Ltd
lyrasship@aol.com

Mare Maritime Company S.A.

Marine Transport Lines Inc
a Crowley Company
www.mxtl.com / www.crowley.com

Marinvest AB
office@marinvest.se

Metrostar Management Corp
star@metrostar.gr

Minerva Marine Inc
www.minervatank.com

Mitsui O.S.K Lines Ltd
www.mol.co.jp

Multi Trading Shipmanagement Ltd
multi@softway.gr

N.J. Goulandris Limited

Naviera F. Tapias S.A.
www.ftapias.com

Neda Maritime Agency Co Ltd

Novorossiysk Shipping Company
www.novoship.ru

Olympic Shipping & Management S.A.
contact@olyship.com

Pétromarine S.A.
www.petromarine.fr

Petroships Pte Ltd

Premuda
www.premuda.net

Rederi AB Brevik
www.r-brevik.se

Rigel Schiffahrts GmbH & Co KG
www.rigel-hb.com

Rudolf A. Oetker
www.rao-shipping.com

SBM Production Contractors Inc
www.singlebuoy.com

Sea Oil Shipping Ltd
www.seaoilshipping.com

Seatramp Tankers Inc
chartering@seatramp.com

Sociedad Naviera Ultragas Ltda
www.ultragas.cl

Société de Services Maritimes S.A.
care@careoffshore.com

Soponata
www.soponata.pt

Stelmar Tankers (Management) Ltd
www.stelmar.com

Stena Group
www.stena.com

Stolt-Nielsen Transportation Group
www.sntg.com

Sun Enterprises
email@sunernterprises.gr

Tai Chong Cheang Steamship Co (H.K.) Ltd
www.tccgroup.com.sg

Tankerska Plovidba
www.tankerska.hr

Teekay Shipping Corporation
www.teekay.com

The Great Eastern Shipping Co Ltd
www.greatship.com

www.jjuc.no

Thenamaris Ships Management Inc
www.thenamaris.gr

Thome Ship Management Pte Ltd
www.thome.com.sg

Tokyo Marine Co Ltd
www.tokyomarine.net

Tradewind Tankers
www.tradewindtankers.com

TransPetrol Services N.V.
operations@trapet.com

www.tschudi-eitzen.com

Ugland Nordic Shipping
www.uns.no

Unicom Management Services (Cyprus) Ltd
www.unicom-cy.com

Unicorn Lines (Pty) Ltd

Vopak Chemical Tanker Services B.V.
www.vopak.com

V.Ships Switzerland SA
www.vships.com

Wah Kwong Shipping Holdings Ltd
wk@wahkwong.com.hk

Westfal-Larsen Management AS
westfal@wlco.no

Wilh. Wilhelmsen ASA
www.wilh-wilhelmsen.com

# INTERTANKO ASSOCIATE MEMBERS

Aarus Maritima S.A.
www.aarus.com

American Bureau of Shipping
www.eagle.org

ABS Nautical Systems LLC
www.abs-ns.com

Abu Dhabi National Tanker Co.
www.adnatco.com

Alessandro Archibugi & Figlio
www.archibugi.com

Arab Maritime Petroleum Transport Co
www.amptc.net

Argent Shipping Limited
argentship@argentship.co.uk

Barber Ship Management Sdn Bhd
www.barbership.com

Bonyad Shipping Agencies Co
www.bosaco-iran.com

BP Shipping Ltd
www.bp.com

Bryggen Shipping & Trading A/S
post@bryggen.no

Bulls Tankrederi A/S
unnisol@bullstank.com

Bureau Veritas
www.bureauveritas.com

Canega Shipping Services
www.canega.com

www.capital-shipbrokers.co.uk

Chamber of Shipping of BC
www.chamber-of-shipping.com

Charles R. Weber Company, Inc.
www.crweber.com

www.clarksons.co.uk

www.confitarma.it

Det Norske Veritas
www.dnv.com

DVB NedshipBank
www.nedshipbank.com

E.A. Gibson Shipbrokers Ltd
www.eagibson.co.uk

Economou International Shipping Agencies Ltd
www.economou.gr

ECP Service Corporation
www.ecpservice.com

Coastal Tankships USA

El Paso Marine
www.elpaso.com

Fearnleys A/S
www.fearnleys.com

Fortum Shipping
www.fortum.com

Frachtcontor Junge & Co.
www.frachtcontor.com

G.M. RICHARDS ENTERPRISES, INC.

G. M. Richards Enterprises Inc
www.gmreshipagent.com

THE GMS GROUP

Gallagher Marine Systems
www.gallaghermarine.com

Gard Services
www.gard.no

GRAYPEN

TANKER

AGENCY
SERVICES
UK/IRELAND

Graypen Limited
www.Graypen.co.uk

Green Award Foundation
www.greenaward.org

Groupama Transport
www.groupama-transport.com

Gulf Agency Company Ltd
www.gulfagencycompany.com

Gunclean Toftejorg AB
www.gunclean.toftejorg.com

Hamworthy KSE Svanehøj A/S
www.svanehoj.com

Hong Kong Shipowners Association
www.hksoa.org.hk

IDESS Maritime Centre Inc
www.idess.com

Institut Français de la Mer
http://ifm.free.fr

Katradis Marine Ropes Industry S.A.
www.katradis.com

Korean Register of Shipping
www.krs.co.kr  -  www.krclass.org

Kuwait Oil Tanker Company S.A.K.
www.kotc.com.kw

laycan AS
www.laycan.com

Lloyd's Register of Shipping
www.lr.org

LORENTZEN & STEMOCO

Lorentzen & Stemoco AS
www.lorstem.com

Mallory Jones Lynch Flynn & Assoc Inc
www.mjlf.com

Marine Response Alliance LLC
www.marineresponsealliance.com

Maritime & Port Authority of Singapore
www.mpa.gov.sg

Medco Shipbrokers S.L
medcotk@seneca.net
medco@medcoshipbrokers.com

Middle East Shipping Company Ltd
Republic of Yemen
www.mideastshipping.com

Moran-Gulf Shipping Agencies
www.moranshipping.com

MTI Network
www.mtinetwork.com

Naess Shipping (Holland) B.V.
naesship@naess.nl

Nippon Kaiji Kyokai (ClassNK)
www.classnk.or.jp

Nor-Ocean Tank AS
tank@nor-ocean.com

www.odingroup.com

P.F. Bassøe A/S & Co
www.pfbassoe.com

Petrobras Transporte S/A
www.petrobras.com.br

Port Autonome de Marseille
www.marseille-port.fr

Post & Co (P & I) B.V.
Rotterdam

Poten & Partners, Inc.
www.poten.com

Rocargo Services Bonaire N.V.
Aruba, Bonaire, Curacao
rocargoshipping@rocargo.com

Russian Maritime Register of Shipping
www.rs-head.spb.ru

Saab Marine Electronics AB
www.tankradar.com

Saga West Africa Network
shipping.tramp@fr.dti.bollore.com

Seawaves Shipping Services Co Ltd
seawaves@dpimail.net

Shell International Trading & Shipping Co. Ltd
www.shell.com/shipping

Shipmanagement Expert Systems S.A.
www.vardakis.com

Shoreline Mutual Insurance
www.mutrisk.com/shoreline

Simpson, Spence & Young Ltd.
www.ssyonline.com

SOVCOMFLOT
www.sovkomflot.com

224

Stocznia Szczecinska S.A.
www.sssa.com.pl

TankOil Chartering & Brokerage
tankoil@sky.net.co

The International Association of Ports and
Harbors (IAPH)
http://www.iaphworldports.org

www.shipindia.com

The Swedish Shipowners' Association
www.sweship.se

TURMEPA
www.turmepa.org.tr

# INTERTANKO Members

Finaval SPA
Finbeta SpA
First International Shipping Corp Ltd
First Olsen Tankers Ltd AS
Fouquet Sacop Group
Fratelli d'Amico-Armatori SpA
G D'Alesio SAS
Gadot Yam Ltd
General Maritime Corporation
German Tanker Shipping GmbH & Co KG
Gestioni Armatoriali Srl
Glafki (Hellas) Maritime Company
Greenwich Ship Management & Brok SA
Groton Pacific Carriers Inc
Halfdan Ditlev-Simonsen & Co
Halkidon Shipping Corporation
Hanseatic Shipping Company Ltd
Heidenreich Marine ( Far East ) Pte Ltd
Heidenreich Marine Inc
Hiltveit Associates Inc
Histria Shipmanagement SRL
Hong Kong Ming Wah Shipping Co Ltd
Iino Kaiun Kaisha Ltd
International Andromeda Shipping
International Tanker Management Norway AS
Interorient Navigation Co Ltd
IPSIS
Iver Ships AS
Jahre Dahl Bergesen AS
Jahre-Wallem AS
John T Essberger GmbH & Co
Kawasaki Kisen Kaisha Ltd
Kent Line Limited
Knutsen OAS Shipping A/S
Kristen Navigation Inc
Kristian Gerhard Jebsen Skipsrederi A/S
Krupp Seeschiffahrt GmbH
Kyklades Maritime Corporation
Kyoei Tanker Co Ltd
Latvian Shipping Company
Laurel Sea Transport Ltd
Liquimar Tanker Management Inc

Lorentzens Skibs A/S
Lundquist Shipping Company
Malaysia International Shipping Corp Bhd
Mare-Denholm Ltd
Marine Management Services MC
Marine Transport Corporation
Marinvest AB
Maritrans Inc
Maryville Maritime Inc
Medcare Shipping SA (Hellas)
Mega Tankers ASA
Meiji Shipping Co Ltd
Metrostar Management Corp
Minerva Marine Inc
Mitsui OSK Lines Ltd
Mosvold Shipping AS
Motia Compagnia di Navigazione SpA
Multi Trading Shipmanagement Ltd
NS Lemos & Company Limited
Naviera F Tapias SA
Neda Maritime Agency CoLtd
Neptune Orient Lines Ltd
Nereus Shipping SA
Niarchos (London) Limited
Nippon Yusen Kabushiki Kaisha
Nissho Shipping Co Ltd
Norbulk Shipping UK Ltd
Norse Management (UK) Ltd
Novorossiysk Shipping Company (Novoship)
Ocean Shipholdings Inc
Ole Schrøder & Co A/S
Olympic Shipping & Management SA
OMI Corp
Ondimar Transportes Maritimos
Orpheus Marine Transport Corp of Piraeus
Orsa Tanker Isletmeciligi Ve Denizcilik San
Overseas Maritime Carriers SA
Paradise Navigation SA
Parakou Shipping Ltd
Paralos Maritime Corporation SA
Pegasus Ocean Services Ltd
Petromarine SA

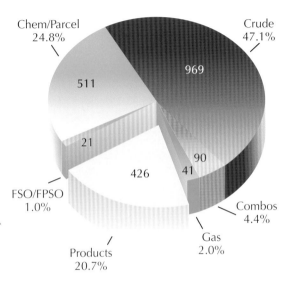

## Membership covering all types of tankers
### By number of tankers

Crude 47.1% — 969
Chem/Parcel 24.8% — 511
Products 20.7% — 426
Combos 4.4% — 90
Gas 2.0% — 41
FSO/FPSO 1.0% — 21

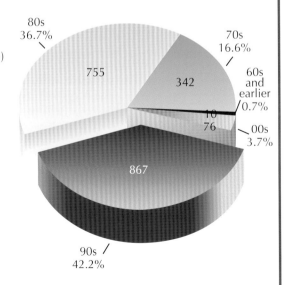

## Age distribution by number
### Average age 13.5 years

90s 42.2% — 867
80s 36.7% — 755
70s 16.6% — 342
00s 3.7% — 76
60s and earlier 0.7% — 10

Company

Petroships Pte Ltd
PGS Production AS
Pioneer Tankers Shipping Corp
PLM International Inc
Pratibha Shipping Company Ltd
Premuda Societá di Navigazione
Prime Marine Management Inc
Primorsk Shipping Corporation
Qatar Shipping Company SAQ
Quantum Tankers A/S
Rasmussen Maritime Services AS
Rederi AB Brevik
Rederi AB Väderö
Reederei "Nord" Klaus E Oldendorff Ltd
Reliance Industries Ltd
Rigel Schiffahrts GmbH & CO KG
Rigel Shipping Canada Inc
Roxana Shipping SA
Rudolf A Oetker
Sanmar Shipping Corporation
Saudi Maritime Holding Co
SBM Production Contractors Inc
Scinicariello Ship Management SpA
Scorpio Ship Management SAM
Sea Oil Shipping Ltd
Sea Trade Shipping Corp SA
Seabulk A/S
Seacrest Shipping Co Ltd
Seatramp Tankers Inc
Seatrans DA
Seaworld Management & Trading Inc
Services et Transports Management
Shinwa Kaiun Kaisha Ltd
SIB Società a Responsabilità Limitata
SK Shipping Co Ltd
Socatra
Sociedad Naviera Ultragas Ltda
Société de Services Maritimes SA
Stealth Maritime Corp SA
Stelmar Tankers (Management) Ltd
Stena Bulk AB
Stolt-Nielsen Inc
Styga Compania Naviera SA
Sun Enterprises Ltd

Tai Chong Cheang Steamship Co(HK)Ltd
Taiheiyo Kaiun Company Limited
Tankerska Plovidba
Tarntank Rederi AB
Team Tankers Shipping AS
Teekay Shipping (Canada) Ltd
The Great Eastern Shipping Co Ltd
The J J Ugland Companies
Thenamaris Ships Management Inc
Theodora Tankers BV
Thome Ship Management Pte Ltd
Tokyo Marine Co Ltd
Tomasos Brothers  Inc
Torvald Klaveness & Co AS
Tradewind Tankers CA
Transman Shipping Enterprises
TransPetrol Services NV
Traschimar SAM
Tsakos Energy Navigation Ltd (TEN)
Tsakos Shipping & Trading SA
Tschudi & Eitzen A/S
Tschudi & Eitzen Sembawang Pte Ltd
Tschudi & Eitzen Ship Management Denmark A/S
UCT United Chemical Transport GmbH
Ugland Nordic Shipping ASA
Unicom Management Services (Cyprus) Ltd
Unicorn Lines (Pty) Limited
Unique Shipping (HK) Limited
Universe Maritime Ltd
VShips Switzerland S A Geneva
Valles Steamship (Canada) Ltd
Varun Shipping Company Limited
Viken Shipping AS
Vinalmar SA
Vopak Chemical Tanker Services BV
W W Marpetrol SA
Wah Kwong Shipping Holdings Ltd
Wallem Shipmanagement Limited
Western Shipping
Westfal-Larsen Management AS
Wilh Wilhelmsen ASA
World Tankers Management Pte Ltd
Yuyo Steamship Co Ltd

# INTERTANKO Associate Members

Company

A C M Shipping Limited
A M B and Partners SrL
A/S Inventor Shipping
Aarus Maritima SA
ABS Nautical Systems LLC
Abu Dhabi National Tanker Co
AC Shipping Ltd
Agemar CA
AGF Marine Aviation Transport
Agip Petroli SpA
Alessandro Archibugi & Figlio srl
Alexia Shipping Ltd
American Bureau of Shipping
Anglo Maritime Shipbrokers
Arab Maritime Petroleum Transport Co
Arendal Maritime College
Argent Shipping Limited
Asociación de Navieros Españoles
Assuranceforeningen GARD
Assuranceforeningen SKULD (Gjensidig)
Atlas Marine Services Co SAE
Auxitrol SA
B Skaugen Shipping AS
BE Moors Ltd
Banchero-Costa & Co SpA
Barber Ship Management Sdn Bhd
Barry Rogliano Salles
Barwil Agencies AS
Becoblohm Maracaibo CA
Besora Oil Services SL
BHP Transport & Logistics Pty Ltd
Biehl & Co Inc
BlueCalm Marine Services
Bonyad Shipping Agencies Co
BP Shipping Ltd
Braemar Tankers Ltd
Bravo Chem SRL
Brookwater Ltd
Bryggen Shipping & Trading A/S

Bureau Veritas Marine Division
Burke & Novi Shipping SRL
California Maritime Academy
Camafrica Tanker Ltd
Cambiaso & Risso Srl (Head office)
Canadian Shipowners Association
Canega Shipping Services
Capital Shipbrokers Ltd
Cargo Maritime
Carmelo Caruana Company Limited
Castalia Partners LLC
Catoni Maritime Agencies SA
Chamber of Shipping of British Columbia
Charles R Weber Co Inc
Chartering Solutions
Chevron Shipping Company LLC
Christiania Bank og Kreditkasse
Cincotta Shipping Agency
CLS*
Compañia Española de Petróleos SA (CEPSA)
Confederazione Italiana Armatori
Consulmar SL
Corbett & Holt LLC
Credit Agricole Indosuez
D Koronakis SA
Dalian Ocean Shipping Co (COSCO Dalian)
Den norske Bank ASA
Det Norske Veritas
Deutsche Schiffsbank AG
Dietze & Associates LLC
Ditas-Deniz Isletmeciligi ve Tankerciligi
DNV Petroleum Services Pte Ltd
DOW Hydrocarbons and Resources Inc
Drug Testing International
Dubai Shipping Company LLC
Dudley & Asociados
DVB NedshipBank nv
E A Gibson Shipbrokers Ltd
E N Bisso & Son Inc

## Company

ECM/Hudson Maritime Services LLC
Economout Int Shipping Agencies Ltd
ECP Service Corporation
El Paso Marine
Elder Dempster Agencies (Nigeria) Ltd
Embiricos Shipbrokers Limited
Environmental Protection Eng
Equant
Equiva Trading Company
Fairdeal Group Management SA
Fearnleys A/S
Fender Care Marine & STS Transfer Services Ltd
Ferrotank Srl
Flota Petrolera Ecuatoriana FLOPEC
FONASBA
Fortum Oil and Gas Oy
Frachtcontor Junge & Co
G M Richards Enterprises Inc
GAC Shipping Ltd AB (Head Office)
Galbraith's Ltd
Gallagher Marine Systems Inc
Gard Services AS
Genel Denizcilik
Genoa Sea Tankers Srl
GEODIS Africa Services
Germanischer Lloyd
Gjensidige Nor Forsikring
Global Transport Inc
Globe Wireless
GN Comtext International
Gothenburg Port Authority
Graypen Limited
Green Award Foundation
Groupama Transport
Gunclean Toftejorg AB
H Clarkson & Co Ltd
Hamworthy KSE Svanehøj A/S
Hanjin Shipping Co Ltd
Hasting Tanker AB
Herbert Engineering Corp
Hill Betts & Nash
Hong Kong Shipowners Association
Ibérica Marítima Barcelona SA

IDESS Maritime Centre (Subic) Inc
Ince & Co
Indian Register of Shipping
ING Bank NV
Inge Steensland A/S
Institut Francais de la Mer (IFM)
International Assoc of Class Society
International Marine Consultants
International Marine Transportation Ltd
International Shipping Enterprise
ISACOL SA
Islamic Republic of Iran Shipping Lines (IRISL)
ISLAND SHIPBROKERS (PTE) LTD
Italia Chartering SRL
JLT Risk Solutions Limited
Johan G Olsen Shipbrokers A/S
Jørgen Jahre Shipping AS/Bulls Tankrederi A/S
JSC "LUKOIL- Chernomorye"
Kanoo Shipping Agencies Division SA
Katradis Marine Ropes Industry SA
Koch Shipping Company
Korean Register of Shipping
Kusttankers Interesseforening
Kuwait Oil Tanker Company SAK
Landskrona Ship Agents AB
Lars Lindebäck Shipping AB
Laycan ASA
Leif Høegh & Co ASA
Lemle & Kelleher LLP
Leth Suez Transit Ltd AS
Levelseas Limited*
Liberian International Ship & Corporate Registry
Lintec Testing Services Ltd
Lloyd's Register of Shipping
Lorentzen & Stemoco as
LTB - Corretagem Maritima Lda
LUKtrans Shipping Co ltd
Lyondell-Citgo Refining Company Ltd
Mallory Jones Lynch Flynn & Assoc Inc
Manubito Limitada (Head office)
Marathon Ashland Petroleum LLC
Marine Press of Canada*
Marine Response Alliance

| | |
|---|---|
| Marine Spill Response Corporation | Port Autonome de Marseille |
| Maritime and Port Authority of Singapore | Post & Co (P & I) bv |
| Marittima Ravennate SpA | Poten & Partners Inc |
| Marjan Shipping Services Ltd | Pres-Vac Engineering A/S |
| Massachusetts Maritime Academy | Quality Maritime Services SA - QMS SA |
| Matsui & Co Ltd | RS Platou Shipbrokers as |
| McQuilling Brokerage | Raffles Shipbrokers (S) Pte Ltd |
| Medco Shipbrokers SL | Rajah & Tann |
| Medscreen Ltd | REPSOL YPF Trading and Transport |
| Middle East Navigation Aids Service (MENAS) | Richardson Lawrie Associates |
| Middle East Shipping Company Ltd | Riley-Sherman Shipping Agency Inc |
| Milbros Shipping AS | RINA SpA |
| Moore Stephens | Robin Maritime Inc |
| Moran-Gulf Shipping Agencies | Rocargo Services Bonaire NV |
| MTI (Maritime Technical International) | Rotterdam Municipal Port Management* |
| Multiport Ship Agencies Network | Royal Fleet Auxiliary |
| Naess Shipping (Holland) bv | Russian Maritime Pilots' Association |
| Naggar Shipping Co | Russian Maritime Register of Shipping |
| National Iranian Tanker Co | Saab Marine Electronics AB |
| National Response Corporation | SAGA West Africa Network |
| Navigation Maritime Bulgare | Sarda Marittima Srl |
| Navion ASA | Seascope Shipping Limited |
| Nippon Kaiji Kyokai (ClassNK) | Seatown Shipbroking Pte Ltd |
| Nor-Ocean Tank AS | Seawaves Shipping Services Co Ltd |
| Norsk Hydro ASA | Servicios Navieramar CA |
| North of England P&I Association Limited | Shell International Trading & Shipping Co Ltd |
| Norton Rose | Shipmanagement Expert Systems SA |
| Nurminen Port Agency OY | Shoreline Mutual Insurance |
| Nyship Chartering | Sigma Coatings* |
| O - J Libæk & Partners A/S | Simpson Spence & Young Shipbrokers Ltd |
| O'Brien's Oil Pollution Service Inc | Sinbad Chartering Co AB |
| Odin Marine Inc | Sinclair Roche & Temperley |
| Okendo Maritima SL | Singaport Cleanseas Pte Ltd |
| P F Bassøe A/S & Co | Skymar Maritime Services |
| Parekh Marine Agencies Pvt Ltd | Smit International Norway A/S |
| PDV (UK) SA | Sovchart SA |
| Pérez y Cía (Cataluña) sa | SOVCOMFLOT |
| Petrobras Transporte S/A - Transpetro | Steamship Association of Louisiana |
| Petromar Schiffahrts- und Befrachtungsgesellscha | Stentex (UK) Ltd |
| Petro-Nav Inc* | Stephenson Harwood |
| Philippine Petroleum Sea Transport Assn | Stockholm Chartering AB |
| Philippine Shipowners' Association | Stocznia Szczecinska Porta Holdings SA |
| PMI Trading Ltd | Strømme Teco ASA |

Company

Sun Company Inc
Tankoil Chartering and Brokerage
Telemarine Ltd
TeRo Co Ltd
Texaco Oil Trading & Transp - Maritime Inspection
The Britannia Steam Ship Ins Ass Ltd
The Institute of Chartered Shipbrokers
The Institute of Shipping Analysis
The International Association of Ports and Harbor
The London Steamship Owners' Mutual Ins
The Royal Bank of Scotland plc
The Shipowners Insurance and Guaranty Company Ltd
The Shipping Corporation of India Ltd
The Standard Steamship Owners' P&I Assn
The Steamship Mutual Underwriting Association
The Swedish Club
The Swedish Shipowners' Association
The West of England Ship Owners Mutual
Thocomar Shipping Agency
Titan Maritime Industries Inc
Tomas Ruiz SA de CV
TotalFinaElf Group
Trade Sea Shipbroking Pte Ltd
Transmarine Navigation Corporation
Tripul Lda
TS Tanksystem SA
TURMEPA
UK Hydrographic Office
UK P&I Club
Union of Greek Shipowners
United Messaging Systems AS
United Ocean Ship Management Pte Ltd
Vela International Marine Limited
Ventspils Free Port Authority
Vinodol CA
VISMA ASA
Vopak Tanker Chartering Belgium NV
Waterfront Shipping Co Ltd
Western Petroleum SA*
Worms Services Maritimes
Zihni Shipping Agency SA

*Subject to Council approval

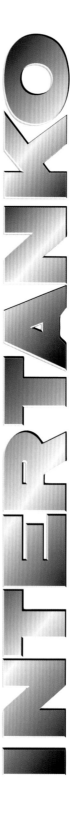

# Acknowledgments

The initiative to publish 'A Century of Tankers' came from INTERTANKO's Communication and PR Committee Chairman, Paul Slater, First International Corp, who, together with the Committee members John Damilatis, Kyklades Maritime Corporation; Philip Embiricos, Embiricos Shipbrokers; Steven A Hillyard, formerly Chevron Shipping Corporation; Jack Kitchura, ABS Nautical Systems LLC; Dimitris N. Lyras, Lyras Shipping Company; Iouri A. Peskov, Novorossiysk Shipping Company; Stefano Rosina, Premuda Societa di Navigazione; Harald Svensen, B+H Equimar Singapore Pte; and Francis Vallat, FV Marine, provided valuable support and guidance throughout the project.

A number of people in the industry were kind enough to read draft chapters, make constructive suggestions and provide additional material. For their help and advice we thank:

Capt. Sir William Codrington, Bt., formerly World-Wide Shipping Agency Ltd; Colin Cridland, Simpson, Spence and Young; Philip Embiricos, Embiricos Shipbrokers; Capt. Bruce Ewen, formerly World-Wide Shipping Agency Ltd; John Ferguson, formerly Lloyds Register of Shipping; William Gray, Gray Maritime Co; Tim Gunner, INTERTANKO Consultant; Westye Høegh, Leif Høegh & Co ASA; Erric Kertsikoff, Eletson Corporation; Hans Laurin, Laurin Maritime; Stefan Nystrom, Stolt-Nielsen Inc; Ken Marshall; Iouri A. Peskov, Novorossiysk Shipping Company; Hirohiko Tanaka, Tokyo Marine Co Ltd; and Stewart Wade, American Bureau of Shipping.

Further valuable information and useful insights into many specialized aspects of the industry were generously provided and for this we are most grateful to:

Kristin Arendt, A P Møller; Hans Chr. Bangsmoen, Wilh. Wilhelmsen ASA; Ina Borch; Lars Carlsson, Concordia Maritime; Karen Check, World-Wide Shipping Agency; Fred Cheng, formerly Chairman, Golden Ocean; Joe Cruise, John D. McCown; Pierre de Livois, Tanker Structures Cooperative Forum; Alan Doig, Shell International Trading and Shipping Co Ltd; Svante Domizlaff, John T. Essberger & Co; Lawrence Dunn; Richard du Moulin, Marine Transport Lines; Svein Eriksen, Bergesen DY ASA; John Fields, Iver Ships AS; George Foustanos, Argo Shipping Review; Otto Fritzner, Stolt-Nielsen Inc; Annika Grell, Stena Bulk; Jarle Hammar, Fearnleys AS; Gøran Hammarberg, INTERTANKO Consultant; Capt Rolf Fabricius Hansen, Tschudi & Eitzen; Gelina Harlaftis, University of Piraeus; Lars Härneman, Varvshistoriska Föreningen, Gothenburg; Barb Hestermann, Louisiana Offshore Terminal; Bruce Hutton, V.Ships UK Ltd; Per Jessing, Maritime Forum; Michael Julian, Australian Maritime Safety Agency; Andy King, Bristol Industrial Museum; S. Konishi, ClassNK; Hege J. Kruse, Bergesen DY ASA; Gerhard Kurz, Seabulk International Inc; Nils Kvodal; Roger Lankester, Friends of the Earth; Donald Liu, American Bureau of Shipping; Raymond H C Lo, Hong Kong Shipowners Association; Morten Lovstad, Stolt-Nielsen Inc; Valerie Lyons, Stolt-Nielsen Inc; Lars Erik Marcussen, Maersk Broker UK; Brendan Martin, E.A. Gibson Shipbrokers; Capt Torvald Mjøs, Leif Høegh; Jan Eric Møller, Sandefjord Blad; William O'Neil, IMO; Mike Osborne, Shell International Shipping and Trading; Christian Ostersehlte, Howaldtswerke-Deutsche Werft AG; Else Marie Ottemo, Jahre Dahl Bergesen;

Basil Papachristidis, Papachristidis Holdings Ltd; Sigrid Pedersen, Andreas Ugland & Sons AS; Morgens Peterson, Poten and Partners Inc; Robert Porter, Worldscale Association; Claes Rechnitzer, Dannebrog Rederi AS; Keiichi Sakamoto, Ishikawajima-Harima Heavy Industries Co Ltd; Øyvind Thureson, Sandefjord Maritime Museum; Martin Stopford, H. Clarkson Co Ltd; David Taylor, National Maritime Museum, Greenwich; Paul Tomas, Vitol Services Ltd; Chen Tze Penn, Maritime and Port Authority of Singapore; George R. Uhlich, Jr, The Ludwig Group, Inc; Ane Varden, Tschudi & Eitzen Ship Management AS; Evert Jan van Drent, Europort; Emmanuel Vordonis, Thenamaris Ship Management Inc; Ernst Vossnack; Malcolm Walker, Niarchos (London) Ltd; Captain Graham Westgarth, Teekay Shipping (Canada) Ltd; Capt C. C. Wong, Associate Maritime Company (HK) Ltd.

Also the following organizations: Amsterdam Maritime Museum; Bergen Maritime Museum; Imperial War Museum; Oslo Maritime Museum; The Royal Institute of Naval Architects; Tyne and Wear Museum.

Thank you to the INTERTANKO staff, many of whom read draft material and provided valuable contributions, including: Peter M Swift, (Managing Director), Minerva Alfonso, Anders Baardvik, Steinar K Digre, John Fawcett-Ellis, Kristain R. Fuglesang, Adele Garnett, Gurinder Singh Gill, Julia Hoerenz-Liseth, Gunnar A Knudsen, Petter Markussen, Dag Næstvold, Susan J Owen, Adrian Pedley, Theodore Plessas, Erik Ranheim, Svein A Ringbakken, Dragos Rauta, Howard Snaith, Jan Svenne, Ann Sæther, Donna Tang-de Leon, Milly Tseng and Tim Wilkins.

Thank you also to Daniella Cottew and Leia Doherty for patiently preparing many drafts and amendments during the course of the book's production.

A special thank you, in particular, goes to Clarice Tan from INTERTANKO and Chris Skinner from Creative Decisions. Clarice for her dedicated work in collating funnels and logos from INTERTANKO's Members and Associate Members and Chris for his patient and tireless work on the technical and computer graphics for the book.

* * * * * * * * * * * * * * * * * * * * * * * * * * * *

Managing Editor, Sally Woulfe, Communications Manager, INTERTANKO

Editorial Consultants:
Andrew Guest, Shipping Journalist and Mike Corkhill, Technical Journalist

# List of illustrations

Acknowledgement is gratefully made to those have given permission for the reproduction of illustrations and photographs for this book. We are also grateful to the people and organisations who kindly gave us material which, unfortunately, due to design and layout considerations we were unable to include.

**Chapter 3**

Page 64, Side launch of Promachos, *courtesy Dorian (Hellas) S.A.* Page 65, Sitakund, *courtesy Tschudi & Eitzen Holding AS.* Page 66, crude oil seaborne trade 1938, *courtesy Fearnleys AS.* Page 67/68/69, B P Newton launching/sea trials, B P Newton as Notraship, *courtesy Tschudi & Eitzen.* Page 70, Swordfish aircraft landing on Merchant Aircraft Carrier and MAC ship Rapana, *courtesy Shell.* Page 71, Battle of the Atlantic, *courtesy Imperial War Museum.* Page 72, Høegh Ray, *courtesy Leif Høegh & Co ASA.* Page 73, Ohio under tow, *courtesy National Maritime Museum Greenwich.* Page 74, Fires being brought under control on San Demetrio, *courtesy Kanal + Image UK.* Page 75, San Demetrio, *courtesy National Maritime Museum Greenwich.* Page 76, Various photos of Biskaya, *courtesy John T. Essberger.* Page 78/79, Advertisements from Fairplay, *courtesy Fairplay Lloyds Register.* Sketch protective hood. Page 80, Liberty ships. Page 81, T-2 tanker Schenectady, *courtesy of US Navy Archives.* Page 82, Henry Kaiser and President Roosevelt, *courtesy US Naval Historical Center: NH46486.* Page 83, HMS Hemione refueling from RFA Dingledale, *courtesy Imperial war Museum.* Page 84, Chart growth in tanker dwt 1900-60, *courtesy SSY Consulting & Research Ltd.* Page 85, Velutina, *courtesy Shell.*

**Chapter 4**

Page 86, Universe Ireland, *courtesy Foto Flite.* Page 87, Idemitsu Maru, *courtesy Foto Flite.* Page 88, Daniel K Ludwig, *courtesy The Ludwig Group Inc.* Page 90, Sketch Suez Canal development. Page 91, Map Suez Canal, Graph Suez Canal Oil Flows, *courtesy Suez Canal Authority/SSY Consultancy & Research Ltd.* Page 93, Naess Sovereign, *courtesy Foto Flite.* Page 95, Chart growth in tanker numbers 1900-70, Nisseki Maru, *courtesy Ishikawajima-Harima Heavy Industries Co. Ltd (IHI)/'A ClassAct'.* Page 97, Aristotle Onassis and Tina Onnasis, Stravros Niachos and World Concord, *courtesy George Foustanos, Argo Shipping Review.* Page 99, World Chief, *courtesy World-Wide Shipping.*

**Chapter 5**

Page 100, Yamatogawa. Page 101, Tanker in lay-up *photo Torsten Andreas.* Page 103, Chart crude oil seaborne trade 1973 *courtesy Fearnleys AS,* oil price development 1970-80, growth in tanker dwt 1970-80, *courtesy SSY Consultancy & Research Ltd.* Page 104, Tigre, *courtesy Wilh. Wilhelmsen ASA.* Page 106, Graph tanker fleet by flag *courtesy SSY Consultancy & Research Ltd.* Page 108, Bulbous bow *photo Reg Wright,* Scrapping, *courtesy BIMCO.* Page 109, Scrapping, *artist Brian Entwisle.* Page 110, Kristine Mersk, *courtesy A P Moller.* Page 111, Vietnamese boat people *photo Jan Eric Møller, Sandefjord Blad.* Page 112, Jahre Viking. Page 114, Shuttle Tanker. Page 115 LOOP Marine Terminal, *courtesy Loop Business Development.* Page 116, World Petrobras, *courtesy Capt Bruce Ewen.* Page 117, Tanker in the Gulf War. Page 118, World Petrobras after the attack, *courtesy Capt Bruce Ewen.* Page 119, Seawise Giant in a ball of flames.

*courtesy LR Fairplay*. Page 153, London Pride. Page 154/155, Charts crude oil seaborne trade 1885 to 2000, *courtesy Fearnleys AS*. Page 156, Sketch types of modern oil tanker. Page 157, Tankers and other man made structures.

**Chapter 9**
Page 158, Ryushsan, courtesy Mitsui OSK. Page 159, Safety *photo Reg Wright*. Page 160, Cargo discharge. Page 163, Load on top, *courtesy Shell*. Page 164, Torrey Canyon, *courtesy Imperial War Museum*. Page 165, Chart casualty statistics, *courtesy ITOPE*. Page 166, Arosa. Page 166, Shinoussa, *courtesy Eletson Corporation*. Page 167, Clean seas *photo Reg Wright*. Page 169, Globtik Toyko, *courtesy Foto Flite*.

**Chapter 10**
Page 170, Sabine. Page 171, Construction of double hull, *courtesy Litton Ship Systems/ARCO Marine Inc*. Page 172, Front Viewer. Page 173, Bulbous bow *photo Reg Wright*. Page 174, Loaded tanker at sea. Page 175, Futura. Page 176, Turbinia, *courtesy Imperial war Museum*. Page 177, Shin-Aitoku Maru, *courtesy Japanese Marine Equipment Association (JSMEA)/'A Class Act'*. Page 178, Engine room from a modern tanker. Page 179, Engine Room, *courtesy Thenamaris Ships Management Inc/photo Studio Vrettos*. Page 181, Navion Munn. Page 182, Manhattan. Page 183, Training with models and simulators. Page 184, Product tanker features. Page 186, VLCC features. Page 188, Liquified Natural Gas Tanker. Page 190, Historical development in tanker size and dimensions, *courtesy Lloyd's Register of Shipping*.

**Voyage of modern tanker**
Page 196, Berge Stadt. Page 197, Crew, *courtesy Bergesen d.y. ASA*. Pages 198/205 *Various photographs Teekay Shipping, Bergesen d.y. ASA, Reg Wright*.

**At the start of the new millennium**
Page 206, *Various photographs courtesy Teekay Shipping, Commission des Communautés Européennes and Reg Wright*.

Page 233, Toula Z. Page 236, Tabriz, *courtesy Wilh. Wilhelmsen*. Page 242, Einar, *courtesy Tschudi & Eitzen*. Page 247, Fertility L. Page 250, Berge Banker. Page 255, Nordscot, *courtesy DS Norden*.

*Every effort has been made to obtain permission for the reproduction of illustrations and photographs in this book; apologies are offered to anyone it has not been possible to contact.*

# Glossary

**AFRAMAX** *(American Freight Rate Association)*
Approximately - 80,000/105,000 dwt - term for a tank ship of standard size

**AFT**
The section of a vessel towards the stern.

**AMIDSHIPS**
Midway between the forward and aft sections of a vessel.

**ARABIAN LIGHT CRUDE OIL**
The world's most prolific crude oil frequently used as a 'marker crude' by which the prices of other crude oils are fixed by comparing their quality with Arabian Light.

**BALLAST**
When a tanker is not carrying oil it has to carry sea water as ballast to ensure adequate stability and propeller immersion so that it can proceed safely.

**BARREL**
A standard petroleum unit of measure defined as 42 US gallons, equivalent to 34.97 UK gallons or 159 litres.

**BILL OF LADING**
A negotiable document which gives title to a cargo, acknowledges receipt and indicates the port of destination.

**BULKHEAD**
Longitudinal or transverse structural partitions which strengthen the hull and sub-divide it into compartments.

**BUNKER FUEL**
Any fuel which is loaded into the bunker tanks for use in powering a vessel. Often referred to as 'bunkers'.

**CABOTAGE**
Reservation of the coastal trade of a country to ships sailing under the flag of that country.

**CAPESIZE**
Term to describe large ships which are too wide to negotiate the Panama Canal.

**CASE OIL**
Rectangular metal cans holding five US gallons, usually packed in pairs in wooden cases, which superseded barrels for oil transportation before oil was carried in bulk.

**CHICKSANS**
Cargo loading / discharging equipment situated on oil jetty.

**CLEAN**
In oil terms products such as light or middle distillates (gasoline's, naphtha's, kerosene's, gas oils) as opposed to dirty products (fuel oils, bituminous, crude oils).

**COFR**
Certificate of Financial Responsibility, required under the US Oil Pollution Act of 1990.

**COFFERDAM**
This sub-division of a tanker into its many tanks is achieved by the use of cofferdams which are oil tight bulkheads.

**COMPOSITE SHIP**
An iron framed wooden hull ship.

**DISPLACEMENT**
The term is used for the weight of a ship i.e. when a ship floats in water it is the weight of water displaced by a ship.

## EXPANSION TRUNKING

Continuous trunking across the top of a vessel's tanks to allow for expansion of the oil cargo.

## FORE-PEAK TANK

Situated in the forward part of the vessel below the deck store and chain locker, used for sea-water ballast.

## FREEBOARD

The distance of a vessel from deck to waterline.

## INERT GAS

Inert gas replaces air in the tanks and reduces the oxygen content to a level which cannot support combustion (less than eight per cent oxygen).

## IMO

International Maritime Organisation; a specialist agency of the United Nations providing for inter-governmental cooperation on shipping issues.

## IOPC Fund

International Oil Pollution Compensation Fund.

## ISM

The International Safety Management Code which provides for the audit and certification of shipowner and shipboard safety systems.

## ITOPF

The International Tanker Owners Pollution Federation Ltd which provides advice on all aspects of preparing for and responding to oil spills from tankers.

## KNOT

Measure of speed for ships, i.e. one nautical mile (1,852 metres) per hour.

## LAY-UP

A vessel which is not available for immediate charter can be put into lay-up, in which it is immobilised in a safe location. Vessels enter lay-up during prolonged periods of unemployment.

## LIGHTERING

A procedure for discharging part of a vessels' cargo into other vessels, so that it may enter a port which could not take it when fully laden.

## Mbd

Million barrels daily (oil production)

## NEWBUILDINGS

This term describes the orderbook for ships under construction, to distinguish them from the existing fleet

## OAPEC

Organisation of Arab Petroleum Exporting Countries

## OCIMF

Oil Companies International Marine Forum is a voluntary organisation of oil companies with interests in the shipment of crude oil and oil products.

## OPA 90

The US Oil Pollution Act of August 1990.

## OPEC

Organisation of Petroleum Exporting Countries.

## PORT OF REFUGE

A port not included in the vessel's passage plan but which could provide a safe haven in an emergency.

### PUMP ROOM

Area where cargo pumps and related equipment are located on a tanker. Protected by oil-tight bulkheads, the pump room it is normally situated between cargo tanks and machinery spaces.

### SBT

Segregated ballast tanks for tankers.

### SCANTLINGS

The quality and thickness of steel plating used in tanker construction.

### SIRE

Ship Inspection Reports Programme; a database of ship inspection reports submitted by charterers and administered by OCIMF.

### SOLAS

Safety of Life at Sea, an IMO Convention concerned with the safe design and operation of ships.

### STCW

Standards of Training, Certification and Watchkeeping for Seafarers. An IMO Convention that specifies minimum performance standards for the certification of masters, deck and engineer officers and seamen.

### SUMMER TANKS

In early tankers, the expansion tanks served as spaces that could be filled with oil to bring a vessel to the loading mark in summer.

### TONNAGE

Gross Tonnage - A figure representing the total of all the enclosed spaces within a ship, arrived at by means of a formula which has as its basis the volume measured in cubic metres. Abbreviated to GT. The gross tonnage has replaced the gross register tonnage.

Net Tonnage - A figure representing the total of all the enclosed spaces within a ship available for cargo, arrived at by means of a formula which has its base the volume measured in cubic metres. Abbreviated to NT. The net tonnage has replaced the net register tonnage.

Deadweight - Difference between a ship's loaded and light displacements, consisting of the total weight of cargo, fuel, fresh water, stores and crew, which a ship can carry when immersed to a particular load line, normally her summer load line. The deadweight is expressed in tons or tonnes. Abbreviated to DWT.

### ULLAGE

The space in tanks not occupied by oil. Ullage figures are quoted as a measure of the ability of a tank or tanks to hold further stocks.

### USCG

The United States Coast Guard.

# Index of tankers

# Index

# Index

**INTERTANKO**

The International Association of Independent Tanker Owners

**INTERTANKO OSLO**
Bogstadveien 27B
PO Box 5804 Majorstuen
0308 Oslo, Norway
Tel:  +47 22 12 26 40
Fax: +47  22 12 26 41
oslo@intertanko.com

**INTERTANKO LONDON**
Baltic Exchange
38 St Mary Axe
London, EC3A 8BH, UK
Tel:  +44 20 7623 4311
Fax:  +44 20 7626 7078
london@intertanko.com

**INTERTANKO ASIA**
5 Temasek Boulevard
#12-07 Suntec City Tower 5
Singapore 038985
Tel:  +65 333 4007
Fax: +65 333 5004
singapore@intertanko.com

**INTERTANKO USA**
801 North Quincy Street
Suite 200, Arlington,
VA 22209
USA
Tel:  +1 202 320 0457
washington@intertanko.com

**www.intertanko.com**